# SUPPLY CHAIN
# NETWORKS
## and
# BUSINESS PROCESS
# ORIENTATION

*Advanced Strategies
and Best Practices*

# The St. Lucie Press/APICS Series on Resource Management

## Titles in the Series

**Applying Manufacturing
Execution Systems**
*by Michael McClellan*

**Back to Basics:
Your Guide to
Manufacturing Excellence**
*by Steven A. Melnyk
and R.T. "Chris" Christensen*

**Enterprise Resources
Planning and Beyond:
Integrating Your Entire
Organization**
*by Gary A. Langenwalter*

**ERP: Tools, Techniques,
and Applications for
Integrating the Supply Chain**
*by Carol A. Ptak
with Eli Schragenheim*

**Integrated Learning
for ERP Success:
A Learning Requirements
Planning Approach**
*by Karl M. Kapp,
with William F. Latham
and Hester N. Ford-Latham*

**Integral Logistics Management:
Planning and Control of
Comprehensive Business Processes**
*by Paul Schönsleben*

**Inventory Classification
Innovation: Paving the Way
for Electronic Commerce and
Vendor Managed Inventory**
*by Russell G. Broeckelmann*

**Lean Manufacturing:
Tools, Techniques,
and How To Use Them**
*by William M. Feld*

**Macrologistics Management:
A Catalyst for
Organizational Change**
*by Martin Stein
and Frank Voehl*

**Restructuring the
Manufacturing Process:
Applying the Matrix Method**
*by Gideon Halevi*

**Basics of Supply Chain
Management**
*by Lawrence D. Fredendall
and Ed Hill*

**Supply Chain Management:
The Basics and Beyond**
*by William C. Copacino*

**Handbook of
Supply Chain Management**
*by Jim Ayers*

# SUPPLY CHAIN NETWORKS
## and
# BUSINESS PROCESS ORIENTATION

## *Advanced Strategies and Best Practices*

## Kevin P. McCormack
## William C. Johnson
### with William T. Walker

The St. Lucie Press/APICS Series on Resource Management

APICS®

The Educational Society for Resource Management

$S^t_L$

## ST. LUCIE PRESS

A CRC Press Company

Boca Raton   London   New York   Washington, D.C.

## Library of Congress Cataloging-in-Publication Data

McCormack, Kevin (Kevin P.)
    Supply chain networks and business process orientation : advanced strategies and best practices / Kevin McCormack, William Johnson ; with William T. Walker.
        p.   cm. — (APICS series on resource management)
    Includes bibliographical references and index.
    ISBN 1-57444-327-5
    1. Business logistics. 2. Business networks. I. Johnson, William C. (William Charles), 1954- II. Walker, William T. III. Title. IV. Series.

HD38.5 .M395 2002
658.7′2—dc21
                                                     2002068207

**Visit the CRC Press Web site at www.crcpress.com**

# DEDICATIONS

To Susan, the angel, from the dreamer.

**Kevin McCormack**

To my late mother, who left a legacy of benediction
by the giving of herself to her children.

**Bill Johnson**

# CONTENTS

1   **Introduction** .......................................................................................**1**
    Summary ............................................................................................ 5
    References .......................................................................................... 7

2   **Business Process Orientation — From Vertical Integration
    to Networked Communities** .......................................................**9**
    An Overview of the BPO Concept ................................................. 10
    Functional Orientation: How Did We Get Here? ......................... 12
    Process and Value Creation .......................................................... 13
    Business Process Orientation in the 1990s — Technology Enablement ... 16
    Business Process Orientation in the 1990s — Organizational Design ....... 19
    BPO: From Concept to Measurement ........................................... 21
    The Impacts of BPO ....................................................................... 23
    Business Process Orientation and the Networked Corporation ................. 26
    Summary .......................................................................................... 28
    References ........................................................................................ 29

3   **BPO and the Supply Chain Performance** ..............................**31**
    Supply Chain Management and BPO ............................................ 31
    Data Collection ............................................................................... 34
    Finding the Relationships .............................................................. 35
    Relating BPO to Supply Chain Performance ............................... 40
    Summary .......................................................................................... 42

4   **BPO and Supply Chain Management Maturity** .....................**45**
    Process Maturity and SCM ............................................................. 45
        Process Maturity Concepts and Foundations ......................... 45
        Assessing Supply Chain Network Maturity using BPO ......... 48
            SCM Maturity Levels ........................................................... 50
            BPO Components in the SCM Maturity Model ................. 52
    Using the SCM Maturity Model ..................................................... 56

Case 1: Ad Hoc — "Shore Up the Chassis Before You Race the Car" .................................................................................... 57
    Basic Process Documentation .......................................... 59
    Basic SCM Best Practices ................................................ 59
    Basic SCM ....................................................................... 60
    Basic Process Jobs .......................................................... 60
    Basic SCM Measures ....................................................... 60
    Basic Operations Strategy ............................................... 60
    Conclusion ...................................................................... 61
Case 2: Defined — "Expand the Chassis and Turbocharge the Engine with Advanced Measurements" ............................... 61
    Basic Process Structure ................................................... 61
    Basic Operation Strategy ................................................ 62
    Balance is a Problem ...................................................... 62
Case 3: Integrated — "Patch a Few Holes in the Chassis and Push to the Next Level" .................................................... 63
    Basic SCM Jobs .............................................................. 64
    Basic SCM Measures ....................................................... 64
    Advanced Process Structure ............................................ 64
SCM Maturity and Business Performance ................................ 64
Conclusion and the Extended Supply Chain — The Next Frontier .......... 66
References .............................................................................. 67

**5 The Extended Supply Chain and the Internet — The Bridge to a Supply Chain Network ...................................... 69**
Introduction .......................................................................... 69
Background ........................................................................... 70
Scope and Organization of Our Study .................................... 72
Defining the Concepts and Measures ..................................... 73
    Internet Technology Usage .............................................. 73
    Integrating Practices ....................................................... 73
    Measures ......................................................................... 74
Data Gathering and Results .................................................... 77
    Sample ........................................................................... 77
    Analysis of Data ............................................................. 77
Results and Findings .............................................................. 81
Conclusions and Implications ................................................. 83
References .............................................................................. 84

**6 Interactions and Relationships in the Networked Economy .......................................................................... 87**
Introduction .......................................................................... 87
Interaction Costs — Unbundling the Corporation .................... 88
More Than Just Communication .............................................. 91
Information Exchange and Network Alignment ......................... 94
Building Stronger Network Bonds — The Ties that Bind ........... 96

Trust .................................................................................................. 96
Commitment ..................................................................................... 97
Cooperation ...................................................................................... 98
Dependence ...................................................................................... 98
Summary ............................................................................................ 99
References ........................................................................................ 101

**7   Unbundling the Corporation: A Blueprint for Supply Chain Networks ..................................................................................103**
Understanding Supply Chain Networks ....................................... 103
Identifying the Main Thread and Business Strategy Alignment ........ 104
Classifying the Supply Chain Players ....................................... 107
Tracing the Flows through the Network — Physical, Information, and Cash .......................................................................... 109
Network Dynamics — Static, Switched, and Chaotic ...................... 112
Building BPO within a Supply Chain Network ......................... 114
The APICS SCM Principles and BPO ....................................... 115
Integrating BPO with Network Design ............................................ 117
Build a Competitive Infrastructure ........................................... 117
Leverage Worldwide Logistics ................................................. 119
Integrating BPO with Network Operations ..................................... 122
Synchronize Supply with Demand .......................................... 122
Measure Performance Globally ............................................... 125
Driving Value through High BPO Maturity .................................... 127
Summary .......................................................................................... 128
References ........................................................................................ 129

**8   The Challenges of Building a Networked Supply Chain ......131**
Introduction .................................................................................... 132
The SC Network Model ................................................................... 132
Building the Model .......................................................................... 134
Concepts and Components ........................................................ 134
Measuring SC Network Performance ....................................... 135
Situational Factors .................................................................... 137
SC Network Situational Factors — Internal .............................. 137
SC Network Situational Factors — External (Environmental) .... 140
Applying the Model to an SC Network ........................................... 141
The Focus of the Model ............................................................ 141
Using the Model to Create Alignment within the SC Network ......... 142
Conclusions ..................................................................................... 144
References ........................................................................................ 145

**Case 1: Herding Cats across the Supply Chain ....................147**
*Ram Reddy and William C. Johnson*
Background ...................................................................................... 147
Defining the Problem ...................................................................... 148

Proposed Solution.................................................................................. 149
The 800-pound Gorilla Approach — Role of the Channel Master......... 150
Collaborative Team Approach — A Win–Win Focus............................... 151
What Happened?.................................................................................. 152
The Lessons Learned............................................................................ 152
Case Questions.................................................................................... 154
References............................................................................................ 155

## Case 2: Envera™ — Creating Value through Supply Chain Optimization in the Chemical Industry ...............................157
*Richard Chvala and William C. Johnson*

History................................................................................................. 157
Envera's Value Development and Deployment....................................... 158
    Explanation of Value Chain Economics........................................... 158
Origin of the Envera™ — Business-to-Business (B2B) Exchange ........... 159
Developing and Launching Envera — First Steps ................................. 162
Transforming Chemical Industry Supply Chains.................................... 163
Forces of Change................................................................................. 164
Benefits of Supply Chain Etransformation............................................ 166
The Challenges and Competitive Responses......................................... 167
Case Study Questions........................................................................... 168

## Appendix A: Final Survey Questions.....................................169

Exhibit A.1 BPO Survey Questionnaire ............................................... 169
    Process View (PV)......................................................................... 170
    Process Jobs (PJ) .......................................................................... 170
    Process Management and Measurement Systems (PM).................... 170
    Interdepartmental Dynamics (ID)................................................... 171
        Interdepartmental Conflict ..................................................... 171
        Interdepartmental Connectedness .......................................... 171
    Organizational Performance (OP) .................................................. 172
        Measures of Esprit de Corps.................................................. 172
        Overall Performance (5 = excellent, 1 = poor)......................... 173
    General Questions Needed for Analysis and Reporting of Results .. 173
Exhibit A.2 Supply Chain Assessment Survey......................................... 175
    Supply Chain Management............................................................. 175
    Decision Process Area: Plan (Includes P1: Plan Supply Chain, and
    P0: Plan Infrastructure) ................................................................ 175
    Decision Process Area: Source (Includes P2: Plan Source)............. 177
    Decision Process Area: Make (Includes P3: Plan Make) .................. 178
    Decision Process Area: Deliver (Includes P4: Plan Deliver) ............ 179
    Common Themes Within Each Supply Chain Decision Process
    Area: Strategies, Tactics and Philosophy Components that are
    Common Across the Supply Chain.................................................. 181
    Relative Performance..................................................................... 182
    General Questions Needed for Analysis and Reporting of
    Results............................................................................................ 183

**Appendix B:** Regression and Coefficient Alpha Analysis
Results .................................................................................185

**Appendix C:** Extended Supply Chain vs. Internet Usage
Correlation Results..............................................................189

**Appendix D:** SC Network Model and Situational Factors
— Detailed Survey Questions .............................................191
Exhibit D.1: SC Network Model Components and Outcomes —
Detailed Survey Questions ........................................................... 191
Process View (PV) ........................................................................ 192
Process Jobs (PJ)........................................................................... 193
Process Management and Measurement Systems (PM)............................ 193
Process Structures (PS)................................................................. 193
Process Values and Beliefs (PVB) ................................................ 194
Technology Support (TS) .............................................................. 194
Overall Performance (5 = Excellent, 1 = Poor)............................ 195
Measures of Supply Chain Network Esprit de Corps..................... 195
Internal Situational Factors — Supply Chain Network Power
Measures ...................................................................................... 195
    Expert Power ......................................................................... 195
    Referent Power ...................................................................... 196
    Legitimate Power ................................................................... 196
    Legal Legitimate Power ......................................................... 196
    Reward Power......................................................................... 196
    Coercive Power....................................................................... 196
    Other Measures ...................................................................... 197
        Commitment............................................................... 197
        Conflict ....................................................................... 197
        Conflict Resolution ................................................... 197
        Cooperation ............................................................... 197
        Trust............................................................................ 198
        Performance ............................................................... 198
Competitive Edges Survey Instrument ........................................ 198
    External Situational Factors — (Environmental Factors).................... 199
        Market Turbulence ................................................... 199
    Competitive Intensity............................................................. 200
    Technological Turbulence...................................................... 200

**Glossary** ..............................................................................201

**Index**..................................................................................213

# PREFACE

Given the dot.com collapse and the recent Enron bankruptcy, one might conclude that the promises of the so-called new economy have been overstated. Yet, despite the litany of failed Internet pure plays and Enron's unexpected demise, the Internet has transformed the way the business is being conducted. Yes, the basics still matter and cost cutting is appropriate, but today the basis for value creation has undergone a major shift.

The traditional vertically integrated corporation is no longer the most effective vehicle for value creation. Ford Motor Company was the quintessential example of this. At one point, the company owned steamships, power plants, forests, and virtually every other input critical to building an automobile. The vertically integrated structure worked well for auto manufacturers for a time in order to achieve economies of scale and productivity, but these companies have squeezed out about as much productivity as they can.

In today's networked economy, one company makes the car's wheels, another makes the engine, another makes the seats, and another makes the body, all of which flow through the value-added community that the auto company created. In the end, the auto company and the consumer both benefit. The automobile consumers get a better quality product, delivered precisely when and how they want it, at a much better cost. The auto company can respond to customers far more quickly than ever before. Ford currently produces only about 35% of its own parts and out sources the rest.

Ford is not the only old economy firm capitalizing on the power of the network. In fact, many traditional firms are not only surviving, but thriving by transforming their core business architectures around the Net. Smart companies are focusing on their core competencies and outsourcing the remainder of their nonessential processes.

xiv ■ Supply Chain Networks and Business Process Orientation

The Internet is slashing transaction costs as well as the cost of sharing knowledge, collaborating, and meshing business processes among supply chain partners. Value-added communities are replacing traditional vertically integrated industries; they are created through external networks that connect companies and their supply chain processes, which we have defined as the *supply chain network.*

Using the power of Internet technologies, extended supply chain configurations are evolving that will reshape traditional supply chains into networks or business-webs.[1] These network configurations reflect the interconnected roles and activities within a cross-enterprise supply chain. The historical legal and organizational structures are no longer the basis of competition. The evolving interconnected supply chain webs are the new business-to-business (B2B) configurations and the key competitive levers in the new economy.

We strongly believe that the "glue" for building these networked communities is a business process orientation (BPO), a concept introduced in our earlier book *Business Process Orientation: Gaining the e-Business Competitive Advantage.* BPO serves as a powerful organizing principle for firms competing in the networked economy. BPO is not simply a new business fad, but an entirely new way of thinking or viewing an organization. Nor is BPO simply a new business operations strategy, but instead a broad framework for organizing work and information flows that ultimately help organizations build superior customer value.

We are convinced that survival in the Internet economy will depend largely on a firm's ability to integrate with its supply chain partners both relationally and systematically. Rarely can product or service features provide a long-term competitive advantage; however, value created through the activities and processes performed in supply chain networks is more sustainable. Even where competitors can match individual processes or activities, they cannot match the integration or "fit" among these activities, which is a distinguishing characteristic of supply chain networks.

This book demonstrates how building a process-oriented organization results in improved supply network performance. *Supply Chain Networks and Business Process Orientation: Advanced Strategies and Best Practices* was written to help business practitioners and academics understand the impact that well-defined and carefully integrated processes have on supply chain network performance. The bulk of our insights and conclusions are drawn from actual research conducted among consumer, B2B, and services-based companies. Our research suggests that company-to-company supply chains have begun to interact with their partners using the Internet.

---

[1] Tapscott, D., Ticoll, D., and Lowy, A. (2000), *Digital Capital: Harnessing the Power of Business Webs,* Boston: Harvard Business School Press.

They are sharing data and sending digital orders. In some cases, the companies we studied were establishing collaborative planning initiatives with their supply chain partners.

The book is organized into three sections. The first section consists of eight chapters, beginning with an introduction and a history of supply chain networks (Chapters 1 and 2). Next, we present our research model and explain how the various measures of BPO relate to supply chain performance using the Supply Chain Operation Reference (SCOR) Model (Chapter 3). Chapter 4 discusses how BPO relates to supply chain maturity and presents some anecdotal results of our field research. Chapter 5 offers a definition and proposed measures of the *extended supply chain* and reviews the results of a benchmarking research project completed by U.S. and European firms. Chapter 6 focuses on enabling factors in supply network integration in terms of information and people flows. Chapter 7 is written by contributing author Bill Walker, who brilliantly presents a template for identifying and organizing supply chain network actors. Finally, Chapter 8 discusses the challenges in building a supply chain network and offers a model to use as a guide.

The second section of this book offers two excellent case studies on the challenges of supply chain network integration ("Herding Cats across the Supply Chain"), as well as the synergies realized from its formation ("Envera").

The last section of the book contains appendices that provide the details behind our research and conclusions.

Finally, notice that the book cover includes a conceptual picture of a supply chain network superimposed on the symbol used in our first book on BPO. This symbolizes the competing and complimentary forces within an organization, functional orientation versus business process orientation. Together, these forces represent BPO applied to a new, networked organizational form and thus represent the essence of this book

The picture of a hierarchy symbolizes the vertical or functional orientation and a picture of people running toward the customer represents the horizontal or business process orientation. These two conditions are opposite and complimentary and must both be present in healthy organizations and in healthy networks. By balancing a network's functional and process orientation and maintaining that balance, leaders can tap into an energy reservoir or "esprit de corps." This, we believe, is the glue that holds the network together and the fuel that runs its engine. The illustration used on the cover of this book was designed to communicate this idea.

We hope you enjoy reading this book and we welcome your comments. Feel free to contact either Kevin McCormack at (205) 733-2096 or KMccorm241@aol.com, or Bill Johnson at 1-800-672-7223 (ext. 5109) or billyboy@huizenga.nova.edu.

# THE AUTHORS

**Kevin P. McCormack, Ph.D.** has over 25 years of business leadership and consulting experience in manufacturing, high tech, and information technology services industries in the United States and Europe with companies such as Kraft, Philip Morris, Texas Instruments, Microsoft, and Sapient. He holds engineering and chemistry degrees from Purdue University, an M.B.A., and a doctorate in business administration. He is president of DRK Research and Consulting LLC, and is a published researcher and author. His last book, *Business Process Orientation: Gaining the e-business Competitive Advantage,* is available from CRC Press at www.crcpress.com.

McCormack is a member of the American Society for Quality (ASQC), the Supply Chain Council (SCC), the American Marketing Association (AMA), the American Production and Inventory Control Society (APICS), the Council of Logistics Management (CLM), the Institute for Operations Research and the Management Sciences (INFORMS), and the Institute for Business Forecasting (IBF). He can be reached via e-mail at Kmccormack@drkresearch.org.

**William C. Johnson, Ph.D.** is a Full Professor of Marketing in Nova Southeastern University's Huizenga Graduate School of Business and Entrepreneurship. He teaches several marketing courses at both the master's and doctoral levels. Johnson has consulted with the soft drink, healthcare, personal care, telecommunications, and industrial chemical industries. He has also worked with a variety of small businesses in Broward County in dealing with their marketing problems. Johnson earned his Ph.D. in Business from Arizona State University in 1985.

Johnson has taught in higher education for over 19 years. During that time he has published widely in such journals as *The Journal of Applied Management and Entrepreneurship, International Journal of Value-Based Management, Journal of Food Service Research, Management Decision, Journal of Business and Industrial Marketing, Computers and Industrial Engineering International Journal, Marketing Education Review, The Journal of Marketing in Higher Education, Marketing News, International Business Chronicle, Arizona Business Education Journal, The Marketing Connection, Industrial Engineering International Journal,* and *Beverage World.* He has also coauthored three textbooks: *Total Quality in Marketing; Designing and Delivering Superior Customer Value: Concepts, Cases and Applications;* and *Business Process Orientation: Gaining the e-business Competitive Advantage,* published by CRC LLC St. Lucie Press, Boca Raton, FL. He has conducted international education seminars to business people from Brazil, Taiwan, Thailand, Indonesia, and China. He can be reached via e-mail at billyboy@huizenga.nova.edu.

 **William T. Walker, CFPIM, CIRM** is a supply chain architect for Agilent Technologies. He has worked both sides of the interface between supply chain management and new product development for over 33 years within Hewlett-Packard's Test & Measurement group, now the EPSG group of Agilent Technologies. Walker is accomplished in developing and optimizing international supply chains. He has firsthand experience in leading worldwide product line transfers and was instrumental in developing design for supply chain guidelines. He was awarded a U.S. patent for his early work in new product development. Walker is a Logistics Forum Top 20 Logistics Professional for 2000 award winner, a member of the Logistics Forum Advisory Board, and the ASCET Editorial Advisory Board. He co-developed the Principles of Supply Chain Management and authored APICS courseware on "Build a Competitive Infrastructure" and "Leverage Worldwide Logistics" (APICS CD-ROM #01640). He is co-author of *Supply Chain Management: Principles & Techniques for the Practitioner* (APICS Book #07015), and his definitions for "supply chain," "trading partner," and "nominal trading partner" are now published in the *APICS Dictionary, Tenth Edition.* His articles on defining supply chain management, numerous proceedings, and presentations on advance supply chain management topics have an international following. Walker is past president of the APICS Educational & Research Foundation, where he collaborated on setting education strat-

egy, and is a past APICS vice president of Education-Specific Industry Groups, where he held oversight on education developed for the Aerospace & Defense, Process, Repetitive, ReManufacturing, Small Manufacturing, and Textile/Apparel SIGs. He is APICS certified at the Fellow level, and holds BSEE and MSIE degrees from Lehigh University. He can be reached via e-mail at billwalker@primeisp.net.

# ACKNOWLEDGMENTS

The authors acknowledge and thank the following individuals for their help in completing this book:

Katie Kasper, Director DRK Research and Consulting LLC, for her help in the SCM Maturity Model and Extend Supply Chain research and her help in writing Chapter 5.

Dr. Archie Lockamy III, Professor of Operations Management at the Samford University School of Business, for his help in the research behind the Supply Chain Network Management Model in Chapter 8.

Ram Reddy, President of Tactica Consulting, for his contribution to the Case Study, Herding Cats Across the Supply Chain, which was based on his article.

Richard Chvala, formerly a member of Envera and now Senior Consultant at the Strategic Marketing Group, for his contribution to the Envera case study.

# 1

## INTRODUCTION

*It's not a hyperbole to say that the "network" is quickly emerging as the largest, most dynamic, restless, and sleepless marketplace of goods, services, and ideas the world has ever seen.*

**Lou Gerstner**
Former Chief Executive Officer
IBM

Traditionally, business-to-business (hereafter, B2B) supply chains were comprised of discrete activities, with each supply chain member "holding one leg of the elephant." Each member sought to add value for its immediate customer, yet with little regard for "total value effect" of the entire supply chain. The early days of supply chain management focused only on the management of suppliers, often by use of coercion, by the large companies that dominated the chain. Management's objective was to work with a supplier who could provide low-cost, high-quality, and on-time delivery.

However, the days when the focus was on managing the supply chain of a single company are over. Today, these processes can and often do transcend company boundaries and involve cross-company planning and implementation within the supply chain network. Figure 1.1 illustrates that the goal of supply chain management is to serve customer needs in the most effective and efficient way by shifting from control and efficiency to establishing knowledge and solutions-based supply chain relationships. Integrated supply chain management involves designing, managing, and integrating a company's own supply chain with that of its suppliers and customers. Integrated supply chain management encompasses all activities associated with the flow and transformation of products from the raw

1

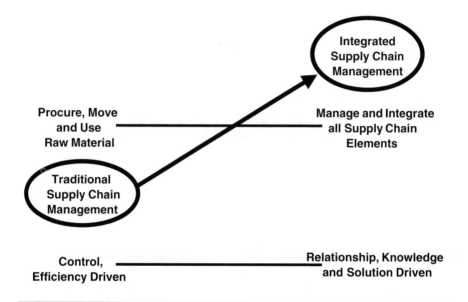

**Figure 1.1   Traditional vs. Integrated Supply Chain Management (Adapted from Srivastava, Shervani, and Fahey, *J. Mark,* 1999. With permission.)**

materials stage through delivery to the end customer.[1] Companies that will survive in the e-economy will have the ability to, according to Rosabeth Moss Kanter, "connect the dots" (i.e., constantly exploring the evolving partner universe and then linking the separate actors through seamless integration[2]). We agree with Kanter and would further maintain that businesses must view and manage their supply chain processes as chains of activity performed by different organizations across the network.

Interactions (i.e., the searching, coordinating, and monitoring that people and companies do when they exchange goods, services, and ideas) are the key activities of managing a supply chain or what is now becoming a trading partner network. They are the friction of the economy. They represent a major cost of managing a supply chain, representing 80% of a supply chain manager's activity. Overall, they represent 51% of total labor activity in the United States or one-third of Gross Domestic Product (GDP).[3] Supply chains and vertically integrated businesses, the ownership of suppliers and sometimes customers, were organized based upon transaction costs and efficacy of these interactions. Companies and entire industries were designed to minimize the total costs of transformation and interaction.

Now a major shift is under way, where computing, networking, interaction technology standards, as well as capacity and cost of interactions, have changed dramatically. The rate at which data can be transmitted has increased fourfold during the last decade and will increase 45-fold during the next. As a node is added in a network, the scope of interactions increases exponentially. It is estimated that these trends will increase overall interaction capability by a factor of ten and reduce interaction costs by a factor of five or more.[4] This has been an earthquake that has shaken every industry, causing major fractures. Global giants are breaking into pieces or unbundling into groups of outsourced business processes.[5] Companies that were once single entities are now networks of hundreds of independent trading partners. Virtual companies based on newly formed networks are also quickly forming, thus changing the competitive structure of almost every industry. The supply chain or trading partner network has now become the dominant organizing principle, not the corporation, joint venture, or keiretsu of the 1980s. This is what we call the networked economy.

Two "old economy" durable goods manufacturers, such as Whirlpool and Maytag, have already demonstrated, in a small way, the potential of supply chain network formation and integration.

Whirlpool, the world's largest appliance manufacturer, has begun introducing radically new measures that will strip out costs and improve supply chain performance. For example, at one of its dishwasher plants in Ohio, Whirlpool has installed an "Integrated Supplier Management" system based on IBM's technology. A network of its suppliers uses the Internet-based method to see what parts the factory needs, confirm that the factory has received the shipment, and determine when the payment will be received. The factory can use the system to conduct auctions on basic commodities, such as masking tape. Whirlpool figures that the 70% savings it expects to achieve will come from the reduction of interaction costs from this kind of supply chain network integration.

Maytag has also realized significant gains from supply chain network integration. For example, it has recently built a network with retailers and consumers in what Maytag calls a "seamless supply chain on the Internet." Using cart-to-cart technology, a consumer can visit Maytag.com, choose a product and then purchase it from any one of about 3,000 participating dealers. The reduction in interaction costs, or friction, is significant, not to mention the improved customer and retailer satisfaction.

These networks of companies are organized and lead by a network *orchestrator,* or the dominant company, usually the one close to the demand or customer. In the previous two examples, Maytag and Whirlpool were the orchestrators of the network. What holds these networks together is not cross-holdings of debt or equity, but an information standard that enables network participants to interact with significant cost savings. The network orchestrators set the standards and operating rules for the network and enforce them. In the best functioning networks, the orchestrators also ensure the distribution of rewards. This keeps the network together for the long term. These networks have been shown to earn significantly greater value than their peers, as well as outperform other top companies inside and outside of their industries.[6] Cisco, the most mature of the network "companies," has lead the building of the Cisco Connection On Line, a network of both customers and partners. Cisco's revenue per employee, one measure of interaction costs, is more than twice that of their industry peers and Cisco's market value, even in the market free fall of 2001 was over four times that of its industry peers.[7] The Cisco network alone is estimated to have produced financial benefits to Cisco, the orchestrator, of $1.3 billion dollars as of the end of 2000 and helped move customer satisfaction to an all-time high.[8] Over 90% of Cisco's business is transacted over the Internet, and 70% of service inquiries are resolved online.

The road to full supply chain network integration is often evolutionary rather than revolutionary. Phillippa Collins writes that, from an information perspective, supply chain integration includes four stages:

1. Push out static information one way over a Web browser or other form of communication
2. Dynamic information, but still one way
3. Dynamic data in both directions and some integration in terms of applications being used with integration into back-office systems
4. Full network integration — two-way flow of information, which is fully integrated into the back-office systems, and into the supplier and customer[9]

From an information standpoint, our research has suggested that most industry supply chains today have progressed only to Stage 2, with only a handful reaching Stage 3 and the rare few reaching Stage 4. At this level, all key business processes are online and aligned within the network. Interoperability is enabled by process standardization and information standards, such as electronic data interchange (EDI), and Internet-based standards, such as ebXML and RosettaNet,[10] but information and system integration is not yet in place to build a supply chain network. Organizational learning can play a key role in facilitating this integration.

## USING LEARNING TO SPEED THE PROCESS OF SUPPLY CHAINS OPTIMIZATION

Organizations that optimize their supply chains can reduce costs with suppliers, streamline internal processes, and better serve their customers. Organizational learning is a powerful tool for promoting supply chain integration. One learning organization, Strategic Management Group (SMG), has launched a computer simulation, delivered via classroom or Internet learning, to speed the business process orientation of companies striving to advance their supply chains.

Developed in partnership with supply chain consultants Genesis Solutions, SMG's *Optimizing the Supply Chain* solution supports cost-effective implementation of supply chain initiatives and faster adoption of enterprise-wide organizational challenge.

As companies launch initiatives to improve supply chain operations, there is often a gap in understanding between the executives initiating the change and the people directly affected by it. Closing the gap increases the likelihood of a successful implementation, shortens project cycle time, and reduces project risk.

*Optimizing the Supply Chain* helps organizations align around supply chain best practices, including

- Strategic sourcing and supplier management
- Operations and logistics
- Customer relationship management and channels
- Information technology
- Change management

A major challenge facing supply chain network actors is the multiple levels of integration required to maximize network effectiveness and efficiency. Alignment of strategies is as critical as ever and common goals and objectives need to be broadly accepted by members of the entire network trading partners. The esprit de corps so desperately sought by leaders of single corporations now must be built across dozens of companies. The business processes that were difficult to integrate across the internal functions of a single company now must cross multiple company boundaries. Interfunctional cooperation, a major issue with business process performance, must now be intercompany cooperation.

Business process orientation (BPO), a concept that has been shown in our earlier book to improve interfunctional cooperation and in turn business process performance, can be applied to this new organizing form, the network. BPO has been shown to increase levels of esprit de corps within companies, and it can also have this effect within a network of companies.[11] We believe, and demonstrate in this book, that BPO is a key ingredient in building the new networked businesses and is a key to the networked economy.

Alignment is not just between information systems and process activities. The BPO components of process jobs, structures, measures, and values and beliefs need to be aligned between network members as well. This BPO alignment between functions within companies has been shown to lead to improvements in interfunctional cooperation, company performance, and esprit de corps, and will have the same effect within the network.

However, as with the Collins information integration stages, building a network that is aligned and integrated at the process and organizational level must come in stages. In Chapter 4 we profile firms and their supply chain network integration stages when we review the concept of supply chain maturity and BPO.

In order to achieve their intended effectiveness efficiencies, these networks must interoperate on many levels. Alignment of strategies is as critical as ever, and common goals and objectives need to be broadly accepted by members of the entire network trading partners. The esprit de corps so desperately sought by leaders of single corporations now must be built across dozens of companies. The business processes that were difficult to integrate across the internal functions of a single company now must cross multiple company boundaries. Interfunctional cooperation, a major issue with business process performance, must now be intercompany cooperation.

Business process orientation (BPO), a concept that, in our earlier book, has been shown to improve interfunctional cooperation and, in turn, business process performance, can be applied to this new organizing form — the network. BPO has been shown to increase levels of esprit de corps within a company, and it can also have this effect within a network of companies.[11] We believe, and demonstrate in this book, that BPO is a key ingredient in building the new, networked businesses and a key to the networked economy.

Alignment is not just between information systems and process activities. The BPO components of process jobs, structures, measures, and values and beliefs need to be aligned between network members as well. This BPO alignment between functions within a company has been shown to lead to improvements in interfunctional cooperation, company performance, and esprit de corps, and will have the same effect within the network.

As with the Collins information integration stages, however, building a network that is aligned and integrated at the process and organizational level must come in stages. In Chapter 4, we profile firms and their supply chain network integration stages when we review the concept of supply chain maturity and BPO.

## SUMMARY

As we enter the 21st century networked economy, dramatic shifts in technology and network cost and capabilities are changing the dynamics of the economy. Industries, companies, and supply chains are fracturing, unbundling, and reforming based on the new economics of interactions. Tenfold interaction capability increases and fivefold reductions in interaction costs are today's reality, with exponential improvements predicted for the future.

New ways to organize and manage supply chains and business relationships, based upon these interaction economics, are being deployed that are drastically changing the competitive landscape. Integrated, interoperating trading partner networks with thousands of independent companies are operating and acting as one.

We believe that corporate survival in the networked economy will depend both on the effectiveness of internal processes and their integration and alignment with supply chain partners and customers. Cross-network supply chain management will serve as the coordinating mechanism for process integration among supply chain partners where "fit" forecloses competition. Competitors can match individual processes or activities but cannot match the integration or fit of these activities within a cohesive network. In order to move forward in building a networked economy business or an e-corporation, however, the network must first commit to becoming business process oriented *across the network*. This commitment is critical because it will guide the hundreds of decisions about jobs, investments, and process ownership, which are key ingredients of customer focus and accountability.

Finally, with the future competitive landscape shifting from competition among companies to competition among trading partner networks, understanding and mastering process design and change will become more critical than ever. To succeed, companies will have to weave their key business processes into hard-to-imitate strategic capabilities that distinguish them from their competitors in the eyes of customers. This was the premise of our earlier book *Business Process Orientation: Gaining the e-Business Competitive Advantage*. This new book should help practitioners to "connect the dots" by offering insights on how to achieve greater integration within their supply chain networks and realize the performance possible with today's interaction economics.

This book provides a conceptual foundation in the first four chapters by reviewing the concept of BPO in Chapter 2, describing how BPO relates to supply chain management in Chapter 3, and presenting the concept of supply chain network maturity in Chapter 4.

Chapter 5 demonstrates the impact and opportunities of BPO in supply chain networks by reporting the results of ongoing benchmarking research on extended supply chain networks. Chapter 6 highlights supply chain opportunities in the networked, frictionless economy.

Chapter 7 begins the "how to" section of the book by offering a framework for organizing a supply chain network and classifying trading partners. Chapter 8 presents a model to use in building networked supply chains and offers situational factors that influence the success of these networks.

Finally, we conclude with case studies and tools for analyzing supply chain networks, contained in the appendices, to aid both the instructor and practitioner in the application of the BPO concept.

The goal of this book is to build upon the foundations of the first book and provide strategies, tactics, and methods that help make the network economy everything envisioned by the founders of the Internet, along with our vision of what BPO can help achieve. This combined vision is one of connected communities with a common purpose and high levels of esprit de corps, working together on activities of value, and sharing their knowledge as well as sharing in the rewards of this community.

## REFERENCES

1. Handfield, R. and Nicholas, E., Jr. (1998). *Introduction to Supply Chain Management*. NJ: Prentice Hall.
2. Kanter, R.M. (2001). *e-Volve*. Boston: Harvard Business School Press.
3. Butler, P. (1997). A revolution in interaction, *The McKinsey Quarterly*, 1.
4. Butler, P. (1997). A revolution in interaction, *The McKinsey Quarterly*.
5. Hagel, J. and Singer, M. (March/April 1999). Unbundling the corporation, *Harvard Bus. Review*.
6. Hacki, R. and Lighton, J. (July 2001). The future of the network company, *The McKinsey Quarterly*.
7. Hacki, R. and Lighton, J. (July 2001). The future of the network company, *The McKinsey Quarterly*.
8. Grosvenor, F. and Austin, T. (July/August 2001). Cisco's eHub Initiative, *Supply Chain Manage. Review*, 28.
9. Collins, P. (June 2000). E-logistics 2000, re-thinking the supply chain, *Manage. Services*, 44, 6.
10. www.rosettanet.org.
11. McCormack, K. and Johnson, W. (2000), *Business Process Orientation: Gaining the e-business Competitive Advantage*, Delray Beach, FL: St. Lucie Press.

# 2

---

# BUSINESS PROCESS ORIENTATION — FROM VERTICAL INTEGRATION TO NETWORKED COMMUNITIES

Traditionally, auto companies dating back to the River Rouge plant of Ford Motor Company, put lumber, steel, and leather in one end and took Model Ts out the other. The idea was to have a very big company, with a lot of factories and a big capital base. Companies like that could control all aspects of their production and make what they wanted with high levels of productivity and reduced costs. The Rouge was the largest single manufacturing complex in the United States, with peak employment of about 120,000 during World War II. Here, Henry Ford achieved self-sufficiency and vertical integration in automobile production — a continuous workflow from iron ore and other raw materials to finished automobiles. The complex included dock facilities, blast furnaces, open-hearth steel mills, foundries, a rolling mill, metal stamping facilities, an engine plant, a glass manufacturing building, and a tire plant.

For a time, the vertically integrated structure worked well for auto manufacturers in order to achieve scale economies and productivity; but these companies have squeezed out about as much productivity as they can. Automotive companies, which were once original equipment manufacturers, have now become vehicle brand owners. They have started outsourcing the parts (in Ford's case, it now buys two-thirds of its auto components), and they have found that, in some cases, they can outsource the manufacturing of the whole car! These value-added communities are external networks that cover both the supply chain and processes, such as financial, marketing, accounting, and human resources services.

Moreover, very sophisticated businesses have been created around supplying these services.

One outsourced company makes the car's wheels, another makes the engine, another makes the seats, and another makes the body — all of which flow through the value-added community that the auto company created. In the end, the auto company and the consumer both benefit. The automobile consumers get a better-quality product, delivered precisely when and how they want it, at a much better cost. The auto company can respond to customers far more quickly than ever before.

We strongly believe that the "glue" for building these networked communities is a business process orientation (BPO), a concept introduced in our earlier book, which serves as a powerful organizing principle for firms competing in the networked economy. We presented empirical evidence in our earlier work showing that building a process-oriented organization results in improved business performance. BPO is not simply a new business fad, but an entirely new way of thinking or viewing an organization. Nor is it simply a new business operations strategy, but instead a broad framework for organizing work and information flows that ultimately help an organization build superior customer value.

This chapter presents a history and overview of the BPO concept along with a discussion of how a BPO is linked to survival in the e-business, networked world of today.

## AN OVERVIEW OF THE BPO CONCEPT

The orientation of a firm or an organized group of firms, known as the network, has a base point of reference for the people in the organization that is a critical aspect of all the business drivers. This "way of looking at the world" drives strategy, decisionmaking, investments, and selection of employees and leaders. A study of U.K. manufacturers attempting to examine business orientations in these firms identified the following types and descriptions of orientations:[1]

**Production:** Concentrate on reducing costs, achieving high production efficiency and productivity, and increasing production capacity.

**Product:** Make products with good quality and features, improve them over time, and then try to sell them.

**Selling:** Concentrate on promoting and selling what we can make.

**Market:** Identify changing customer wants, and develop products to serve the customer better than the competitors.

**Competitors:** Identify the closest rivals, learn their strengths and weaknesses, forecast their behaviors, and develop marketing strategies to capitalize on their weaknesses.

Business process orientation (BPO) was significantly missing from the previous list. Why? Did this orientation not exist, or was it just not defined enough to measure and talk about?

Most of what has been written about business process orientation during the last two decades is in the form of success stories concerning new forms of organizations. Although, in most cases, empirical evidence was lacking, several examples of these new forms had emerged during this period that were presented as high-performance, process-oriented organizations needed to compete in the future. Leading thought leaders, such as Deming, Porter, Davenport, Short, Hammer, Byrne, Imai, Drucker, Rummler-Brache, and Melan, have all defined what they view as the new model of the organization. Developing this model requires a new approach and a new way of thinking about the organization, which will result in dramatic business performance improvements. This "new way of thinking" or "viewing" the organization has been generally described as business process orientation.

During the 1980s, Michael Porter introduced the concepts of interoperability across the value chain and horizontal organization as major strategic issues within firms.[2] Edward Deming developed the "Deming Flow Diagram" depicting the horizontal connections across a firm, from the customer to the supplier, as a process that could be measured and improved like any other process.[3] In 1990, two researchers, Thomas Davenport and James Short, proposed that a process orientation in an organization was a key component for success.[4] In 1993, Michael Hammer, who led the "reengineering" craze of the 1990s, also presented the BPO concept as an essential ingredient of a successful reengineering effort. Hammer described the development of a customer-focused, strategic business process-based organization enabled by rethinking the assumptions in a process-oriented way and utilizing information technology as a key enabler.[5] Dr. Hammer offers reengineering as a strategy to overcome the problematic cross-functional activities that are presenting major performance issues to firms. The apparent conflict between a functional focus (who I report to) versus a horizontal focus (who I provide value to) is offered by Hammer as being brought back in balance by adding a BPO to the organization.

As the "connectivity" craze of this decade (virtual corporations, networked organizations) replaces the reengineering craze of the 1990s, business process performance and the horizontal nature of corporations has risen to a new level of importance. Companies are extending outside of their legal boundaries and building networks as a normal way of organizing. Not only vertical integration but partnering, functional outsourcing, business process outsourcing, alliances, and joint ventures are all yesterday's requirements for success. The new realities of business require greater flexibility, responsiveness, and lower transaction costs, not only within but also across companies, without the leverage of company ownership. A BPO helps firms realize these goals through superior intra- and interprocess integration.

## FUNCTIONAL ORIENTATION: HOW DID WE GET HERE?

A functional orientation, or the focus of people within an organization on their departments, their bosses, and only their tasks within their departments, still dominates the thinking within organizations today. What lead up to this functional mentality in business?

Let us start at the beginning. Adam Smith first described the concept that industrial work should be broken into its simplest tasks. This became the basic organization model of business for almost 200 years. The modern business enterprise has gone through only two major evolutions since the Civil War in the United States.[6] Around the turn of the century, management came to be viewed as work in its own right. Up until that time, management was indistinguishable from ownership. J.P. Morgan, Andrew Carnegie, and J.D. Rockefeller began the restructuring of the railroads and American industry using the basic principles of Adam Smith and the new concept of management work or hierarchy. Twenty years later, DuPont began the second evolution by restructuring the family business into the modern corporation. Henry Ford, followed by Alfred Sloan, began to redesign their companies based on a business model characterized by command and control, centralization, central staff, the concept of personnel management, and budgets and controls. This model was tightly defined and controlled, ultimately giving rise to the functionally oriented organization model of today.

Business performance, as defined by return on assets (ROA), was achieved with this model by leveraging size and division of labor. This allowed organizations to maintain highly paid, scarce skills as well as effectively gather and deploy natural resources and labor — two major success factors for enterprises of that time. The hierarchy of skilled managers was necessary to coordinate the functional activities, manage the information flow, and interface with the other functions in the organization. The better the focus and coordination of the company resources, the more profitable the business.

The organizational chart in Figure 2.1 best illustrates the functional view. This chart shows which people have been grouped together for operating efficiency as well as reporting relationships. What is not shown is the customer and the "what," "why," and "how" of the business. The value-added work that is performed to satisfy a customer is invisible in this view. "Out of sight, out of mind" is an old saying that describes the

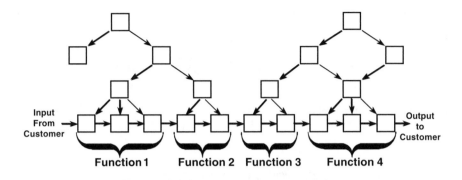

**Figure 2.1    The Typical Organizational Chart**

problem. Using this as the primary way to view an organization resulted in organizations that were focused on the boss and the functional task, yet rarely were they characterized by internal coordination of functions working together to satisfy customers.

Thus, the greatest opportunity for performance improvements lies in the functional interfaces — the points where the "baton" is being passed from one function to another. Phrases such as "fall between the cracks" or "somebody's dropped the ball" are commonly used in today's organization to describe a missed hand-off between functions. This often results in poor quality, high costs, and dissatisfied customers, not to mention the frustration and poor morale of the people that work within these organizations.

Too often, the focus of these organizations is on power and authority, not the activities that bring value to the customer from the customer's perspective. Turf wars between functional kingdoms often appear to be the priority in functionally oriented organizations instead of doing what is needed to serve the customer.

## PROCESS AND VALUE CREATION

The concept of improving these functional interactions by "viewing" the business differently is evident in Edward Deming's philosophy, captured by "The Deming Flow Diagram" (see Figure 2.2).[7]

The flow diagram takes a BPO and describes a business as a continuous process connected on one end with the supplier and on the other to the customer. A feedback loop of design and redesign of the product also connects to both customers and suppliers. Deming's fourteen points and elimination of the seven diseases describe the strategies for optimization of the flow diagram and, therefore, the creation of superior customer value and superior profitability.

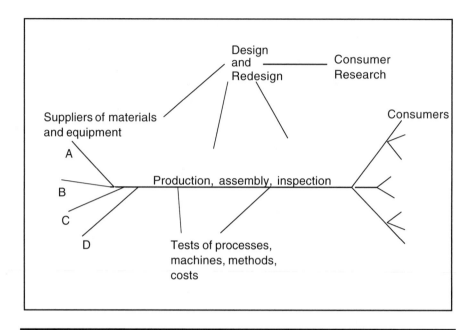

**Figure 2.2 The Deming Flow Diagram (Adapted from *Out of Chaos,* Walton, 1986. With permission.)**

Porter introduced the "value chain" concept as a systematic way of examining all the activities a firm performs and how they interact to provide competitive advantage (see Figure 2.3). This chain is composed of "strategically relevant activities" that create value for a firm's buyers. Competitive advantage comes from the value a firm is able to create for its buyers that exceeds the firm's cost of creating it.

A firm gains competitive advantage by performing these strategically important activities more cheaply or better than competitors. According to Porter, a firm is profitable if the value it commands exceeds the costs involved in creating the product.

A major way to develop competitive advantage in this value chain is described by Porter as managing linkages. Linkages are relationships between the way one value activity is performed and the cost of performance of another. Optimization and coordination approaches to these linkages can lead to competitive advantage. The ability to coordinate linkages often reduces cost or enhances differentiation. The ability to recognize and manage linkages, which often cut across conventional organizational lines as well as legal company boundaries, can yield a significant competitive advantage. The linkages between supplier and customer value chains can also be a source of competitive advantage. Competitors can usually match individual processes in the firm's value

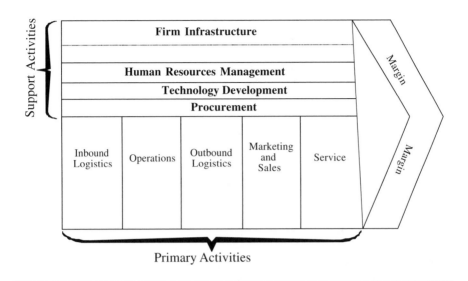

**Figure 2.3 The Generic Value Chain (Adapted from Porter, M.E. (1985).** *Competitive Advantage: Creating & Sustaining Superior Performance.* **New York, NY: The Free Press. With permission.)**

chain, but cannot necessarily match the "integration" of these activities across the industry supply chain.

The organizational structure often defines the linkages in a value chain. Integrating mechanisms must be established to ensure that the required coordination takes place. Information is essential for the optimization of these linkages and is rarely collected or connected throughout the chain. Porter suggested that a firm might be able to design an organization structure that corresponds to the value chain, and thus improving a firm's ability to create and sustain competitive advantage through coordination, minimization, and optimization of linkages.

The value chain is an important tool for helping organizations to identify the processes that are most likely to produce added value and optimize the linkages among those processes. A closer match between organizational structure and how processes are organized will promote greater internal coordination and a more positive organizational culture. A BPO — how processes are viewed, measured, and managed — helps firms get closer to both their internal and external customers. Well-designed processes can unlock tremendous value not only in a firm's internal value chain, but also across the industry supply chain, leading to more committed customers.

The Porter value chain, and the suggestion that a firm organized around this structure can gain a strategic competitive advantage, positioned the concept of BPO firmly as a key competitive strategy.

## BUSINESS PROCESS ORIENTATION IN THE 1990S — TECHNOLOGY ENABLEMENT

Hammer started the reengineering movement in 1990 when he declared war on the old organizational model with his article "Reengineering work: Don't automate, obliterate," published in the *Harvard Business Review*.[10] His premise was that the old model, built in the 19th century, is no longer relevant and something entirely different was needed.

This new model would be accomplished by looking at fundamental processes of the business from a cross-functional perspective and enabling a radical new way of operating using information and organizational technology. Radically new processes would drive dramatic changes in jobs and organizational structures. This, in turn, would require radical changes in the management and measurement systems that would shape the values and beliefs of the organization. These values and beliefs of the organization would finally support and enable new business processes by reflecting the important performance measures of the new process.

Hammer defined a business process as a collection of activities that takes one or more kinds of input and creates an output that is of value to the customer. A reengineered business is composed of strategic, customer-focused processes that start with the customer and emphasize outcome, not mechanisms. This is the heart of the enterprise: how a company creates value and represents the real work.

Process thinking is described as cross-functional, outcome-oriented, and essential to customer orientation, quality, flexibility, speed, service, and reengineering. A company is defined not by its products and services, but by its processes. Managing a business means managing its processes. These processes are classified as value adding, enabling, asset creating, and governing. Figure 2.4 is an example of a company, Texas Instruments Semiconductor Division, viewed as a process according to Dr. Hammer.[9]

The construction of this map not only creates a process "view" of a business but it creates a process vocabulary that is essential for cooperation and coordination within the firm. This map makes business processes visible that were once invisible.

Information technology enables the new organization to use the organizational technology components to build a high-performance, customer-focused, empowered, flat, results-oriented, continuous-improvement-oriented, and process-oriented organization. This organization model, according to Hammer, would result in dramatic increases in business performance and profitability.

Davenport provided the foundation for this technology-oriented area of investigation by describing a revolutionary approach to information technology in business — how a business was viewed, structured, and

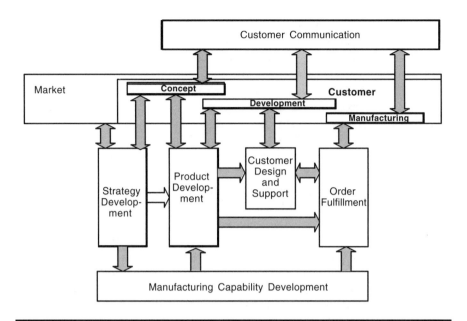

**Figure 2.4 Texas Instruments High-Level Business Process Map (Adapted from Hammer, M. and Champy, J. (1993). *Reengineering the Corporation: A Manifesto for Business Revolution*, first ed. New York: HarperBusiness. With permission.)**

improved.[10] Davenport suggested that business must be viewed according to key processes, not in terms of functions, divisions, or products. One of Davenport's major propositions was that the adoption of a process view of the business with the application of innovation to key processes will result in major improvements in process cost, time, quality, flexibility, service levels, and other business objectives, thus leading to increased profitability. Davenport further defined a process perspective as a horizontal view of business that cuts across the organization, with product inputs at the beginning and outputs and customers at the end.

Building on the work of Davenport and others, we proposed in our earlier book that firms adopt a process orientation, beginning first with a process view. A process view facilitates the implementation of cross-functional solutions and the willingness to search for process innovation, thus achieving a high degree of improvement in the management and coordination of functional interdependencies. A process view is the first key step in building a BPO. It removes the "out of sight, out of mind" factor. Viewing the organization in terms of processes and adopting process innovation, as explained by Davenport, inevitably entails cross-functional and cross-organizational change. Just the identification and definition of these processes often leads to innovative ways of structuring work.

BPO also involves elements of structure, focus, measurement, ownership, and customers. The functional structure has hand-offs between functions that are frequently uncoordinated. The functional structure also does not define complete responsibility and ownership of the entire process. No one is managing the entire ship, only pieces of it. This is expensive, time-consuming, and does not serve customers well. Davenport defines a process-oriented structure as deemphasizing the functional structure of business. A process structure, which is a dynamic view of organizational "connections," orders these processes in such a way as to deliver superior value.

Clearly defined process owners are also positioned as a critical dimension of the new model and are the individuals charged with acting as customer advocates. Process ownership is also discussed as an additional or alternative dimension of the formal organization structure. The difficulty in process ownership is that strategic business processes usually cut across boundaries of organizational power and authority as defined by the formal functional organization chart. Davenport suggested that, during periods of radical process change, process ownership should be granted precedence. This will, in theory, grant the process owner legitimate power and authority across the interfunctional boundaries.

Finally, processes can and should be measured. Processes, unlike hierarchies, have cost, time, output quality, and customer satisfaction measurements and emphasize *how* work is done, instead of which products or services are delivered. Davenport's process approach also implies adopting the customer's point of view, and a measure of customer satisfaction with the process output is probably *the* priority measure of any process.

From an information technology perspective, the key enabler of Davenport's proposal is that the interfaces between functional or product units can be improved or eliminated, and sequential flows across functions can be made parallel through rapid and broad movement of information.

During the 1990s, many studies examined the issue of reengineering and business processes. The focus on business improvement during this decade was clearly on business process reengineering, that is, reorienting the organization toward processes, customers, and outcomes as opposed to hierarchies. In most of the studies of technology-oriented reengineering, reorienting of the people and the organization was the major challenge and opportunity for business improvement. In a 1996 research study, Coombs and Hull reported the emergence of a "business process paradigm," a heterogeneous collection of theories, concepts, practices for analyzing organizations, and practices for managing organizations.[11] The authors suggested that, although these are as yet heterogeneous, they all share a common view of a fundamental change in managing and thinking about organizations. They are distinguished from previous forms of management and analysis in that the focus is no longer on optimizing the specialist functions within the organization (e.g., operations, marketing, human resource management), but shifts the focus to ways of understanding and managing the horizontal flows within and between organizations.

## BUSINESS PROCESS ORIENTATION IN THE 1990S — ORGANIZATIONAL DESIGN

John Byrne's powerful article comparing vertical and horizontal corporations was instrumental in showing the need for research in process design.[12] Byrne described the vertical organization as one where members look up to bosses instead of out to customers. Loyalty and commitment is given to functional fiefdoms, not the overall corporation and its goals. Too many layers of management cause slow decision making and lead to high coordination costs. The answer, according to Byrne, is the *horizontal corporation*. This type of corporation uses reengineering or process redesign is used to achieve greater efficiency and productivity. Bryne popularized the term "horizontal organization" and provided a prescriptive definition of a business process oriented model. Byrne indicates that companies such as AT&T, Dupont, General Electric, and Motorola are all moving toward this model, along with many other firms.

What does the horizontal corporation look like? First, both hierarchy and functions are eliminated, and employees work together in multidisciplinary teams that perform core processes such as product development. It is suggested that an organization of this type would only have three or four layers of management between the chairman and the "staffers" in a given process. Dupont's goal is to get everyone focused on the business as a system in which the functions are seamless in order to eliminate the "disconnects and hand-offs." Former General Electric Chairman, John Welch, spoke of building a "boundary-less" company to reduce costs, shorten cycle time, and increase responsiveness to customers. Managers in this organization would have "multiple competencies" instead of narrow specialties, and would function in a group to allocate resources and ensure coordination of processes and programs. Byrne sited numerous examples of companies that are organizing around market-driven business processes and realizing cost reductions of 30% or more.

Other organizational design strategies were based on the premise that organizations behave as adaptive processing systems that convert various resource inputs into product and service outputs, which they provide to receiving systems or markets. These organizations are based upon process-oriented structures, measures, rewards, and resource allocation, especially investments.

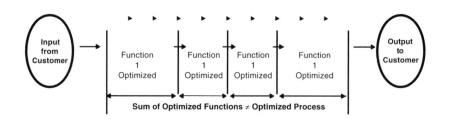

**Figure 2.5 The "Silo" Suboptimization Phenomenon**

Rummler and Brache, leaders in the process-oriented performance management field, suggested that the investment and budgeting policies designed by using a functional orientation often resulted in functional optimization that suboptimizes the organization, and business process as a whole.[13] A person in a functional silo will focus on what is best for his or her function, many times at the expense of other functions. This means that while the individual function benefits, oftentimes the firm as a whole loses. Figure 2.5 visually depicts Rummler and Brache's hypothesis of suboptimization.

To address the suboptimization phenomenon, Rummler and Brache suggested organizing jobs, structures, measures, investments, budgets, and rewards around horizontal processes. This process-oriented organizational design is offered as the improved model of business performance. In fact, during the 1990s, Rummler and Brache built a sizable consulting practice by helping firms implement this model.

Along this same line, Melan, from IBM, published several articles in the quality literature suggesting that the principles of process management can be used successfully in manufacturing.[14] Melan suggested "viewing the operation as a set of interrelated work tasks with prescribed inputs and outputs." This provides a structure and framework for understanding the process and relationships, and for applying the process-oriented tools used successfully in manufacturing.

Various tools have been introduced that facilitate a process orientation. They include:

Process measurement and control
Statistical process control
Cycle time analysis and optimization
Line balancing
Variability analysis and reduction
Continuous process improvement

However, these tools are successful only when a process-oriented framework is first in place.

## BPO: FROM CONCEPT TO MEASUREMENT

As previously discussed, the virtues of process orientation have been widely reported. When we began our research, however, we found that the concept had only been generally defined, and had not been measured or tested in order to statistically determine its impact on an organization. We concluded that, although there appears to be a general consensus as to the key elements of business process orientation, no one to date had developed and tested this concept.

If you cannot clearly define, describe, and measure something, you will not know if you ever have it. If you cannot determine the impact of it, you may not even be sure you want it. In other words, you cannot manage what you cannot measure. With this in mind, we undertook a multiyear research study in 1996 to develop and test a valid and reliable BPO measure, as well as confirm the impacts on an organization.[15]

We began by reviewing popular business press and interviewing experienced practitioners and experts, both in the United States and Europe, to help define BPO and its major components. Various statistical techniques (e.g., domain sampling, coefficient alpha analysis, and factor analysis) were used to produce a more parsimonious measure of BPO and to elicit its major dimensions.

We used key informant research (selecting participants based on their understanding of a subject) to investigate the process orientation of selected organizations in the United States during 1998. Once the data were collected and analyzed, a consensus of two definitions of BPO appeared to surface:

*An organization that is oriented toward processes, outcomes, and customers as opposed to hierarchies*

*An organization that emphasizes process and a process-oriented way of thinking*

These two definitions were then combined to most accurately represent the BPO construct. Thus, the final definition of BPO that would be used in all future research can be stated as follows:

*An organization that, in all its thinking, emphasizes process as opposed to hierarchies with special emphasis on outcomes and customer satisfaction*

The results of our research produced three key elements of BPO:

**Process View** — the cross-functional, horizontal picture of a business involving elements of structure, focus, measurement, ownership, and customers

**Process Management and Measurement** — measures that include aspects of the process such as output quality, cycle time, process cost, and variability compared with the traditional accounting measures

**Process Jobs** — jobs that focus on process, not functions, and are cross-functional in responsibility (e.g., "product development process owner" instead of "research manager")

Our goal was to measure BPO within organizations as well as its impact on organizational performance, which required a valid and reliable measure. Factor analysis techniques were used during this initial stage to produce a final BPO measurement or survey instrument (see Appendix A). The resulting survey instrument consists of the three elements listed previously and questions that relate to each element. Process view (PV) has three questions, process management and measurement (PM) has five questions and process jobs (PJ) has three questions.

Why are these 11 questions necessary? Two answers exist — one statistical and one intuitive. The statistical answer is that factor analysis, of course, is a well-proven data reduction and summarization technique used to analyze the interrelationships among a large number of variables; it is then used to mathematically identify the common underlying dimensions (factors). This technique gets at the statistical "root" of the concept.

In order to identify these final 11 questions using statistical analysis, we started with approximately 200 questions from five different categories, which represented the proposed components of BPO:

1. A *process view* of the business
2. *Structures* that match these processes
3. *Jobs* that operate these processes
4. *Management and measurement systems* that direct and assess these processes
5. Customer-focused, empowerment, and continuous-improvement-oriented *values and beliefs* (culture)

Factor analysis was performed on the data and the component categories were reduced to three, thus reducing the questions to the final survey count of 11. After confirmatory factor analysis, the final questions were also retested using coefficient alpha measures, a statistical test used to examine the validity of a measure.

As for the "intuitive" aspect of the final questions, we had several BPO experts from around the world look at the "face validity" or "Does this make sense?" aspect of the final questions. All the experts felt that the final questions and categories represented BPO.

A Likert scale was used for this survey instrument in order to measure agreement with the question in regard to the participant's organization. This scale consists of the following:

1. Completely disagree
2. Mostly disagree
3. Neither agree nor disagree
4. Mostly agree
5. Completely agree
6. Cannot judge

In our research using this BPO instrument, participants are asked to respond to statements to which company personnel could agree or disagree on varying levels. For example, under "Process Jobs," participants were asked to indicate their level of agreement on the statement: "Jobs are multidimensional and not just simple tasks."

## THE IMPACTS OF BPO

In order to further test the instrument and answer the question of whether BPO is related to improved organizational performance and long-term health, four potential outcome variables were selected (see Figure 2.6: overall business performance, interfunctional conflict, interdepartmental connectedness, and esprit de corps. These factors were selected based upon their use in previous research, where they had also been significantly defined and measured.[16]

The internal organizational impacts of BPO proposed are *interfunctional conflict* and *interdepartmental connectedness*. Interfunctional conflict is defined as tension among departments arising from the incompatibility of actual or desired responses. Interdepartmental connectedness is the degree of formal and informal direct contact among employees across departments. An increase in conflict across functions is thought to be a negative internal organization factor. Incompatible goals and tension between individuals in different functions, such as sales and manufacturing, have been shown to negatively impact organizational performance. An increase in connectedness across departments, as measured by the easy flow of communication between departments and a low level of tension between members of each department, has been shown to contribute to improved organizational performance.[16] Implement-

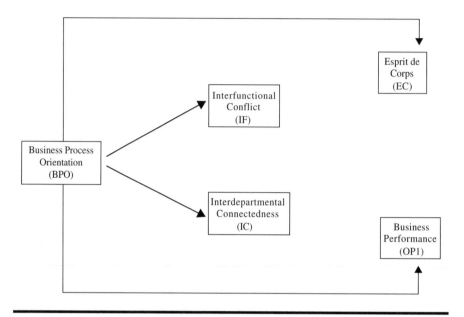

**Figure 2.6   BPO and the Impacts on an Organization**

ing BPO as a way of organizing and operating in an organization can improve internal coordination and break down the functional silos that exist in most companies. This increase in cooperation and decrease in conflict has been shown by research to improve both the short-term and long-term performance of an organization

Organizational performance can vary greatly among companies competing in similar markets. Moreover, industries apply different performance metrics, making cross-industry comparisons difficult. For example, the retail industry uses rapid inventory turns as a key performance metric in measuring good performance, while the defense industry defines good performance as something very different. For this reason, we selected a self-report rating system to measure overall performance of the organizations studied. Key informant self-ratings closely approximate quantitative measures of performance and can also be used to compare organizations in different industries. Research has also shown that key informants can accurately and honestly position their organizations on an objective performance scale.[18] Using a 5-point rating scale, each participant in our research was asked to rate their organization's performance as well as that of their competitors.

Esprit de corps within an organization is a well-known indicator of organizational health and a predicator of superior business performance. It has been said to be the glue that holds a group together. The term esprit de corps means "solidarity," not "team spirit" as is commonly thought, and is defined as:[19] a set of enthusiastically shared feelings, beliefs, and values about group membership and performance.

Esprit de corps manifests itself as a strong desire to achieve a common goal even in the face of hostility. At the work group level, esprit de corps is said to exist when individuals in the same department or team enthusiastically share values and goals.

Esprit de corps is strongly associated with the military. In the book *Battle Studies, Ancient and Modern,* the famous French infantry officer Colonel Ardant du Picq said that official discipline can be replaced by social controls exhibited by a small group of soldiers over time and

> *... includes confidence in [his] comrades and the fear of reproaches and retaliations if he [the soldier] abandons them in danger; his desire to go where others go without trembling more than they ... in a word esprit de corps.*[20]

If esprit de corps is a concept powerful enough to make soldiers go into battle knowing their odds of survival are strongly against them, then it can be a powerful alignment mechanism strengthening any organization.

Esprit de corps has been the subject of thousands of leadership books, tapes, and speeches. Unfortunately, the restructuring and downsizing of the 1980s and 1990s destroyed this spirit, and organizations have spent many millions of dollars in an attempt to rebuild it. Many leadership heroes and gurus have earned their reputations by building this spirit of enthusiasm and credit their successes as a leaders to this ability. Witness Southwest Airlines, the number one airline in almost every performance and customer satisfaction measure. A strong esprit de corps instilled by its charismatic leader, Herb Kelleher, has made Southwest profitable for 26 straight years with an average earnings before interest, taxes, depreciation, and amortization (EBITDA) margin of 22.6%.[21] In order to gather data for our research, we administered the BPO measurement instrument to over 100 domestic and international manufacturing companies. These firms represented a broad cross-section of industries, ranging in size from approximately $100 million to several billion in annual sales.

The results of our research (see Figure 2.7), along with the details contained in our earlier book on BPO, demonstrated that BPO is critical in reducing conflict and encouraging greater connectedness within an organization while improving business performance. Moreover, companies with strong measures of BPO achieved better overall business performance.

More important, our research also clearly demonstrated that high BPO led to a more positive corporate climate, including higher esprit de corps and connectedness as well as less internal conflict. Companies structured into broad process teams instead of narrow functional departments have

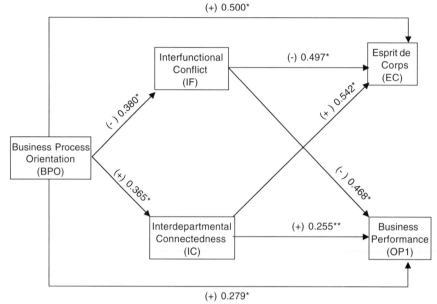

**Figure 2.7   Regression results — Impacts of BPO on an Organization**

less internal conflict and stronger spirit. This spirit, esprit de corps, is the competitive engine for any organization. This was a very powerful finding and answers the "Why BPO?" question.

## BUSINESS PROCESS ORIENTATION AND THE NETWORKED CORPORATION

The completion of the interstate highway system in the United States ushered in the age of transportation by significantly reducing the transportation "friction;" it made every business a national business. What the interstate highway system did for public transportation, the Internet has done for commerce. This universal information network has significantly reduced interaction friction; companies and markets are now global, and every customer is an informed consumer. The Internet is connecting customers, suppliers, and resellers in ways not even imagined a few years ago. In short, the Internet has helped usher in the new digital economy, with new rules and new realities.

The Internet has the capacity to change everything and is doing so at a far greater speed than the other "disruptive" technologies of the 20th century, such as electricity, the telephone, and the automobile. "In five years' time, all companies will be Internet companies or they won't be companies at all," says Andy Grove, chairman of Intel.[22] Changes in interaction costs (i.e., the money and time expended whenever people and companies exchange goods, services, or ideas, as driven by the Internet) have been proposed to unbundle the vertically integrated corporation, creating networks of outsourced business processes.[23] This unbundled network of processes, people, and technology is demanding new strategies to replace the ones that managed the vertically integrated corporation's supply chain.

These networked companies, explained more fully in a later chapter, are organized and lead by a network *orchestrator,* the dominant company, usually the one close to the demand or customer. What holds these networks together is not cross-holdings of debt or equity, but a standard that enables network participants to interact with significant interaction cost savings and a high level of interfirm connectedness. The network orchestrator sets the standards and operating rules for the network and enforces them. This aligns the individual companies in the network and builds a common horizontal orientation. The high-performing networks also focus on common goals and have very high levels of network esprit de corps, a key result of BPO. It has been proven that these networks earn significantly greater value than their peers and outperform other top companies inside and outside of their industries.[24] For example, Cisco, the premiere example of a networked corporation, had twice the revenue per employee than that of other industry leaders at the time of this writing.

In a presentation to Wall Street analysts, Lou Gerstner of IBM described the new "dot-com" companies as "fireflies before the storm — all stirred up, throwing off sparks." But he continued, "The storm that's arriving — the real disturbance in the force — is when the thousands and thousands of institutions that exist today seize the power of this global computing and communications infrastructure and use it to transform themselves. That's the real revolution."[25] This means building the networked e-corporation.

What does this mean for BPO? As this storm drives the corporation to perform at even greater levels and focus outward on the customer, improvement efforts and activities must include a strong horizontal and value-added focus. With effortless globalization enabled by the Internet, competition has increased exponentially. Corporations can no longer afford internally focused people and functional processes that serve the functional fiefdom, yet bring little or no value to the customer. We strongly believe, and our research has confirmed, that competition in this networked world will be largely driven by a horizontal or BPO.

For example, hundreds of companies are now forming that exist solely around a business process: e-procurement. This totally business-process-

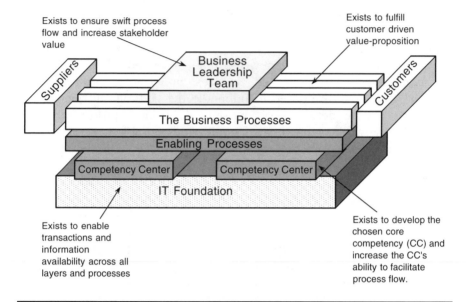

**Figure 2.8   The BPO Networked Corporation**

oriented organization can operate at efficiencies that are 10–20 times that of the functional, internally focused model. These are only the first of the many BPO networked corporations yet to come.

What do these BPO networked corporations "look" like? From our research, we offer our vision in Figure 2.8 as one possibility.

This totally horizontal view ignores traditional ownership boundaries and geographies. This view could include hundreds of legal entities and span the globe. The functions only exist as competency centers, and these could also be different legal entities. The leadership is in the form of a team representing the stakeholders — the legal shareholders as well as customers, suppliers, and participants in the networked corporation.

It is apparent from this brief description and "view" of the networked corporation that BPO is the fundamental orientation guiding the building and operation. Therefore, creating higher levels of BPO within an organization, or a network of organizations, becomes even more important today.

## SUMMARY

Our conclusion on this journey from the functionally oriented organizations of Adam Smith to our vision of the BPO networked corporation outlined in Figure 2.8 is that there is an unstoppable dynamic driving this change. The reduction in interaction costs and increase in globalization, caused by the Internet, is breaking up yesterday's models of organizing companies. Vertical integration and acquisitions as methods of dominating a market are no longer working, and virtual or networked corporations are now dominant. In order for this new, networked organizational form to be successful, intercompany conflict must be reduced and connectedness increased. Network or multicompany esprit de corps is also appearing as the new competitive advantage. From our research, we have shown that these are all proven outcomes of BPO. Therefore, increasing and aligning the levels of BPO within the networked corporation will be key to winning and possibly survival in this new environment.

Chapter 3 discusses the application of BPO to the supply chain, the critical network configuration of companies that is used to deliver products and services.

# REFERENCES

1. Payne, A.F. (May/June 1988). Developing a marketing-oriented organization, *Business Horizons,* 46-53.
2. Porter, M.E. (1985). *Competitive Advantage: Creating & Sustaining Superior Performance.* New York, NY: The Free Press.
3. Walton, M. (986). *The Deming Management Method.* New York: Perigee Books.
4. Davenport, T.H. and Short, J.E. (1990). The new industrial engineering: Information technology and business process redesign, *Sloan Manage. Review,* 31, 11-27.
5. Hammer, M. and Champy, J. (1993). *Reengineering the Corporation: A Manifesto for Business Revolution,* first ed. New York: HarperBusiness.
6. Drucker, P.F. (1989). *The New Realities.* New York: Harper and Row.
7. Walton, M. (1986*). The Deming Management Method.* New York: Perigee Books.
8. Hammer, M. (July-August 1990). Reengineering work: Don't automate, obliterate, *Harvard Business Review,* 104–112. reprint no. 90406.
9. Hammer, M. and Champy, J. (1993). *Reengineering the Corporation: A Manifesto for Business Revolution,* first ed. New York: HarperBusiness.
10. Davenport, T.H. (1993). *Process Innovation: Reengineering Work through Information Technology.* Boston: Harvard Business School Press.
11. Coombs, R. and Hull, R. (1996). The wider research context of business process analysis. Working Paper, Center for Research on Organizations, Management and Technical Change. Manchester School of Management, U.K.
12. Byrne, J.A. (December 13, 1993). The horizontal corporation, *Business Week,* 76-81.
13. Rummler, G.A. and Brache, A.P. (1990). *Improving Performance: How to Manage the White Space on the Organization Chart.* San Francisco: Jossey-Bass.
14. Melan, E.H. (1985). Process management in service and administrative operations, *Quality Prog.,* 52-59.
15. McCormack, K. and Johnson, W. (2000*). Business Process Orientation: Gaining the e-business Competitive advantage.* Delray Beach, FL: St. Lucie Press.
16. Jaworski, B.J. and Kohli, A.K. (July 1993). Market orientation: Antecedents and consequences, *J. Mark.,* 57, 53-70.

17. Jaworski, B.J. and Kohli, A.K. (July 1993). Market orientation: Antecedents and consequences, *J. Mark.,* 57, 57.
18. Rodgers, E.W. and Wright P.M. (Fall 1998). Measuring organizational performance in strategic human resource management: Problems, prospects and performance information markets, *Human Resource Manage. Review.*
19. Boyt, T.E., Lusch, R.F., and Schuler, D.K. (Spring 1997). Fostering esprit de corps in marketing, *Mark. Manage.,* 6, 1.
20. du Picq, A. (1946). *Battle Studies, Ancient and Modern.* Harrisburg, PA: Military Service Publishing Co.
21. (June 1999). How Herb keeps Southwest hopping, Money, *61.*
22. (Staff). (June 26, 1999).The net imperative, *The Economist.*
23. Hagel, J and Singer, M. (March/April 1999). Unbundling the corporation, *Harvard Business Review.*
24. Hacki, R and Lighton, J.(July 2001). The future of the network company, *The McKinsey Quarterly.*
25. (Staff). (June 26, 1999). The real revolution, *The Economist.*

# 3

---

# BPO AND THE SUPPLY CHAIN PERFORMANCE

This chapter describes the application of business process orientation (BPO) concepts in the supply chain using the Supply Chain Council's model as a framework. This model, called the Supply Chain Operations Reference or SCOR™, focuses on four key process areas in a supply chain: *Plan, Source, Make,* and *Deliver.* The results of several years of investigation into U.S. and European supply chains using a BPO-based survey instrument are presented. The results clearly outline the components of BPO that are major contributors to improving supply chain performance.

## SUPPLY CHAIN MANAGEMENT AND BPO

During the past several years, the concept of supply chain management (SCM) has been maturing both in terms of theory and practice. Terms such as integrated SCM, supply chain optimization, and supply chain collaboration have become the focus and goal of many organizations in the United States and around the world. Global SCM has also emerged as a key competitive strategy.

SCM is often described as coordinating the activities of different people, departments, and companies. By most accounts, it requires a horizontal view of the business and its partners that cuts across the organizational boundaries in order to manage product inputs at the beginning and outputs and customers at the end. In Chapter 2, we described this as managing the linkages and dependencies in the value chain. Michael Porter, Harvard Business School's leading strategy thinker, positions this as a path to competitive advantage. SCM obviously involves the BPO-related concepts of "connectedness" and "conflict" and good SCM should relate to superior performance. Therefore, we posed the following question, which guided our research efforts:

> *How is supply chain management influenced by a business process orientation?*

The initial challenge we faced in our study was in developing a clear, simple definition of the main concept of SCM. A review of the popular business press literature revealed that SCM was becoming another "buzzword" that appeared to lack a clear, simple definition. As we have said with BPO, if you cannot define something in simple terms, you do not really know what it is. With that in mind, the definition we used in this project was first the result of decomposing SCM into its constituent parts:

**Supply chain** — the global network used to deliver products and services from raw materials to end customers through an engineered flow of information, physical distribution, and cash (from *APICS Dictionary Tenth Edition*, p. 115, 2002.)

**Management** — the process of developing decisions and taking actions to direct the activities of people within an organization; planning, organizing, staffing, leading and controlling (from Peter Drucker).

The final definition used in this study combined the previous two statements to read as follows:

**Supply Chain Management** — the process of developing decisions and taking actions to direct the activities of people within the supply chain toward common objectives.

Before we could begin this study, we had to develop detailed definitions and operational measures for the practice of SCM. To accomplish this, we conducted interviews and focus groups with supply chain experts and practitioners. We asked them to indicate what they do in managing the supply chain and whether or not they feel it makes a difference. Their answers and our follow-up questions were organized generally around the components of BPO but slightly expanded (see Figure 3.1). These categories were specific to SCM and generally related to the proposed BPO components of SCM such as process view, process jobs, process structures, process values and beliefs, process management and measures, information technology support, and SC-specific best practices.

This is a slight expansion of the final BPO components list mentioned earlier, but represents the concept before our earlier data reduction tech-

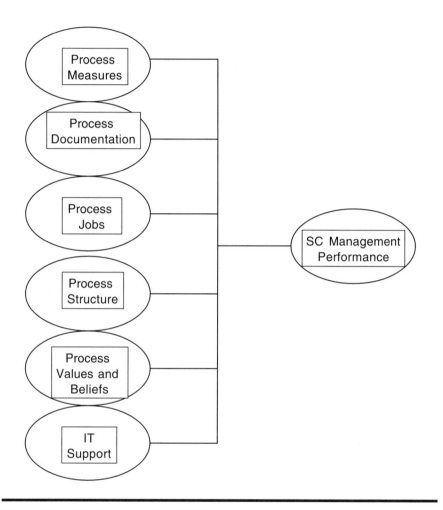

**Figure 3.1   BPO Components of SCM**

niques reduced the list to the top three. As we conducted the interviews, we felt that the earlier list was a better way to organize the BPO components of SCM. The results of these focus groups and interviews were used to build an initial list of survey questions to be used in this research study. This initial list was further reduced through expert reviews and testing. Duplicate questions were eliminated and wording was adjusted as required.

We wanted to investigate the impact of the BPO SCM variables on performance. To do this, we needed a performance measure to which everyone could relate and one that would permit cross-industry comparisons. We chose several subjective self-assessment measures similar to those in our original research on BPO. First, we asked participants about the performance of their individual SCM processes of *Plan, Source, Make,*

**Figure 3.2 Supply Chain Operations Reference (SCOR) Model Version 4.0**

and *Deliver.* We did this by asking them to agree or disagree with the statement, "Overall this decision process performs very well." We also asked the participants to rate the overall performance of their supply chains by rating the performance from 1 to 5 in several different categories (see Table 3.5 later in this chapter).

The unit of analysis was "the company." The sampling framework used in our study was constructed from the Supply Chain Council's SCOR model (see Figure 3.2).

Figure 3.2 represents a process model only; it does not clearly show company boundaries or company-to-company structures, but focuses on the basic processes involved in any supply chain. This model breaks the supply chain into the core processes of *Plan, Source, Make,* and *Deliver* components (and return in Version 5.0), and is further defined by more detailed process models within each component area. This "common language" for supply chains offers the opportunity for cross-functional and cross-company communication and collaboration, and is proposed as the preferred supply chain language for the examination of BPO impacts on the supply chain. For this reason, the SCOR model served as the basis for studying the impact of BPO on SCM performance.

## DATA COLLECTION

Participants were selected from the membership list of the Supply Chain Council. The members of the council are generally viewed as experts in supply chain design and operations, with most of them in a supply chain leadership position. The "user" or practitioner portion of the list was used as the final selection because this represented members whose firms were in the business of supplying a product, instead of a service; they were also considered as generally representative of supply chain practitioners instead of consultants. This list consisted of 523 key infomants representing 90 firms.

Hard copy questionnaires were sent to these key informants. Informants were asked to complete the questionnaires and return them within 2 weeks. Data from these surveys were entered, cleansed, and analyzed.

**Table 3.1  Sample Profile**

| Industry Description | Number of Responses | Response Percentages |
|---|---|---|
| Electronics | 6 | 10.9 |
| Transportation | 2 | 3.6 |
| Industrial Products | 2 | 3.6 |
| Food and Beverage/CPG | 8 | 14.5 |
| Aerospace and Defense | 2 | 3.6 |
| Chemicals | 4 | 7.3 |
| Apparel | 1 | 1.8 |
| Utilities | 10 | 18.2 |
| Pharmaceuticals/Medical | 3 | 5.5 |
| Mills | 0 | 0.0 |
| Semiconductors | 1 | 1.8 |
| Other | 16 | 29.1 |
| Total | 55 | 100% |

**Table 3.2  Respondent Profile by Position**

| Respondent Position | Number of Responses | Response Percentages |
|---|---|---|
| Senior leadership/executive | 19 | 38.0 |
| Senior manager | 10 | 20.0 |
| Manager | 17 | 34.0 |
| Individual contributor | 4 | 8.0 |
| Total | 50 | 100% |

Over 30 firms responded with completed surveys. The industries represented in these responses are listed in Table 3.1.

Table 3.2 lists the organizational positions represented in the completed surveys; there is significant participation at the leadership levels. Table 3.3 lists the functions represented. As expected, there was heavy participation from the traditional supply chain functions of planning/scheduling and purchasing, as well as a large category of "other" reponses. Upon investigation, it was found that this category represented the emerging supply management functions (i.e., Global Supply Chain Team, etc.).

## FINDING THE RELATIONSHIPS

The first step in analyzing the data was to examine the overall characteristics of the companies surveyed. In the survey, general questions were

**Table 3.3  Respondent Profile by Function**

| Respondent Function | Number of Responses | Response Percentages |
|---|---|---|
| Sales | 1 | 2.0 |
| Information systems | 3 | 5.9 |
| Planning and scheduling | 8 | 15.7 |
| Marketing | 0 | 0.0 |
| Manufacturing | 4 | 7.8 |
| Engineering | 0 | 0.0 |
| Finance | 0 | 0.0 |
| Distribution | 4 | 7.8 |
| Purchasing | 9 | 17.7 |
| Other | 22 | 43.1 |
| Total | 51 | 100% |

asked about the overall level of BPO of the company, especially about certain BPO characteristics such as organizational structure, jobs, measures, customer focus, and information technology support. Table 3.4 outlines the results. The responses appear to follow a normal distribution with no one category over or underrepresented, except the responses in the "5" grouping ("completely or entirely"). This was expected and did not influence the relationship results.

We needed to investigate the relationship of the BPO variables to overall supply chain and business performance; therefore, the next step was to analyze the performance distribution of the respondent companies. The response distributions are also shown in the Table 3.5. As in the overall BPO questions, the distribution of the answer to the performance questions was acceptable with no one grouping over or underrepresented. The only exception was that the answers to the overall business performance question were slightly skewed because no one rated his or her own performance as a "1" ("poor").

In the next step of the process of finding the relationships, we investigated the influence of the overall BPO factors shown in Table 3.4 on overall supply chain performance variables shown in Table 3.5. We needed to find the answer to the following question:

*Does BPO influence overall supply chain business performance?*

In order to answer this question, we used correlation analysis. This method identifies the statistically significant relationship between variables. A rating of "0" means no relationship, and "1.0" means a perfect relation-

**Table 3.4   Overall BPO Component (C1–7) Levels (% of Respondents)**

1. Your supply chain processes are documented and defined ...

| Not at all | a little | somewhat | mostly | completely |
|---|---|---|---|---|
| 5.5 | 22.6 | 35.8 | 35.8 | 0.0 |

2. Your supply chain organizational structure can be described as ...

| Traditional Function- | a little | some | mostly | entirely |
| Based | Process | Process | Process | Process-Based |
|---|---|---|---|---|
| 13.5 | 25.0 | 30.8 | 25.0 | 5.8 |

3. Your supply chain performance measures can be described as ...

| Traditional Function | a little | some | mostly | entirely |
| Based | Process | Process | Process | Process-Based |
|---|---|---|---|---|
| 19.2 | 17.3 | 28.8 | 32.7 | 1.9 |

4. People in the supply chain organization can be generally described as ...

| Totally Internally Focused | a little Customer- Focused | somewhat Customer- Focused | mostly Customer- Focused | entirely Customer- Focused |
|---|---|---|---|---|
| 11.3 | 34.0 | 39.6 | 15.1 | 0.0 |

5. Your information systems currently support the supply chain processes ...

| Not at all | a little | somewhat | mostly | completely |
|---|---|---|---|---|
| 1.9 | 17.0 | 54.7 | 24.5 | 1.9 |

6. Does the demand for your product vary?

| Not at all | a little | somewhat | often | always |
|---|---|---|---|---|
| 7.5 | 28.3 | 34.0 | 30.2 | 0.0 |

7. Jobs in the supply chain can generally be described as ...

| "Limited" Task- Oriented | a little Process | somewhat Process | mostly Process | "Broad" Process- Oriented |
|---|---|---|---|---|
| 5.8 | 25.0 | 36.5 | 23.1 | 9.6 |

**Table 3.5 Overall Supply Chain Business Performance (% of Respondents)**

Please rate the overall performance of your business unit last year.

| Poor | Fair | Good | Very Good | Excellent |
|------|------|------|-----------|-----------|
| 1 | 2 | 3 | 4 | 5 |
| 0 | 11.8 | 39.2 | 41.2 | 7.8 |

Please rate the overall performance of your business unit last year, relative to major competitors.

| Poor | Fair | Good | Very Good | Excellent |
|------|------|------|-----------|-----------|
| 1 | 2 | 3 | 4 | 5 |
| 4.1 | 10.2 | 26.5 | 46.9 | 12.2 |

Compared to your major competitors, your overall inventory Days of Supply (DOS) are:

| Poor | Fair | Good | Very Good | Excellent |
|------|------|------|-----------|-----------|
| 1 | 2 | 3 | 4 | 5 |
| 10.0 | 32.0 | 24.0 | 22.0 | 12.0 |

Compared to your major competitors, your overall cash-to-cash cycle times are:

| Poor | Fair | Good | Very Good | Excellent |
|------|------|------|-----------|-----------|
| 1 | 2 | 3 | 4 | 5 |
| 8.9 | 20.0 | 42.2 | 20.0 | 8.9 |

Compared to your major competitors, your delivery performance vs. commit date is:

| Poor | Fair | Good | Very Good | Excellent |
|------|------|------|-----------|-----------|
| 1 | 2 | 3 | 4 | 5 |
| 4.0 | 6.0 | 24.0 | 50.0 | 16.0 |

Compared to your major competitors, your quoted order lead times are:

| Poor | Fair | Good | Very Good | Excellent |
|------|------|------|-----------|-----------|
| 1 | 2 | 3 | 4 | 5 |
| 2.0 | 14.3 | 40.8 | 26.5 | 16.3 |

**Table 3.6    BPO Common Themes Correlated to Overall Performance (Overall Supply Chain Business Performance)**

| Overall BPO Components | Business Performance vs. Competitors | DOS vs. Competitors | Delivery Performance | Order Lead Time vs. Competitors |
|---|---|---|---|---|
| Process structure — C2 | 0.33[a] | 0.43[b] | — | 0.35[a] |
| Process documentation — C1 | — | — | — | 0.29[a] |
| Process values/beliefs — C4 | — | 0.35[a] | 0.37[b] | 0.43[b] |
| Process jobs — C7 | — | 0.39[b] | — | 0.34[a] |
| Process measures — C3 | — | 0.31[a] | — | 0.38[b] |
| IT Support — C5 | — | — | — | 0.37[a] |

[a]  $p < .01$
[b]  $p < .05$

ship. The closer a correlation is to 1, the stronger the relationship. Table 3.6 lists the results of this first test for relationships, correlating the questions in Table 3.4 (Overall BPO Component Levels) with the questions in Table 3.5 (Overall Supply Chain Business Performance).

The performance variable "order lead times versus competitors" appears to be the variable most impacted by BPO in a supply chain. All the correlation coefficients for all the BPO factors were between 0.3 and 0.4. This is a key customer-focused variable that can lead to a competitive advantage and increased margins. These results indicate that BPO can help a company achieve superior process performance in this area.

Overall inventory performance, as measured in days of sales (DOS) versus competitors, is the second-most influenced overall performance variable. Process structure, process values and beliefs, process jobs, and process measures all have correlations between 0.3 and 0.4. This is a major measure of supply chain performance, both of cost and meeting customer product demands. These results demonstrate that BPO can help improve inventory management in a supply chain, one of the most significant challenges in any industry.

Delivery performance is impacted by only process values and beliefs, in this case "customer focus." This makes sense. The more customer-focused an organization is, the more it is going to strive to satisfy the customer, which is the essence of delivery performance.

**Table 3.7   Average Correlation Coefficient of BPO Components and SCM Process Performance**

| Category | Plan | Source | Make | Deliver |
|---|---|---|---|---|
| Process structure | 0.7 | 0.6 | 0.5 | 0.6 |
| Process documentation | 0.6 | 0.7 | 0.5 | 0.5 |
| Process values/beliefs | 0.6 | 0.5 | 0.6 | <0.5 |
| Process jobs | 0.5 | 0.5 | 0.6 | <0.5 |
| Process measures | 0.5 | 0.7 | <0.5 | 0.6 |
| IT support | <0.5 | <0.5 | <0.5 | 0.7 |

*Note:* The closer the correlation coefficient is to 1.0, the stronger the relationship.

Lastly, overall business performance versus competitors was influenced by process structure. A conclusion to be drawn from these data is that a more process-oriented structure leads to better overall performance versus competitors.

Two overall business performance variables were not influenced by BPO: overall business performance in general and overall cash-to-cash cycle time. This makes sense because many elements in addition to SCM, such as financing, accounting, collection, and marketing, affect these two variables.

As a next step in our research, we needed to identify the influence of specific BPO factors on SCM performance. To do this, correlations were performed on the data again, but the specific questions in each SCOR area were used. Responses to the specific survey questions in each SCOR area were organized by BPO component category and were then correlated with overall SCM SCOR process performance. Table 3.7 reports the average of the correlation coefficients indicating the strength of the relationship between SCM process performance and each BPO component. All correlation coefficients were at least significant to a 0.05 level. The results of additional statistical analysis such as regression and coefficient alpha analysis are listed and explained in Appendix B.

For classification purposes, we drew a line between strong and weak relationships: above 0.5 were considered strong relationships, and below 0.5 were considered weak. Correlations for all components other than information technology (IT) support were 0.5 or above in most areas.

## RELATING BPO TO SUPPLY CHAIN PERFORMANCE

As indicated in Table 3.7, *process structure* appears to be slightly stronger than the others. When we asked respondents about this, we discovered that this was indeed true. The structure represents the span of involvement, influence, and authority in an organization. It is the base operating system for an organization. Similar to a computer, if the structure does not allow for multidimensional, cross-functional authority, then it is difficult to operate. This is particularly true in a management function that demands cross-functional action such as SCM. The basic process structure measures represent cross-functional teaming, process integration, and cross-functional authority of the teams. This makes good intuitive sense. If SCM is to be successful, the individuals involved must work as a tightly integrated group with shared authority to both make decisions and take actions.

*Process documentation,* according to our research, is also very strongly related to SCM performance (0.5 to 0.7). This is slightly stronger than our original BPO research. One possible explanation is that, in a cross-functional and possibly cross-company activity such as SCM, the documentation of the process to be used is much more important than in other activities. A clear understanding and agreement of what is to be done appears to be very important in SCM. This is usually achieved through process design and mapping sessions, or review and validation sessions with the team. This is a clear message to those implementing SCM strategies that the time and money invested in designing and documenting the processes are critical to success. Omitting this step or allowing it to be done in an ad hoc way will negatively impact supply chain performance.

*Process values and beliefs,* which represent customer trust, firm credibility, and interfirm collaboration in customer relationships, appear to also be strongly related to SCM performance (0.5 to 0.6). The *Deliver* area, although slightly below 0.5, is still important. Trusting customers enough to team with them and supply critical information is a very important factor in cross-company collaboration. Trust applies in a similar fashion when dealing with suppliers. For example, it is important that functional employees in an organization jointly participate on operations teams with their counterparts from the supplier firms. Our research also shows that believing what you are told and acting upon it is also a critical factor in SCM. Why bother getting forecasts from your customers if you do not believe them or do not act upon them?

*Process jobs* reflect the assignment of broad process ownership. In this research, we measured whether process owners were identified for each SCOR area of *Plan, Source, Make,* and *Deliver,* as well as an owner for the overall supply chain. The correlation results indicate that a strong relationship exists between process jobs and SCM performance. Clearly, creating broad, cross-functional jobs with real overall supply chain authority is a key component of SCM performance.

*Process measures* are also strongly correlated to SCM performance (0.5 to 0.7). This study identified key measures in each SCOR area and respondents were asked about the frequency of use. Measures such as supplier performance to agreements, inventory measures, and customer and product profitability were included in this study. The results clearly show that measures are very important in SCM just as in our original BPO research.

Many software firms and consultants are emphasizing the importance of information technology in SCM, therefore, we considered its role in SCM performance. Our research demonstrates that *IT support,* although strongly related to delivery process performance, is only marginally related to overall SCM performance (<0.5). The strong relationship of *IT support* to the delivery of the SCM process is perhaps because customer order processing and inventory management are usually part of the *Deliver* processes. These are very information-intensive processes and, by definition, very dependent on IT support. Based on the findings of our research, we have concluded that IT investments alone will not substantially improve SCM performance, except in the *Deliver* process area. Therefore, in order to realize a significant return, these investments must be in support of actions to improve the BPO of an SCM organization.

## SUMMARY

The results of our research investigating BPO in the supply chain clearly demonstrate that BPO is important in managing a supply chain for competitive advantage. *Process structure,* the basic architectural design of an organization, is critical. We recommend that when you start with a BPO structure and add the other components, improved performance will follow. *Process jobs,* the authority and responsibility component of BPO, was also related to improved supply chain performance.

Our research has also demonstrated that process-oriented measures and process-oriented values and beliefs are the engine of BPO supply chain performance and critical ingredients of SCM. Although cascading measures used to link people's actions to supply chain performance goals is directly related to performance, it appears to be very difficult to implement. Many of the participants in our research indicated very little progress in this area.

In our first book, we introduced the concept of BPO maturity. We defined maturity as the stages through which an organization progresses in becoming business-process-oriented, ultimately realizing an end goal of being fully process-oriented. A major inspiration for the model comes from Philip Crosby, who developed a maturity grid for the five stages companies go through in adopting quality practices. Crosby suggested that small, evolutionary steps, instead of revolutionary ones, are the basis for continuous process improvement. We have proven that the same holds true for BPO. Each successive step includes more practices involving more functions and more people within a given organization.

A major question, therefore, is: does SCM, because it is influenced by BPO, go through similar stages of maturity? We will examine this question in the Chapter 4.

# 4

---

# BPO AND SUPPLY CHAIN MANAGEMENT MATURITY

A maturity model assumes that progress comes in stages, ultimately reaching an end goal. The supply chain management (SCM) maturity model has a foundation based upon business process orientation (BPO) concepts introduced in earlier chapters. These concepts are based on Philip Crosby's development of a maturity grid for the five stages that companies follow in adopting quality practices, as well as the Capability and Maturity Model developed by Carnegie Mellon University in Pittsburg, PA, for the software development process.

This chapter presents an SCM maturity model that allows managers to quantitatively identify their company's position within this framework of maturity factors and best practices. Using this framework, managers can pinpoint areas of progress and stagnation. It is, in essence, a mall map that tells managers, "You are here." Using the model, managers attempting to build SCM networks will answer two very important questions: "Where are they?" and "How far do they have to go?" A discussion of how to apply the model to benchmark supply chains is also presented in this chapter.

## PROCESS MATURITY AND SCM

### Process Maturity Concepts and Foundations

The concept of process maturity proposes that a process has a life cycle that is measured by the extent to which the process is explicitly defined, managed, measured, controlled and effective.[1] Coincidentally, these represent four of the five components of BPO: process view, jobs, structures, measures, and management systems. Maturity implies increasing levels (breadth and depth) of BPO and, as we have seen in previous chapters,

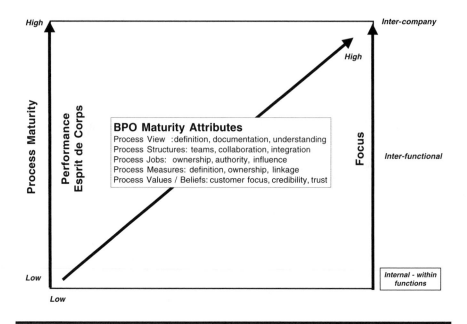

**Figure 4.1    Process Maturity and BPO**

increasing levels of performances and esprit de corps (see Figure 4.1). It also implies growth in capability potential — the richness of the process and the consistency with which it is applied across the organization.

As an organization increases its process maturity, institutionalization takes place via policies, standards, and organizational structures. Building an infrastructure and a culture that supports the methods, practices, and procedures enables process maturity to survive and endure long after those who have created it are gone. This is the fifth component of BPO: process values and beliefs. Continuous process improvement, an important aspect of this culture and BPO, is based on many small evolutionary instead of revolutionary steps. Continuous process improvement serves as the energy that maintains and advances process maturity to new maturity levels.

An additional and very critical factor of process maturity, which we discovered in our research (also shown in Figure 4.1), is focus or *perspective*. As processes mature, they move from an internally focused perspective to an externally focused, system perspective. These processes become aware and interact with the environment in a complementary way. This, we found leads to less conflict and more connectedness with the total system, as well as to improved business performance and esprit de corps. This increase in connectedness with the total system, we feel, will also lead to becoming part of a supply chain network. If fact, it may be a prerequisite for membership in a supply chain network. It is hard

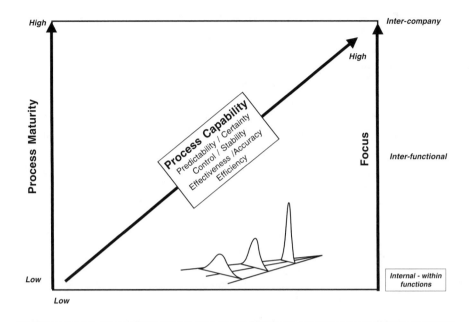

**Figure 4.2   Process Capability and Maturity**

to imagine a network member as a successful contributor if it is not operating at a sufficient SCM maturity level to interact effectively with their environment.

A maturity level represents a threshold that, when reached, will institutionalize a total systems view necessary to achieve a set of process goals. Achieving each level of maturity establishes a higher level of process capability for an organization. This capability, as illustrated in Figure 4.2, can be defined by:

**Control** — described as the difference between target and actual, and the variation (range) around these targets

**Predictability** — measured by the variability in achieving cost and performance objectives

**Effectiveness** — the achievement of targeted results and the ability to raise targets

These are critical aspects of process maturity. As process maturity increases, control of processes improves. The difference between targeted and actual performance is known and decreases as maturity increases. This improving control results in the increasing ability to predict process performance with some level of certainty. The distribution or range of process results gets smaller, as pictured in Figure 4.2.

A tighter-shot group (cluster) of process performance outcomes gathers around the bull's eye. As with a big game hunter or a soldier, this can be a powerful competitive advantage.

Customers of a predictable process develop powerful loyalties and will often pay a premium for this predictability. For example, the fact that some airlines deliver a higher percentage of on-time arrivals allows them to charge higher prices for this predictability. Business customers who rely on this performance are willing to pay for this reliability and will fill these airlines' seats.

A process under control can also be more readily understood and improved, allowing for shifting of targets to higher and higher levels of performance. This ability to continuously move performance to higher and higher levels, with the confidence that it will not degrade, can also serve as a source of competitive advantage. A firm that can take an order and deliver a product in 3 days versus 5 days will often win the business. If the firm can do it every time so that customers come to depend and plan on its performance, it often dominates the market. Southwest Airlines constantly boasts the best on-time performance rating (80%), the best price, and a flight turnaround time of less than 20 minutes, which allows Southwest to dominate the "short-haul" market. Other airlines have poor on-time arrival performance (60–70%) and are often averaging 1 hour or more in turnaround times.

We have developed a BPO maturity model based upon these foundational concepts of process maturity, our BPO research, and leveraging the Capability and Maturity Model developed by the Software Engineering Institute at Carnegie Mellon University. This model was introduced in our first book and has been used to assess numerous organizations' levels of BPO and process maturity.[2] This model and descriptions of each maturity level are outlined in Figure 4.3.

It is important to note that trying to skip maturity levels is counterproductive because each level builds a foundation from which to achieve the next level. An organization must evolve through these levels to establish a culture of process excellence. They can implement an advanced practice at any time; but without the foundation, the stability is in question and these processes often degrade or fail under stress.

## Assessing Supply Chain Network Maturity using BPO

In Chapter 3, we described how we investigated the application of BPO to the SCM processes. In Chapters 5, 7, and 8 we also discuss how BPO can be applied to supply chain networks, resulting in similar positive impacts. Before going any further, however, we need a brief review of some definitions.

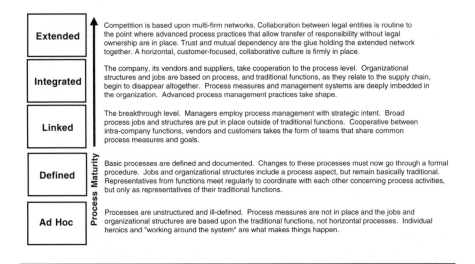

**Figure 4.3   The BPO Maturity Model**

First, what is a process? A *process* is generally defined as a specific ordering of work activities across time and place, with a beginning, an end, and clearly identified inputs and outputs; it is a structure for action.[3] Because we are examining the maturity of the supply chain management process we need to again present the definition of management used in Chapter 3.

> *Management — the process of developing decisions and taking actions to direct the activities of people within an organization including planning, organizing, staffing, leading, and controlling.*

Therefore, as was presented in Chapter 3, the SCM process is:

> *SCM Process — the process of developing decisions and taking actions to direct the activities of people within the supply chain toward common objectives; planning, organizing, staffing, leading, and controlling the supply chain.*

Also presented in Chapter 3 was the process we went through to build a BPO framework for SCM concepts and measures. We used a systematic, rigorous approach similar to that used to develop the BPO concepts, measures, and model described in our earlier book and Chapter 3. First, beginning with the SCM definition and leveraging the existing BPO measurement questions, we developed approximately 145 survey questions representing BPO components of SCM based upon an extensive literature review and interviews. These interviews took place with SCM practitioners by asking them to describe their SCM activities that they felt led to superior performance.

This initial list of survey questions was then organized according to the Supply Chain Council's model for describing and measuring supply chains. This model is intentionally holistic (includes aspects of process, material flows, information flows, and measures) and includes suppliers and *their* suppliers as well as customers and *their* customers. Called the Supply Chain Operations Reference or "SCOR™," the model focuses on the five key process areas: *Plan, Source, Make, Deliver,* and *Return* (in V.5.0).

The questions were then pretested for validation with several Supply Chain Council member companies and well-established SCM experts. SCM best practice questions were then identified through their statistical correlations to supply chain performance. These "best practice" survey questions became the basis of measuring BPO as applied to SCM maturity.

In order to build a process maturity model that would parallel our earlier BPO model, we needed to organize the survey questions into variables or concepts that related to the different maturity levels. The first step was to develop a definition of each level from an SCM perspective. In our discussions with SCM experts and practitioners, we were asked to draw a picture matching each of the levels. Figure 4.4 represents our conceptualization of how process maturity relates to the SCOR model.

### SCM Maturity Levels

The five stages of maturity show the progression of activities toward effective SCM and process maturity. Each maturity level has characteristics, or a personality, which reflects aspects of process maturity such as predictability, capability, control, effectiveness, and efficiency. The following is a brief description of each SCM maturity level.

### Ad Hoc

The supply chain and the SCM practices are unstructured and ill-defined. Process measures are not in place and the jobs and organizational structures are based upon the traditional functions, not horizontal supply chain processes. Individual heroics and "working around the system" are what make things happen. Process performance is unpredictable and targets, if defined, are often missed. SCM costs are high both in dollars and emotional costs. Frustration and burnout are often present in the organization and customer satisfaction is low.

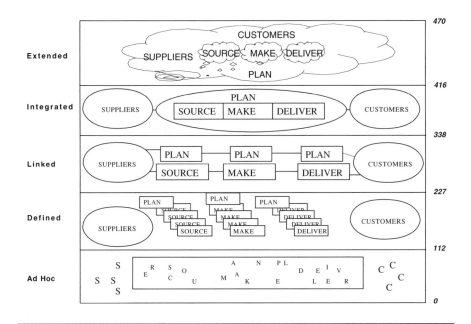

**Figure 4.4 The SCM Maturity Model View**

## Defined

The basic SCM processes are defined and documented. The order commitment, procurement, and other processes, for example, are available in flow charts; changes to these processes must now go through a formal procedure reflecting the foundations of process management. Jobs and organizational structures include an SCM aspect, but remain basically traditional. Representatives from sales, manufacturing, and transportation meet regularly to coordinate with each other, but only as representatives of their traditional functions. Similarly, functional representatives meet to coordinate schedules with vendors and customers. Process performance is more predictable and targets are defined but still missed more often than not. Overcoming the functional silos takes considerable effort due to turf concerns and competing goals. SCM costs remain high, frustration is still present, and customer satisfaction, although better defined, is still low.

## Linked

This represents the breakthrough level. Managers employ SCM with strategic intent and results. Broad SCM jobs and structures are put in place outside and on top of traditional functions. One common indicator is the appearance of the title "supply chain manager." Cooperation between intracompany functions, vendors, and customers takes the form of teams that share common SCM measures and goals, which reach horizontally across the supply chain. Process performance becomes more predictable, and targets are often achieved. Continuous improvement efforts, focused on root cause elimination and performance improvements, take shape. SCM costs begin to decrease, and feelings of esprit de corps take the place of frustration. Customers are included in process improvement efforts, and customer satisfaction begins to show marked improvement.

### Integrated

The company, its vendors, and suppliers take cooperation to the process level. Organizational structures and jobs are based on SCM procedures, and traditional functions, as they relate to the supply chain, begin to disappear altogether. SCM measures and management systems are deeply imbedded in the organization. Advanced SCM practices, such as collaborative forecasting and planning with customers and suppliers, take shape. Process performance becomes very predictable, and targets are reliably achieved. Process improvement goals are set by the teams and achieved with confidence. SCM costs are dramatically reduced, and customer satisfaction and esprit de corps become competitive advantages.

### Extended

Competition is based upon multifirm supply chains. Collaboration between legal entities is routine to the point where advanced SCM practices that allow transfer of responsibility without legal ownership are in place. Multifirm SCM teams with common processes, goals, and broad authority take shape. Trust, mutual dependency, and esprit de corps are the glue holding the extended supply chain together. A horizontal, customer-focused, collaborative culture is firmly in place. Process performance and reliability of the extended system are measured, and joint investments in improving the system are shared, as are the returns. This is the beginning of a functioning supply chain network.

## BPO Components in the SCM Maturity Model

Our next step in developing a usable SCM maturity model was to define the different BPO components from an SCM perspective. As we did this, it became clear that differences existed in the timing of implementing the components. Some SCM components needed to be present before others could be built. For example, a process needed to be described, documented, and understood before measures could be put in place to manage the process. Also, SCM best practices needed a process foundation (a process view) to sit upon or they could not be successfully implemented. Based on these precedence requirements, we found that two major groupings of components were needed: *chassis* and *engine*. Chassis groupings, as with automobiles, provide the framework or foundation for achieving process capability and predictability. Engine groupings provide the power and control mechanisms for achieving higher performance levels and efficiency. Both are required to achieve sustainable maturity levels.

The three *chassis* groupings include:

**Process View** — Documentation of process steps, activities, and tasks comes in both visual and written formats that allow people in different job functions and companies to communicate using the same vocabulary. This grouping includes a broad understanding of the processes across the organization, not just documentation.

**Process Structure** — This is the framework that defines the SCM team and breaks down the old functional "compartments," such as sales and manufacturing, which inhibit enterprise-wide process thinking. Without it, people with "supply chain manager" titles (see *Process Jobs* next) cannot do their jobs. These structures included horizontal teams, partnerships, shared responsibility, and shared ownership.

**Process Jobs** — These jobs include horizontal (cross-functional) instead of vertical responsibility. People participate and take ownership of the whole process. Titles such as "Supply Chain Team Member," "Plan Process Owner," and "Global Supply Chain Manager" are examples.

The three *engine* groupings include:

**Customer-Focused Process Values and Beliefs** — These are the values and beliefs that energize an organization. For instance, they might include *trust* in the customer's sales forecasts and *belief* that fellow team members are completely committed to common goals and continuous process improvement.

**Process Measurement and Management Systems** — The components of this category include process measurement systems, rewards for process improvement, outcome measurements, and customer-driven and team-driven measures and rewards. These serve as indicators to let you know how fast you are going, what direction you are taking, and when you have to put on the brakes.

**Best Practices** — These are tactics used to improve supply chain performance within best practice firms and are very specific. For instance, "Are supplier lead times updated monthly?" or "Do key suppliers have employees on your site?" and "Is a forecast developed for each customer?" The timing of the implementation of these practices is critical. Certain foundations and conditions must be in place before a selected set, one that aligns with the supply chain strategy, can be implemented. Satisfactory implementation of this selected, aligned set of best practices serves as the fuel to higher levels of performance.

The next step in building the SCM maturity model was to identify which groupings were related to which maturity levels. It became clear that certain components were focused on achieving the process goals for specific maturity levels and were only relevant for that level. Some component groupings also appeared to only lay the foundation needed to get to the next maturity level. It also became clear that upper level performance could not be attempted until the lower maturity levels were well established. For example, integrating your demand planning process with your customers, if your process was not defined, capable, or predictable, would be a big mistake. The resulting customer interactions would be unpredictable and poorly focused, resulting in poor performance of both processes as well as a dissatisfied customer. Therefore, this practice appears only in the integrated and extended levels, after a strong foundation of process interaction within the company has been established.

We located the placement of the component groupings by looking at the definition of each level and identifying the grouping and specific survey questions that related to that level of performance. Two distinct levels resulted: basic and advanced. Certain practices needed to be in place to provide a foundation and the stability needed for basic performance; other practices clearly leveraged this foundation and stability to provide advanced performance capabilities. For example, basic process documentation needs to be in place within a company before a benefit can be realized by documenting the supplier and customer interactions, which is part of advanced process documentation. Also, a basic cross-functional team structure within a company must be in place before collaboration with suppliers and customers can be effective. Figure 4.5 illustrates the placement of groupings by maturity level with a high-level description of the practices contained within the grouping. The resulting SCM maturity framework, detailed in Figure 4.5 and based upon the original BPO Maturity Model, provides a visual maturity scorecard that describes not only the maturity level but also the balance of the maturity component groupings. These groupings are the elements that need to be in place and institutionalized in order to realize sustainable performance

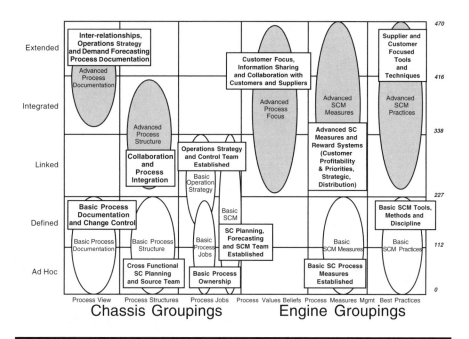

**Figure 4.5 SCM Process Maturity Framework with Groupings and Descriptions**

for that maturity level, and are required foundations for the levels previously described.

With SCM, as with many concepts that are hyped beyond understanding, an organization can get ahead of itself and create an unstable situation. Figure 4.6 depicts a pile of stones that could represent many of the actual SCM maturity models we have seen during the past few years as we applied the model. The stones represent the SCM groupings. Obviously, this pile will tumble with the first upset. Additional stones, similar to the foundation components in the maturity model, should be placed at the base in order to provide the stability that supports a pile this high. The stones at the top, just like the advanced maturity components, need support in order to be successful. The SCM maturity framework in Figure 4.5 can provide this kind of visual insight into SCM maturity and stability for the examination of a specific supply chain, while pointing to critical issues of instability.

The SCM maturity framework also offers a way to organize evolutionary steps in improved SCM into distinct maturity levels that lay successive foundations for increasing SCM process maturity and performance. The SCM maturity model, based upon solid process theory and research, is a framework that represents a path of improvements recommended for SCM organizations that want to increase their SCM process capabilities.

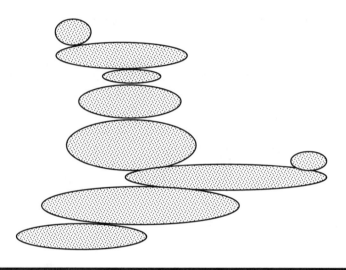

**Figure 4.6    SCM Visual Stability**

The framework also offers highly granular prescriptive detail. Each grouping can be decomposed to a level of detail that can be used to provide specific actions and process recommendations. Using scaled survey questions indicating how often a specific practice is conducted (1 – never, to 5 – always), the framework can also be used as a measure of institutionalization, a critical aspect of process maturity. Institutionalization is when a practice is part of the routine, is completed every time, and is not an exception. This directly relates to the predictability aspect of process maturity. A practice that is a critical component of SCM at a certain maturity level must become institutionalized in order to provide enough stability to support advancement to the next level. Scores of 4 and 5 on the specific survey questions indicate the institutionalization of the practice that is represented by the specific question.

## USING THE SCM MATURITY MODEL

Whether a firm is at the beginning or the middle of its supply chain improvement efforts, the question that must always be confronted at each new milestone is: *What steps should be taken that will most effectively move the process forward?* Or, in tough years with slim budgets, the question is: *What can be done to best keep from losing momentum entirely?*

The Supply Chain Maturity Model can be used to guide the next steps, especially where organizations are trying to incrementally improve processes within planning, sourcing, manufacturing, delivery, or return logistics. Moreover, the model can be used to assess SCM processes by pinpointing gaps and opportunities for SCM improvement activities, and what is necessary to get there.

To determine a company's placement within the framework, key informants, or individuals who are working in the SCM processes, are asked to respond to various SCM maturity survey questions. Questions are organized into SCOR model areas (*Plan, Source, Make, Deliver,* and *Return*) in order to capture the key practices that determine SCM maturity. Answers are given using a five-item Likert-type scale, reflecting institutionalization or the inclusion in the process routine of the specific practice reflected in the question.

1. Never or does not exist
2. Sometimes
3. Frequently
4. Mostly
5. Always or definitely exists

Based on the survey responses, statistical analysis is then used to determine frequencies, mean and standard deviation of the data, and to arrive at numerical scores for each grouping and overall maturity. Each SCM component receives its own summary score, and is plotted on the diagram illustrated in Figure 4.7.

For example, if the basic process documentation component has a total possible score of 30 (6 questions x 5 points maximum per question), and the specific summary score for the supply chain under study is 15, then the oval shown for this component would be 50% filled. This technique provides the powerful visual score card of the current situation and areas of opportunity.

To view how the model works in the real world, we will look at three actual assessment examples of companies at different levels of SCM maturity. We begin with the example that has the most SCM work in front of it and end with a sophisticated SCM example. In each case, the model clarifies the next steps that may not always be obvious.

## Case 1: Ad Hoc — "Shore Up the Chassis Before You Race the Car"

Figure 4.8 illustrates how far this company has to go. It has a total SCM score of 72 out of a possible 470. This puts the company at the Ad Hoc maturity level, which has a top score of 112. At this level, despite use of a few basic SCM tools, overall system performance comes the old-fashioned way: heroic action overcoming a dysfunctional SCM system. Processes are undefined, unstable, and unpredictable. Moving to the next level requires much more definition of the SCM process and organizational

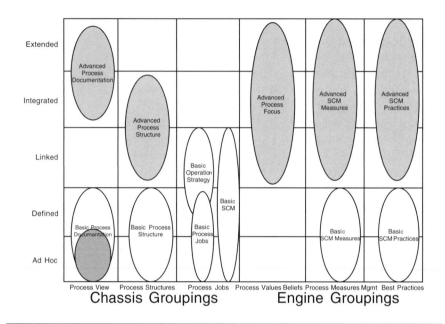

**Figure 4.7  SCMM Plot Example 50% in Basic Process Documentation**

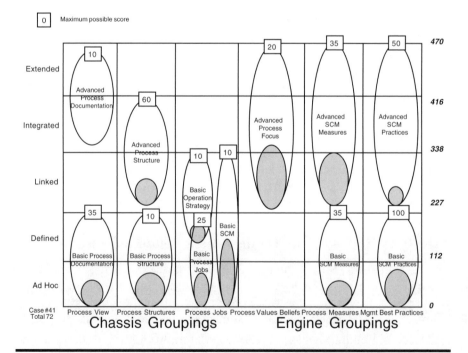

**Figure 4.8  Visual SCMM Map for Case 1 Ad Hoc Maturity Level**

buy-in to those definitions. Figure 4.8 also demonstrates that this company is attempting some advanced components without a strong chassis or foundation. It is trying to pile the stones too high without a good base. The score of 72 is slightly misleading because some of the points are coming from advanced components at the linked level. This indicates an unstable score that may in reality be closer to 50.

The Advanced Process Focus and Advanced SCM Measures ovals are 30% filled, indicating the attempted implementation of externally focused process values and measures. This is a dangerous source of frustration. The SCM team members are held accountable, through these values and measures, for advanced process performance without the foundational components needed for success. It is similar to being asked to drive a Volkswagen "bug" in a high-speed race with lots of tight turns and handling issues that would challenge a Grand Prix racer. This is why we title this example "Shore up the chassis before you race the car."

## Basic Process Documentation

At this stage, a basic foundation needs to be established by defining and documenting the supply chain processes, which also means they must be understood. Having this "visibility" on the front end of the SCM endeavor provides a critical foundation. This company needs a blueprint, such as the Supply Chain Council's SCOR model, from which to borrow process designs and best practices. This basic design process required by this maturity component also implies that a supply chain strategy has been defined. Basic operational decisions must be made in order to build a process view of a supply chain. Are you "Make to Order" or "Make to Stock"? Where will inventory be stored, and how will it be managed? What is the desired order to delivery cycle time needed for this market? These are all very fundamental questions that must be answered when building this process view.

## Basic SCM Best Practices

This company lacks some basic driving skills. It can improve by using historical data and mathematical models to make basic demand (sales) forecasts; the lack of such forecasts is one of the major failings at companies beginning the SCM process. Knowing about the shape of the racetrack and what curves are coming up is a key basic SCM practice at this level. The company can also develop plans at a level of detail needed for decision making across the supply chain and enforce basic schedule discipline; both of these practices contribute to basic predictability/reliability needed to get to the next level.

## Basic SCM

SCM requires the basic ability to respond rapidly to change and to know the system impact of a decision before it is made. This is a real problem in this case with the oval being less than 50% filled. Establishing an SCM team consisting of the functional team leaders that has authority over the entire chain is a critical foundation step needed to bring things under control. The formation of this team makes clear the strategic intent of using SCM to improve performance. It also defines the shared responsibility and ownership for improving the processes as a part of a system instead of parts of the functional silos. Having a forecast that is credible and used to make commitments across the supply chain is also a critical practice lacking in this case. Understanding item and customer characteristics, such as variability, seasonality, buying patterns, and profitability, are also important and need to be addressed. This provides key inputs into developing the controls for a specific supply chain, which is an important step to get to the Defined level.

## Basic Process Jobs

This company also needs to develop a consensus between sales, manufacturing, and other functions on shared SCM goals; it should begin reorganization and job redefinition to create basic ownership for the SCM process. The identification and authorization of process owners in the organization can bring significant stability, and provide the key leadership and ownership needed to go to the next step of process performance.

## Basic SCM Measures

Typically, a company in the Ad Hoc stage would know that it had a certain level of inventory, but would not have broken down the overall aggregate to the product level. Managers need to put themselves in position to answer such questions as: "If I have 122 types of resin, what is my sales aggregate for number 112?" and "What level should it be, and what do I do to impact that number?" Adding process-focused SCM measures with enough granularity would help in this case. Measuring forecast accuracy and supplier performance are also the basic first steps needed here.

## Basic Operations Strategy

Establishing an operations (SCM) strategy team is critical to bring things under control and to move out of Ad Hoc into the Defined level. This team, with cross-functional representation, would develop the specific strategies and tactics needed to support the business and focus the process improvement efforts in the directions needed for improved SCM maturity. Performing adequate analysis of alternatives before changes are made is critically needed in order to control the changes needed for process improvements.

## Conclusion

This case requires that the foundation is built before the house or the chassis needs to be fixed before the car is driven. The company should develop the basic process view, structure, and jobs needed to go forward before considering anything else.

## Case 2: Defined — "Expand the Chassis and Turbocharge the Engine with Advanced Measurements"

This company has performed these basic first steps and is ready to move on, but has some major problems in its foundation components, specifically measurement, process structure, and authority area. The company's score of 140, as in Case 1, is misleading, with much of the score coming from advanced components in the Linked and Integrated levels.

In this case, both basic and advanced documentation representing supplier and customer interrelationships are far advanced. The Advanced Process Focus and Advanced SCM Practices are also advancing into the Integrated level. These practices represent the SCM practices that are being hyped in the press or are contained in a suite of SCM software applications. This usually gets a company into trouble by jumping into these exciting practices without a solid chassis or foundation. Here, Basic SCM Practices (such as the use of mathematical planning models and weekly planning cycles) and Basic SCM Measures are in place, but Basic Process Structure is very low and Basic Operation Strategy does not even exist. These are the key areas that build the bridges that link the supply chain together. This suggests that many of the practices in place are the practices that can be implemented without challenging the traditional power and authority structure.

### Basic Process Structure

In this example, jobs and organizational structures include an SCM aspect, but are still strongly defined by traditional functions. This is a big hole, illustrated by Figure 4.9 and poses a major weakness. Getting to the stage where basic process structures are clearly delineated — with SCM teams formed and exercising authority — is critical to making the shift to the horizontal structures.

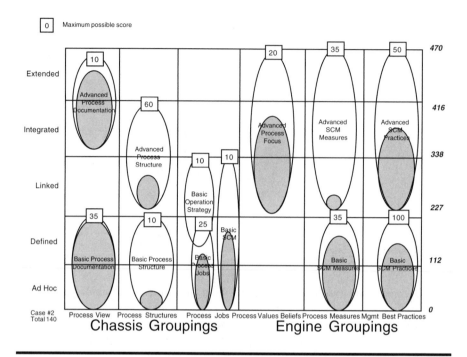

**Figure 4.9   Visual SCMM Map FOR Case 2-Defined Maturity Level**

## Basic Operation Strategy

SCM responsibility needs to broaden and span across the functions. A cross-functional operational strategy planning team should be formed and given broad supply chain authority for the interfunctional decisions necessary to get to the next level. This group is vital. It occupies the optimal management position from which to overcome the natural resistance of managers working out of traditional functional compartments, and to make decisions that benefit the overall supply chain.

## Balance is a Problem

In Figure 4.9, the model appears out of balance, just like the pile of stones. This company is operating at the advanced level in many areas with large holes in its SCM foundation. This instability creates a risk that a shock of some kind, such as a major weather problem, factory outage, or the events of September 11, 2001, will collapse this supply chain, resulting in major problems. Also, this type of imbalance cause high levels of stress with the people working in SCM. They are being asked to perform advanced SCM practices without the proper foundation. This might be because the company has purchased sophisticated SCM software that is driving the advanced practices, which is often the case. This means that they will be constantly dealing with unreliable and unpredictable processes. Firefighting and reacting to the loudest screams will be the order of the day with this supply chain.

## Case 3: Integrated — "Patch a Few Holes in the Chassis and Push to the Next Level"

Case 3 is an excellent example of an SCM system firmly lodged in the Integrated level. This company just needs to patch a few holes in the chassis groupings, and it will then be ready to make the difficult push to the extended level.

At the lofty Integrated level of Case 3, some supplier and customer processes are included in the company's documented processes, as shown by the advanced process documentation group in Figure 4.10. Organizational structures and jobs are firmly process-based and include some members from key suppliers. Collaboration across functions is routine, but collaboration outside of the firm has just begun, generally with

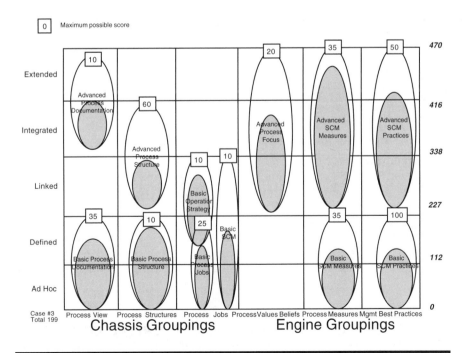

**Figure 4.10   Visual SCMM Map for Case 3 Integrated Maturity Level**

planning processes and decisions. This is a hole that needs to be filled, institutionalizing this external collaboration.

On the engine side of the axis, this example has most of the elements in place. Basic and advanced SCM practices appear mature, and SCM measures and management systems are deeply imbedded in the organization.

### Basic SCM Jobs

The Basic SCM Jobs grouping is less than 50% complete, indicating that a key component is missing. People with the power and authority to make and implement cross-functional SCM decisions are not yet operating at the Integrated level. Broad SCM jobs must be clearly in place and operating effectively before going further. In this case, an overall supply chain strategy and planning process owner must be clearly identified and given authority to select and replace SCM team members. This SCM team also needs some permanent members representing sales and marketing.

### Basic SCM Measures

This is also a hole in the chassis. "Adherence to Plan" measures need to be put in place and the discipline needed to accomplish this must be established. This is a critical area of predictability and must be addressed. Measuring and feeding back supplier performance is also missing here. This practice must be institutionalized in order to maintain the high maturity levels being attempted by this company. This is the foundation for external collaboration envisioned in the Extended level.

### Advanced Process Structure

One area of opportunity is in the Advanced Process Structure area. These are outward-looking practices that build the collaborative bridges for including suppliers and customers in forecasting, demand planning, and operational strategy decision making. Bringing outside partners into these activities will help lift this supply chain to the Extended level, a very difficult step involving cross-enterprise cooperation and collaboration, which is not yet the norm in business.

## SCM MATURITY AND BUSINESS PERFORMANCE

The evidence pointing to improved business performance through supply chain maturity is significant but has often been a subjective assessment. In our research, we have used subjective performance ratings by the key

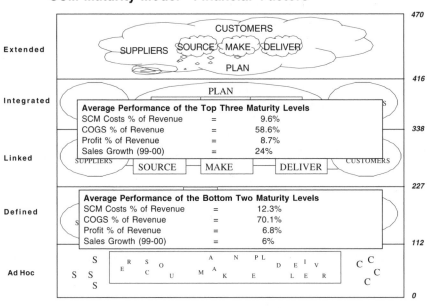

## SCM Maturity Model - Financial Factors

**Figure 4.11    Financial Indicators and SCM Maturity**

informants to indicate performance levels. These ratings have allowed us to identify cross-industry practices that statistically relate to these performance assessments. Thus, these are the practices that relate to performance in a supply chain. We are confident that these practices make a difference in SCM maturity, process reliability, and performance. Bringing the processes under control and making them effective and repeatable has to make a business and market difference. But what is the bottom line impact? Recent research that has been conducted in this area, linking SCM maturity to performance, can provide some of the answers, at least at a high level.

In order to find some of these answers and relate financial bottom-line performance to SCM maturity, we have merged some recent work by The Performance Measurement Group, a company specializing in performance benchmarking, with our BPO and SCM Maturity research. This work captures the financial performance of different supply chains and, through some question similar to our SCM practices, links this performance to maturity levels.[4] Figure 4.11 lists the combined results.

Figure 4.11 illustrates a dramatic difference between the bottom two maturity levels and the top three. SCM costs as a percent of total revenue, for example, are almost 3% lower at the Linked and Integrated levels than at the Defined level. Cost of goods sold (COGS) is almost 12% lower, and profit is almost 2% higher. These are dramatic differences, but what is even more dramatic is the difference in sales growth. The top maturity levels had an average increase in sales of 20% year to year, while the lower levels had only 6%. This would support the premise that process predictability and stability, a key ingredient of process maturity, draws and holds customers. This strongly suggests that the SCM Maturity model can be used as an indicator of financial performance, possibly used to evaluate companies under consideration for acquisition.

We are expanding data collection in this area of financial results and process maturity, but this early study by The Performance Measurement Group apparently supports the value of SCM Maturity. Our initial conclusion is that SCM Maturity makes a big difference in the bottom line.

## CONCLUSION AND THE EXTENDED SUPPLY CHAIN — THE NEXT FRONTIER

The SCM journey is difficult. Without a map and a compass, it is impossible. The SCM Maturity model can be used to assess the current condition of the SCM processes and help the leadership team focus on the areas of improvement that make sense for their unique maturity level. Leaders can avoid "putting the cart before the horse" by using a visual map along with numerical assessments of supply chain network maturity. As improvement progresses, balance can also be maintained by using this tool to periodically assess the SCM processes and the results of the improvement efforts. This can help avoid "building a pile of unstable stones" that collapses at the first upset.

According to our earlier research, the Extended level of supply chain maturity — integrating fully with customers and supply chain partners outside the company's boundaries — had not been reached at any significant level by companies we investigated. The Internet and supporting technologies, however, may have a dramatic impact on this and will soon allow companies to operate at this level.

It may now be possible and affordable to extend outward to suppliers and customers via the Internet, as well as measure the impact of the Internet in supporting this extension. This Extended level was previously envisioned as the ultimate supply chain, with fuzzy process barriers, customers, and suppliers integrated within the processes, and customers in control. In this view, company boundaries or company-to-company structures are almost invisible, and process is the dominant view.

Chapter 5 examines this highest level of SCM Maturity, and presents some of our recent research on the impact of the Internet on SCM.

## REFERENCES

1. Dorfman, M. and Thayer, R.H. (1997). The capability maturity model for software, *Software Eng.*, 427–438.
2. Johnson, W.C. and McCormack, K.P. (2001). *Business Process Orientation: Gaining the e-business Competitive Advantage.* Boca Raton, FL: St. Lucie Press.
3. Davenport, T.H. (1993). *Process Innovation: Reengineering Work through Information Technology.* Boston: Harvard Business School Press.
4. The Performance Measurement Group. (November 6, 2001). Supply Chain Practice Maturity Model and Performance Assessment.

# 5

---

# THE EXTENDED SUPPLY CHAIN AND THE INTERNET — THE BRIDGE TO A SUPPLY CHAIN NETWORK

Internet technologies enable the business-to-business (B2B) or the highest level of supply chain management (SCM) maturity, which is the extended supply chain. How pervasive is Internet usage and what impact is it having on extended supply chains? What practices are impacted the most from this new technology? In this chapter, we offer definitions and measures of the extended supply chain and review the results of a benchmarking research project completed in cooperation with the U.S. and European Supply Chain Councils. Our research found that Internet usage is just beginning in both the United States and Europe, but has significant relationships to cross-company (B2B) integrating practices that are key components of the extended supply chain and SCM performance.

## INTRODUCTION

As we have presented earlier in this book, the impact of the Internet on B2B interactions and practices is anticipated to be significant. The "friction" that was previously a driving force for "bringing external processes and activities in-house" has been dramatically reduced. In some cases, it appears to be easier to work with companies outside of a corporation than with divisions or groups inside the corporation. During our research on this subject, many supply chain managers commented that communicating, obtaining commitments, and receiving results from external suppliers was many times easier than working with an inside supplier. Marketing and sales people have also made this comment about working with customers versus internal departments. How is this affecting the development and maturity of SCM processes?

Some researchers suggest that the supply chain configurations evolving in today's digital economy reshape the historical chain into networks or business webs.[1] These network configurations are proposed to reflect the interconnected roles and activities within a cross-enterprise supply chain, making the historical, legal, and organizational structures no longer the basis of competition. We propose that interconnected supply chain webs are evolving into new B2B configurations that will define new boundaries within which competition will occur. We further propose that a business process orientation (BPO) will be integral to establishing and extending these complex supply chain network connections.

Our research investigated this proposition using the concepts of BPO as they are applied to SCM maturity, which were covered in Chapter 4. In our model, the most advanced level of maturity is the *Extended level,* integrating supply chain partners located outside of company boundaries. To be successful, this level requires a company-to-company technology infrastructure as well as the implementation and institutionalization of core BPO components. This chapter discusses recent research on how BPO is related to extended supply chain integration, proposes and tests a definition of this technology infrastructure (Internet usage), and investigates the impact of Internet usage on the BPO components critical to the Extended level of SCM performance.

## BACKGROUND

B2B interactions, known as the *extended supply chain,* have only recently been proposed and investigated as a business organizing principle. One of the reasons that the extended supply chain has been so poorly understood and inadequately researched is that little agreement exists as to exactly what it is. To date, much of the quantitative research conducted on SCM performance and technology has been in the area of logistics. These studies have focused on the evaluation of the impact of very specific programs such as the use of electronic data interchange (EDI) technologies, vendor-managed inventory, and automatic replenishment programs.[2–4] One exception was a study involving interfirm coordination in food industry supply chains.[5] This study examined the benefits of integrated SCM processes and proposed that SCM extends a firm's capabilities by coordinating operations to encompass source, make, and delivery processes in collaboration with channel partners and suppliers. A shift in channel arrangements from loosely linked groups of businesses to coordinated enterprises is described. The shortfall in this study was that only EDI technology was examined, without considering the role the Internet plays as a "connecting" mechanism.

Forrester Research, an international research firm in Boston, Massachusetts, predicted in December 2000 that enterprises would connect their supply chains to the Internet, thus forming network supply chains (NSCs). They define this as "a network of inter-enterprise supply chain events connected through a private or public eMarketplace."[6] Although they clearly state that few defined practices are in place for this concept, they offer a three-phase approach to achieve NSC status. Phase 1 involves integrating the planning activities, orders, and logistics between members of the NSC; phase 2 involves instituting cooperative advanced planning, scheduling, and synchronization; and phase 3 results in full network supply chains. Forrester offers clear descriptions of the practices needed to achieve phases 1 and 2, yet how to actually reach NSC status is still vague.

AMR Research, a Boston based research firm focusing on manufacturing issues, predicted that electronically connected trading communities will form, driven by the Internet and available Internet-based applications for connecting and interacting.[7] They propose that vendor-managed inventory (VMI), supplier collaboration, collaborative planning, forecasting, and replenishment (CPFR) will be key externally focused programs that will be significantly enabled by the use of Internet technologies.

Much of what has been written concerning the impact of the Internet on SCM practices and performance has been speculative, because Internet usage in this area is not widespread, thus limiting both case study and quantitative research. Most of the case studies suggest the Internet will help create a seamless, integrated supply chain of close collaborative relationships with integrated data and business processes.[8,9] One of the few quantitative studies, completed by Michigan State University, proposes a model consisting of logistic competencies.[10] These are internal integration, customer integration, relationship integration, technology and planning integration, measurement integration, and supplier integration. This study provides solid evidence of the benefit to SCM by extending the supply chain to include suppliers and customers, but does not examine the impact of the Internet on SCM.

Hau Lee of Stanford University in Palo Alto, California, a leading SCM researcher, offers the concept of supply chain integration.[11] An integrated supply chain that makes smart use of information to orchestrate the activities of the chain is described in three levels: level 1 is information sharing, the foundation of supply chain integration; level 2 is coordination; and level 3 is organizational linkages. Although Dr. Lee does not discuss the impact of the Internet directly, it is obvious that levels one and two can be dramatically affected.

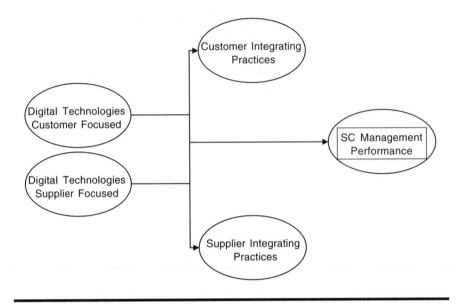

**Figure 5.1  Proposed Variable Relationships**

While much of what has been written supports the benefits of extending the supply chain to form a network of coordinated activities, the impact of the Internet on this goal has not yet been empirically investigated.

## SCOPE AND ORGANIZATION OF OUR STUDY

In addition to investigating the levels of Internet usage as applied to company-to-company interactions, our study attempted to investigate specific research propositions and relationships concerning Internet usage, SCM performance, and extended (B2B) SCM practices. Figure 5.1 depicts the proposed relationships.

We propose that a relationship exists between Internet usage and SCM performance. Further, we propose that a relationship exists between the adoption of cross-company SCM practices (integrating practices) and Internet usage. In other words, we investigated whether the use of the Internet better facilitated and helped institute sound B2B SCM practices, and whether the use of the Internet had an impact on overall SCM performance.

The unit of analysis during our investigation was member firms within an industry supply chain. Specifically, we investigated the interactions between partners that attempted to manage and coordinate the activities in this chain. These interactions cross company boundaries, and are generally referred to as Extended (B2B) supply chain management or extended SCM. Only specific SCM practices that cross company boundaries are included in this study.

## DEFINING THE CONCEPTS AND MEASURES

As we indicated earlier in the book, when a concept such as the extended supply chain cannot be defined, neither can it be measured, and thus there is no way of determining whether such a concept is being practiced. Therefore, we felt the need to precisely define the concepts under investigation. We used current publications, research reports, expert interviews, and the results of our past research to develop a definition of the extended supply chain concept as follows:

> The *extended supply chain* refers to "extending outward beyond company boundaries to customers and suppliers and connecting with them by use of Internet technologies supporting integrating practices."

Based on this definition, we started by first decomposing the extended supply chain concept into its constituent parts: Internet technologies and integrating practices. Our development of a measure for Internet technology usage is discussed next.

### Internet Technology Usage

Internet technologies are the nervous system of the new economy. The pervasive use of these technologies, enabling the integration of company-to-company supply chains, is a critical strategy in building the extended supply chain. These technologies are network-based and communication/information transfer is their main function (e-mail, online chat, file transfer, shared programs). Building upon recent publications, research, and expert interviews, we defined the concept of *Internet technology usage* as:

1. Interaction through e-mail and online chat
2. Gathering of general information about a customer or supplier
3. Placing orders for goods or services
4. Gathering specific interaction data such as usage, forecasts, complaints, or other performance data

### Integrating Practices

Integration is not just communicating across canyons created by an organization's functions, departments or legal structures. Integration is open and somewhat uncontrolled. Sharing the rewards and consequences of actions taken and decisions made is an integrating mechanism within a company and with supply chain partners. Cohabitation, shared employees, shared information, and shared secrets are also key integrating character-istics. For this investigation, integrating practices were further divided into practices that extend *outward to suppliers* and practices that extend *out-ward to customers:*

> Extending *outward to suppliers* is defined as the purposeful inclusion of suppliers in investments, decisions, facilities, social functions, and joint actions.

> Extending *outward to customers* is defined as the purposeful inclusion of customers in investments, decisions, faculties, social functions, and joint actions; it is the flip side of extending outward to suppliers.

As further validation of the definitions proposed in this study, several focus groups and expert interviews were conducted with SCM practitio-ners. There was general agreement that the definitions proposed captured the extended supply chain construct. Next, we needed proper measures to capture these supply chain practices.

## Measures

The measures representing the integrating practices in the extended supply chain were extracted from our earlier research on BPO and SCM (see Chapter 3). This original research developed overall SCM measures through a literature review, and a series of interviews and focus groups with experts and SCM practitioners held from 1996 through 1999. The results of these interviews and focus groups gave rise to the development of a starter list of measures (survey questions) that were later reduced through testing and analysis. These initial survey questions were then linked to the Supply Chain Operations Reference (SCOR™) model from the Supply Chain Council[12] and sent to several experts for evaluation and feedback. Linking the questions to the SCOR model, a recognized common frame-work for describing supply chain processes and activities, provided an easily recognized process context for responding to the survey questions. This initial scale, used to measure supply chain integration, was then tested within a major electronic equipment manufacturer and with several supply chain experts. A 19-item questionnaire was developed using a five-item Likert-type scale measuring the frequency of the practice consisting of:

1. Never or does not exist
2. Sometimes
3. Frequently

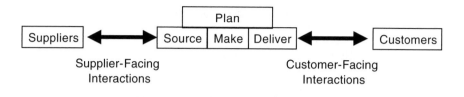

**Figure 5.2 Extended Interactions and the SCOR Model**

4. Mostly
5. Always or definitely exists

The integrating practice measures for the extended supply chain construct were extracted from the original research and broken out by supplier-facing (nine items) and customer-facing (nine items) categories, depicted in Figure 5.2.

We concluded that the selected measures represented specific integrating practices used in SCM between companies interacting within a supply chain. Half were practices used to integrate with a firm's customers, and half were used to integrate with a firm's suppliers.

The numerical designation, next to each question listed in Tables 5.1 and 5.2, indicates the applicable section within each area of the SCOR (*Plan, Source, Make,* and *Deliver*) and the original research question number within that section. For example, P15 refers to the 15th question about the overall supply chain Planning process in the original research. S8 refers to the eighth question about the Source process, and so on.

The Internet usage-specific measures (DT no.) were developed for this study through expert interviews, focus groups, and validation activities. Measure categories were developed, matching the construct definitions along with the starter list of measures developed during the previous

**Table 5.1 Extending Outward to Suppliers**

| | |
|---|---|
| P15 | Does this team (operations strategy team) participate in supplier relationships? |
| S8 | Do you share planning and scheduling information with suppliers? |
| S9 | Do key suppliers have employees on your site(s)? |
| S10 | Do you "collaborate" with your suppliers to develop a plan? |
| S11 | Do you measure, and provide feedback about, supplier performance? |
| M5 | Are supplier lead times a major consideration in the planning process? |
| S6 | Do suppliers manage "your" inventory of supplies? |
| S5 | Do you have strategic suppliers for all products and services? |
| S7 | Do you have electronic ordering capabilities with your suppliers? |

## Table 5.2 Extending Outward to Customers

| | |
|---|---|
| P15 | Does this team (operations strategy team) participate in customer relationships? |
| P25 | Does your demand management process make use of customer information? |
| D9 | Are the projected delivery commitments given to customers credible (from the customer's view)? |
| D4 | Are the customers satisfied with the current on-time delivery performance? |
| M13 | Is your customer's planning and scheduling information included in yours? |
| D3 | Do you track the percentage of completed customer orders delivered on time? |
| D12 | Do you automatically replenish a customer's inventory? |
| P23 | Is a forecast developed for each customer? |
| P6 | Has your business defined customer priorities? |

## Table 5.3 Customer Interaction-Related Internet Usage

| | |
|---|---|
| DT1 | Do your customers interact with you through the Internet (e-mail, online chat)? |
| DT2 | Do your customers gather information about you (and your products) through the Internet? |
| DT3 | Do your customers place orders for your goods and services through the Internet? |
| DT4 | Do you gather customer data (usage, forecast, ideas, complaints) through the Internet? |

## Table 5.4 Supplier Interaction-Related Internet Usage

| | |
|---|---|
| DT5 | Do your suppliers interact with you through the Internet (e-mail, online chat)? |
| DT6 | Do you gather information about your suppliers (and their products) through the Internet? |
| DT7 | Do you place orders for your suppliers' goods and services through the Internet? |
| DT8 | Do you gather supplier data (performance, forecast, ideas) through the Internet? |

research, literature review, and interview results. The scale used for integrating practice measures was also used for Internet usage measures. The resulting measures used in this study are shown in Tables 5.3 and 5.4.

SCM performance, as in our earlier research, was measured using a self-report rating scale completed by the respondents. The questionnaire contained a question in each of the four SCOR model areas, which asked the participants to rate the performance of the specific SCM process on a scale of "1" to "5" by agreeing or disagreeing with the following statement: "Overall, this decision process performs very well." For a total SCM performance score, the individual answers were summed to create one score that was used in the correlation analysis.

## DATA GATHERING AND RESULTS

### Sample

The survey questionnaires used in this study were distributed to Supply Chain Council members in July 2000. Twenty-five companies participated, and 38 usable surveys were returned. Figures 5.3a and 5.4b depict the industry makeup of the respondents, Figure 5.4 the functions, and Figure 5.5 the positions in the sample.

### Analysis of Data

As a general validation review, frequencies and distributions were developed and compared to the overall database compiled from the multiyear study. In general, the U.S. and European samples were evenly matched regarding integrating practices, and were either at or above the mean of the overall database. The conclusion was that the data set included companies that were using integrating practices to a reasonable level.

Regarding Internet usage, Figure 5.6 depicts the results. The horizontal bar shows the mean of the total sample; the diamond denotes the mean of the European sample; the triangle represents the mean of the North American sample; and the percentages indicate the distribution of respondents' answers (1 through 5). In general, the North American sample showed higher Internet usage than Europe, which makes sense. It is generally accepted that the United States is ahead of Europe in this regard.

From the low usage level listed in Figure 5.6, Internet usage appears to be in an early phase of adoption. Basic e-mail interaction is quite common between both suppliers and customers, while taking orders online was surprisingly low. Considering the e-commerce focus during the last few years, it was expected that taking orders online from customers or placing orders online from suppliers would be almost commonplace. Much to our surprise, however, over 50% of respondents never take or place orders on line. The gathering of information about customers and suppliers was also lower than expected. Perhaps this is due to the fact that, in B2B interactions, the set of suppliers and customers is very stable and well known, thus reducing the need for information gathering.

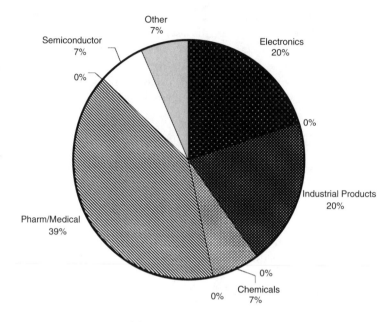

**Europe**

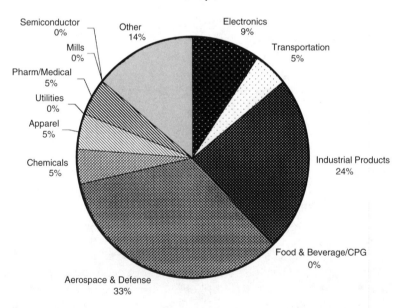

**North America**

Figure 5.3 European and North American Industries in the Sample

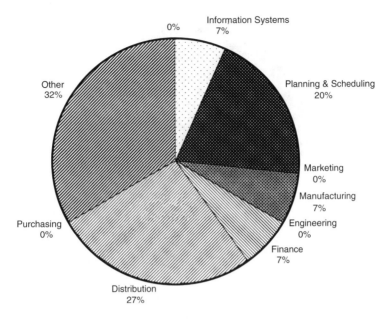

**Europe**

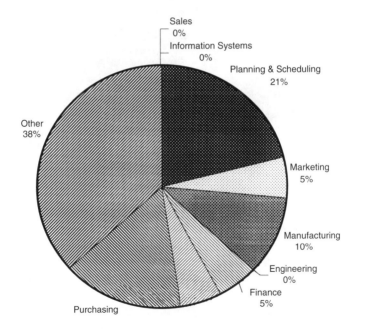

**North America**

Figure 5.4  Functions in the Sample

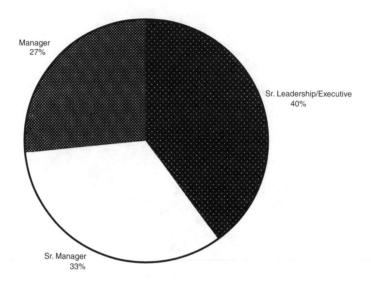

**Europe**

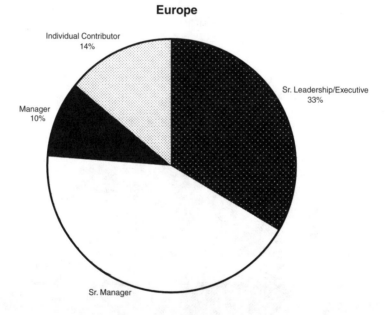

**North America**

**Figure 5.5 Positions in the Sample**

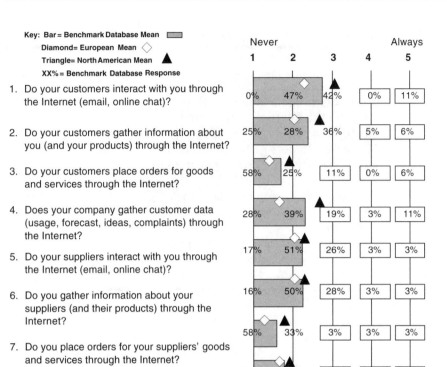

**Figure 5.6 Internet Usage Results**

In order to answer the specific research propositions, a detailed correlation analysis was performed. The results are in Appendix C. Correlation results measure the strength of a relationship from "0" to "1," where "0" is no relationship and "1" is a perfect relationship. The relationships can also be positive or negative, meaning the variables move in opposite directions. Statistical significance was also measured using a Pearson Correlation, two-tailed test. In this study, only correlations above the 95% (0.05) significance level were considered significant.

## RESULTS AND FINDINGS

The correlation results were used to examine two research propositions.

*Proposition 1: A significant relationship exists between Internet usage and SCM performance.*

**Table 5.5 Internet Usage Correlations to SCM Performance**

| Question No. | Question | Correlation | Significance |
|---|---|---|---|
| DT1 | Do your customers interact with you through the Internet (e-mail, online chat)? | 0.364 | 0.05 |
| DT2 | Do your customers gather information about you (and your products) through the Internet? | 0.438 | 0.01 |
| DT4 | Do you gather customer data (usage, forecast, ideas, complaints) through the Internet? | 0.461 | 0.01 |
| DT7 | Do you place orders for your suppliers' goods and services through the Internet? | 0.413 | 0.05 |

Four Internet usage questions were statistically related to overall SCM performance. These are shown in Table 5.5.

Three of the four customer-oriented questions had significant correlations to performance while only one of the four supplier-oriented questions was significant (DT7). This suggests that Internet usage has more of an impact on SCM performance when used in interacting with customers (e-mails, gathering information and data), but not in accepting orders from customers. This is based on the fact that DT3 was not correlated to performance, while DT 1, 2, and 4 were. It also suggests that placing orders with suppliers over the Internet (DT7) has a positive impact on performance, but interacting and gathering information does not (because DT5 and 6 were not correlated to performance). These results suggest a benefit from Internet usage that is slanted toward the supplier role, not a customer, with the exception of efficient processing of orders from a customer with a supplier (DT7).

> *Proposition 2: A significant relationship exists between the adoption of cross-company SCM practices and Internet usage.*

When investigating the relationship between cross-company SCM practices and Internet usage (DT questions), thirteen relationships were significant. Appendix C contains the details.

Some top line analysis suggests that automatic replenishment processes and demand management (forecasting and planning) processes can be positively influenced by Internet use. The results also suggest that interacting with customers through the Internet can influence customer satisfaction with on-time delivery performance. What is most interesting is the negative relationship between question DT3, customers placing orders through the Internet, and a business defining customer priorities. This indicates that the more customer orders you take through the Internet, the less you need to prioritize or rank your customers' orders. It would also suggest that the more orders you take through the Internet, the less you need to expedite, which is the main reason for customer priorities.

Regarding interaction with suppliers, six relationships were significant. Appendix C contains the details.

The emphasis here is that Internet usage strongly influences supplier management of a customer's inventory (question S6) in all supplier-related Internet usage areas. This is consistent with the earlier findings concerning interactions with customers, but is even more significant here. The sharing of planning and scheduling information with suppliers, as well as electronic ordering capabilities were also positively influenced by Internet usage. No other relationships with the nine supplier integrating practices were significant. This is a surprising result because it was expected that measuring supplier performance and collaborating with suppliers to develop a plan is impacted by Internet usage. This indicates that these activities could be successful without Internet technologies.

In summary, both propositions 1 and 2 have considerable support. The data suggest that Internet usage can have a significant impact on cross-company practices in the areas of vendor management inventory (VMI), planning, and demand management. The data also suggest that Internet usage can positively impact overall SCM performance in the extended supply chain.

## CONCLUSIONS AND IMPLICATIONS

In a B2B or extended supply chain, a customer- and process-focused integration of all the SCM aspects is vital. The Internet has provided the ability to easily send and receive information globally. The results of this study suggest that use of the Internet to connect outward to customers and suppliers can influence SCM performance. The results of this study also suggest that a participant in a supply chain may benefit more from extending outward to its customers than back toward its suppliers.

In this study, customers also appear to be more satisfied with on-time delivery performance when information is made available or provided through the Internet. In addition, the results suggest that, when the provided customer information is part of the demand management and the planning and scheduling processes, supply chain performance is positively influenced. The inverse correlation between the use of the Internet and the need for the business to define customer priorities, a key indicator of the practice of expediting orders, suggests that disruptions and unplanned orders are minimized when suppliers leverage the Internet in SCM. Our research suggests that, with the frequent interaction enabled by the Internet, the SCM processes may run more smoothly.

Our research also strongly suggests that Internet usage will enable companies to more easily extend outward to suppliers to share forecasting, planning, and scheduling information. This sharing of demand forecasts can significantly reduce inventory held just-in-case and increase the confidence in suppliers' commitments. Both of these lead to less inventory and improved synchronization of supply chain activities. The results of this study also strongly suggest that connection strategies, such as vendor management inventory, are aided by the use of the Internet. This would further improve the synchronization of a supply chain's activities.

Another observation clearly drawn from this research project is that company-to-company supply chains have begun to interact with their partners using the Internet. They are sharing data and exchanging e-mails. They are providing timely digital orders and some have begun establishing a collaborative effort with their partners. As organizations realize the benefits of supply chain partner collaboration and extending their supply chains, these organizations will no longer view themselves as separate entities, but as partners of their supply chain networks or business webs. This integration of supply chain partners will better position them to fulfill the new customer demands requiring increased agility, versatility, and synchronization of the SCM processes. The extended supply chain is becoming a reality, drawing companies toward the formation of supply chain networks.

Chapter 6 examines these forces in more depth as well as the impact of company-to-company relationships as they form into supply chain networks.

## REFERENCES

1. Tapscott, D., Ticoll, D., and Lowy, A. (2000). *Digital Capital: Harnessing the Power of Business Webs*. Boston: Harvard Business School Press.
2. Daugherty, P.J., Myers, M.B., and Autry, C.W. (1999). Automatic replenishment programs: an empirical examination, *J. Bus. Logistics,* 20, 2, 63–82.
3. Droge, C. and Germain, R. (2000). The relationship of electronic data interchange with inventory and financial performance, *J. Bus. Logistics,* 21, 2, 209–230.
4. Waller, M., Johnson, M.E., and Davis, T. (1999). Vendor-managed inventory in the retail supply chain, *J. Bus. Logistics,* 20, 1, 183–203.
5. Stank, T., Crum, M., and Arango, M. (1999). Benefits of interfirm coordination food industry supply chains, *J. Bus. Logistics,* 20, 2, 21–41.
6. Homs, C. (December 2000). Network supply chains emerge, *The Forrester Report.*

7. AMR Research. (2000). Supply chain strategies outlook: e-business is morphing supply chains. *AMR Research Report on Supply Chain Management for January 2000*.

8. Ljungdahl, L.G. (November/December 2000), What you need to know about the Internet-enabled supply chain. *Supply Chain Management Review*.

9. Kahl, S.J. and Berquist, T.P. (September/October 2000). A primer on the Internet supply chain, *Supply Chain Management Review*.

10. Bowersox, D.J., Closs, D.J., Stank, T.P., and Keller, S.B. (September/October 2000). How supply chain competency leads to business success, *Supply Chain Management Review*.

11. Lee, H.L. (September/October 2000). Creating value through supply chain integration, *Supply Chain Management Review*.

12. Supply Chain Council. (2000). http://www.supply-chain.org.

# 6

## INTERACTIONS AND RELATIONSHIPS IN THE NETWORKED ECONOMY

The Internet has driven the unbundling and reshaping of the integrated corporations of yesterday into value-creating "networks" of suppliers and customers. In the past, the interactions between companies were constrained by the cost and difficulties of communicating using yesterday's technologies. This drove the idea that it was better to contain business activities within a company than to interact with others outside of the company boundaries. With the new digital technologies and the global network we call the Internet, this relationship or business truism has changed dramatically, thus driving the unbundling of the corporation. This chapter discusses this change and the new possibilities for the supply chain.

### INTRODUCTION

The most efficient way to produce anything is to bring together under one management as many of the activities as possible needed to turn out the product. This principle has guided business leaders and strategists for most of the 20th century. Although the concept itself was not developed until after the Second World War, it was actually put into practice 70 or 80 years earlier by John D. Rockefeller.[1] He put exploration, production, transport, refining, and selling into one corporate structure, resulting in the most efficient and lowest-cost petroleum operation, the Standard Oil Trust; it was probably the most profitable large enterprise in business history. Henry Ford, in the early 1920s, also put this concept into practice with the Ford Motor Company. Not only did it produce all parts of the automobile and assemble it, it also made its own steel, its own glass, and its own tires as well as owning the plantations in the Amazon that grew the rubber trees. The company also owned and ran the railroad that carried supplies to the plant and the completed cars from it.

Ronald Coase, who suggested that assembling activities into one company lowers "transactional costs," especially the cost of communications and coordination, developed the theory that informed this practice. For this he received the 1991 Nobel Prize in economics.

Yet this picture has dramatically changed during the past ten years. General Motors, for example, has divested itself of much its manufacturing by spinning off into a separate company called Delphi the making of parts and accessories that together account for 60 to 70% of the cost of producing a car. Rather than owning, or at least controlling, suppliers of parts and accessories, GM will in the future buy them at auction and/or on the Internet through its Covisant business-to-business (B2B) hub. GM is joining a growing list of global competitors who are increasingly functioning as a "syndicate" or "confederacy," which coordinates a diverse network of supply chain partners. The global company of 2025 will likely be held together by a strategy where alliances, joint ventures, and know-how agreements will serve as the building blocks of the confederacy.

Instead of seeing the activities of the firm ending at the edges of individual companies, chains of activities are being performed by different organizations in a coordinated fashion. This requires tremendous process, information, and social integration within the supply chain network of companies.

What is the force driving these actions that seems contrary to the theory and the strategy of most of the successful corporations of the 20th century? The force is, quite simply, the Internet. It has practically eliminated the physical costs of communications and coordination, thus undermining the theory that reduced transactional cost can be achieved only inside the corporation. This means that the most productive and most profitable way to organize is to unbundle.

## INTERACTION COSTS — UNBUNDLING THE CORPORATION

Interaction costs, the money and time expended whenever people and companies exchange goods, services, or ideas, play a crucial role in shaping corporations. These costs are the friction in the economy that drives the way companies organize and the relationships they build. This friction, as well as the capability of the interaction pipeline, has changed dramatically over time. Figure 6.1 puts a historical perspective on this shift.

In the early 20th century, interaction technologies such as the telephone and radio accelerated the trend begun by the telegraph. Rich communi-

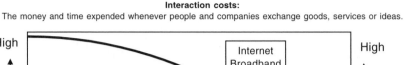

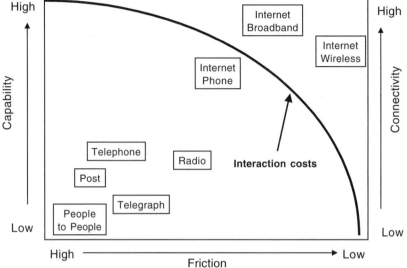

**Figure 6.1   Historical Shift in Interaction Friction and Capability**

cation within and between corporations became possible and affordable. One-to-one conversations became possible on a global scale, replacing the cryptic telegrams that were too often misunderstood. This increase in communication capability helped make the global corporation an effective reality, with almost daily coordination possible. The cost of this communication has also been dramatically reduced. As recently as the 1980s, an international call could easily cost $250. This has been reduced by a factor of ten and is sometimes bundled into a monthly service charge, making it almost invisible.

Another factor that energized the shift in interaction friction is connectivity — the number of possible connections available with which to interact. This connectivity really took off with the worldwide telephone service that we now take for granted. Today, it is not uncommon for a single person to have three business telephone numbers: a voice line, a fax line, and a mobile line. Conference calls with hundreds of participants are now a part of daily business life.

As personal computers became the standard desktop (and mobile) business appliance and the Internet enabled the connection of these appliances to the global telephone system, the interaction capability expanded exponentially. E-mail, file transfers, Web sites and real-time chat dramatically reduced interaction costs. The cost of an e-mail is so minute

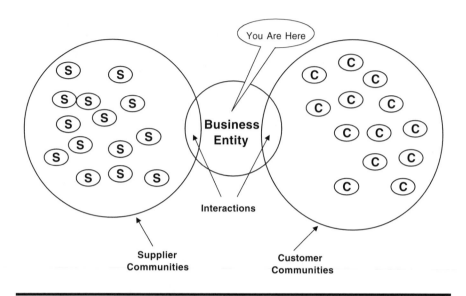

**Figure 6.2   The Corporation of Yesterday**

that it is extremely difficult to measure. Now, with computer-to-computer connectivity easily possible, the interaction capability and connectivity potential is almost unlimited.

What are the impacts of this shift in the equation that allowed Standard Oil to dominate the first part of the 20th century? What has been proposed is the unbundling of the vertically integrated corporation, creating networks of outsourced business processes.[2] Figure 6.2 provides a simple perspective on the corporation of yesterday: the bundled, vertically integrated firm containing as much of the activities as possible within the boundaries of the corporation.

Friction, resulting in communication and coordination costs was the "glue" that apparently held this form together. The theory, and indeed the business reality, that held this form together for most of the 20th century was the understanding that is was easier and less costly to interact within the firm than between outside entities.

As the interaction costs were dramatically reduced and interaction capabilities radically increased, this glue appeared to reverse itself, becoming a force driving the activities apart. In many cases, it was easier and less costly to interact with companies outside of the corporation than with business units inside. The corporation began to break apart. Outsourcing became commonplace; outsourced manufacturing, warehousing, and distribution became the norm. Entire industry segments were created and matured just around these activities. Product development, research, and engineering also became outsourced business activities. This unbundled

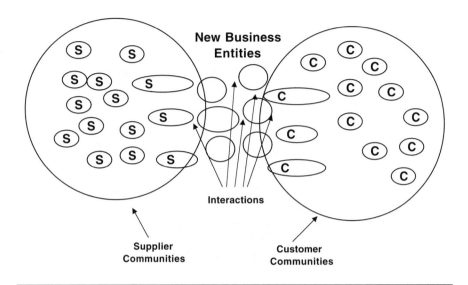

**Figure 6.3 The Unbundled Corporation**

form, represented in Figure 6.3, became the new "truism" of the 21st century. Building and managing this network of companies became the new competitive battleground.

## MORE THAN JUST COMMUNICATION

To manage this network of companies and achieve their intended effectiveness efficiencies, it takes more than just communication. These networks must interoperate on many levels. Alignment of strategies, structures, jobs, and measures is as critical as ever, and common goals and objectives need to be broadly accepted by members of the entire network of trading partners.

Consider how Cisco has achieved this level of integration. For example, its "e-Hub" practically eliminates the need for human intervention; instead, flows of information among Cisco's supply network partners are completely automated (see Figure 6.4). For example, under the Cisco e-Hub, Cisco's demand forecasts are visible to everyone in the supply network, allowing suppliers and manufacturers to better anticipate orders. The network, however, also has a common goal and benefits are shared between members, not just Cisco. Network members have jobs that are focused on the interaction within this network, and they allocate resources to improve the operation of the network processes. These are all key elements of business process orientation (BPO) and, from our research, lead to superior business performance and esprit de corps.

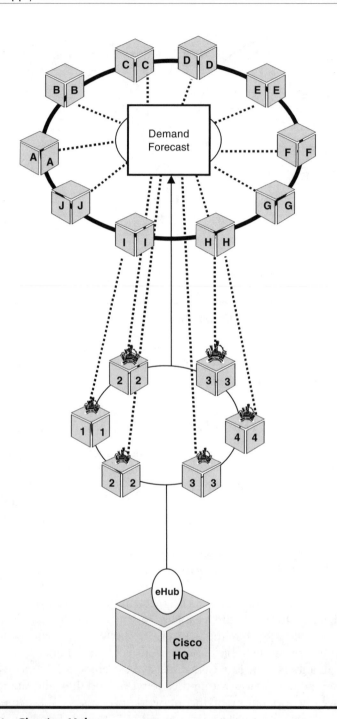

**Figure 6.4    Cisco's e-Hub**

With the unbundling of the corporation, esprit de corps, so desperately sought by leaders of single corporations, now must be built across dozens of companies in a supply chain network. The business processes that were difficult to integrate across the internal functions of a single company now must cross multiple company boundaries. Interfunctional cooperation, a major issue with business process performance, must now be intercompany cooperation.

What are the dimensions of this expansion and the new application of BPO to an entire network of companies? Earlier chapters dealt with the challenges of business process alignment across the supply chain. This chapter focuses on the challenge of integrating not just business processes, but information and "people" flows across firms in the supply chain network.

Alignment is not just between information systems and process activities. The BPO components of process jobs, structures, measures, and values and beliefs need to be aligned between network members as well. It has been demonstrated that this BPO alignment between functions within a company leads to improvements in interfunctional cooperation, company performance, and esprit de corps, and will have the same effect within the network as within the firm.

Our experience is that effective supply chain network integration often fails due to weak relationship bonds. For example, the hierarchy of "bonds" in Figure 6.5 strengthens interorganizational ties in the network

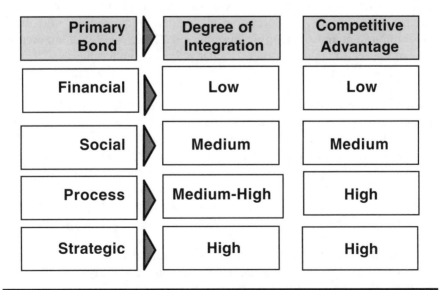

| Primary Bond | Degree of Integration | Competitive Advantage |
|---|---|---|
| Financial | Low | Low |
| Social | Medium | Medium |
| Process | Medium-High | High |
| Strategic | High | High |

Figure 6.5   Levels of Relationship Marketing (Adapted from Berry, L. [1995] On great service. *The Free Press*.)

supply chain. Supply chain actors, with bonds that are based solely on financial or social terms, rarely capitalize on higher degrees of integration or gain a superior competitive advantage. Only recently have we witnessed increasingly higher integration at the process level, which we reported in our earlier book. Integration at the strategic level remains yet an ideal, however, as goals of joint planning and resource sharing have gone largely unfulfilled.

We have already seen that process and systems integration is now possible within the supply chain network, resulting in greater interorganizational connectedness and esprit de corps, as well as improved supply chain performance. This chapter examines the importance of information flows, as well as the development of relationship bonds among the interfirm actors within supply chain networks. The full benefits of supply network integration cannot be fully realized apart from informational and relational alignment. Information exchange, we believe, is a "bridge" to connect network actors, thus enabling the building of strong relational exchanges among these same players.

## INFORMATION EXCHANGE AND NETWORK ALIGNMENT

*Information exchange* is the lubricant that keeps relationships stable and healthy. Where price may attract a relationship, information sustains it. When buyers offer more information, sellers in turn are willing to provide more services, thus creating a win–win situation. Higher levels of integration are based on liberal information exchange, which in turn builds trust and commitment among supply chain players. The reduction of interaction friction, enabled by the Internet, dramatically accelerates this.

McKesson Corporation, a major drug wholesaler, has built a supply chain network representing thousands of independent pharmacies. McKesson invests in this network by helping the independent pharmacies set up accounting and inventory systems, as well as computer ordering systems (i.e., electronic data interchange or EDI). McKesson sets the rules and, most important, the interaction standards that facilitate effective information exchange that make the network function as one. The company also shares in the returns on its investment as a result of building the network. The pharmacies gain value from improved stock planning, resulting in fewer stock-outs and more satisfied customers. McKesson also benefits by creating "captive" retail accounts, which grant McKesson unprecedented access to their sales and financial data.

This information sharing is central to the integration and coordination of supply chains. A common pitfall of poorly managed information flows is the "bullwhip" effect in which demand variability amplification through the supply chain sequence leads to inaccurate forecasts, low capacity

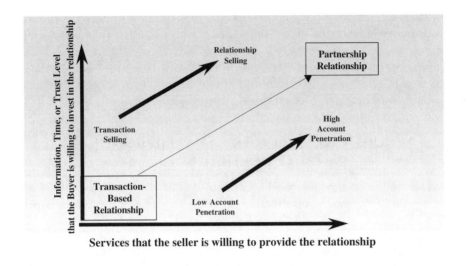

Figure 6.6   Information and Relationships

utilization, excessive inventory, and inadequate customer service.[3] Based on research from the high-technology industry, information sharing can significantly minimize the consequences of this problem.[4] Furthermore, active information exchange between buyers and sellers can also result in product and process innovation. Eric Von Hippel, professor of management of technology at Massachusetts Institute of Technology, found that, in some industries, more than two-thirds of the innovations he studied could be traced back to a customer's initial suggestions or ideas.[5] Consider the fragrance industry, where suppliers are much more involved in new product planning than in the past. One case in point is Vanilla Fields, the blockbuster mass-market scent from Coty. Coty presented Fragrance Resources, one of its suppliers, with a challenge to find "the musk of the Nineties." Fragrance Resources came up with vanilla, but also gave Coty a lot of other marketing information, such as ways that it could position a vanilla fragrance.

In many cases, knowledge exchange between buyers and sellers develops informally over time through interfirm interactions. The key is to use the information obtained to create value for the exchange partners. For example, Fuji and Xerox have attempted to codify this knowledge by creating a "communications matrix," which identifies a set of relevant issues (e.g., products, technologies, markets, and so on), and then identifies the individuals (by function) within Fuji and Xerox who have relevant expertise on that particular issue. This matrix provides valuable information regarding where relevant expertise resides within the partnering firms and helps direct interactions in a much more focused way.

Although information exchange is critical in the unbundled corporation, the long-term result of these interactions is to establish relational bonds among supply chain network actors. Effective supply chain network integration involves many elements, but collaboration, not competition, is a key to the various actors working in harmony to better satisfy customer requirements and achieve superior business performance.

## BUILDING STRONGER NETWORK BONDS — THE TIES THAT BIND

One of the indicators we used to measure BPO was "aligned values and beliefs," which guides supply chain actors as they interact. When supply actors practice opportunistic behaviors, such as taking advantage of another partner, friction is added to the supply network. This friction can grow and actually destroy the network if left unchecked. According to Evert Gummesson, professor and research director of the school of business, Stockholm University, "Effective collaboration in a long-term relationship can only take place if the parties feel like winners, or at least that they gain from a relationship or that it is their best option under the circumstances."[4] In our research, this is defined as network esprit de corps and is strongly related to superior business performance.

Relational bonds are established based on four key behaviors, which we call "relationship enablers." These relationship enablers are the "glue" that binds not simply network firms, but individuals within the supply networks. We propose that these relationship enablers are enhanced by BPO and will minimize relationship decay and strengthen the bonds that lead to long-term supply network relationships. The relationship enablers consist of trust, commitment, dependence, and cooperation (see Figure 6.7).

### Trust

It has been strongly suggested that trust is one factor that plays an important role in facilitating closer buyer–supplier relationships by reducing the tendency of firms to take advantage of each other.[5] A seller can create confidence in the eyes of the buyer by being credible and following up on what he or she promises. For example, Federal Express dominates the overnight delivery market overnight because it promises to have the customer's package there "absolutely, positively, overnight." FedEx's customers rest easy at night knowing that this statement is not simply an advertising slogan, but a pledge to deliver on what the company promises. Further, high levels of trust characteristics during relational exchanges enable both parties to focus on the long-term benefits of the relationship.[6] Perhaps most important, performance outcomes from trust-based relationships will enhance compe-

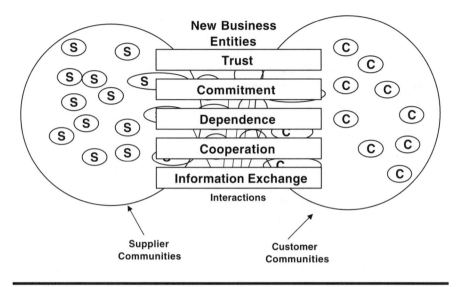

**Figure 6.7   Relationship Enablers**

titiveness and reducing transaction cost.[7] Trust is a fundamental relationship model building block, manifesting four common characteristics:

- A willingness to rely on an exchange partner in whom one has confidence
- One party believes that its needs will be fulfilled in the future by actions taken by the other party
- A party's expectation that another party desires coordination, will fulfill obligations, and will pull its weight in the relationship

The belief that a party's word or promise is reliable, and a party will fulfill his or her obligations in an exchange relationship.[8] Finally, Smeltzer, a noted researcher in the area of relationship marketing, defines trust by stating: "… a trustworthy customer or supplier is one that displays the following characteristics — does not act in a purely self-serving manner, accurately discloses relevant information when requested, does not change supply specifications, standards, or costs to take advantage of other parties, and generally acts according to normally accepted ethical standards."[9]

## Commitment

Besides trust, commitment is another crucial relationship enabler that represents a key construct in both conceptual and empirical models of various interorganizational exchange. Commitment reflects the actions and values of key decision makers regarding continuation of the relationship, acceptance of the joint goals and values of the partnership, and the willingness to invest resources in the relationship. For instance, United Parcel Service and J.C. Penney recently formed a $1 billion partnership in which UPS became Penney's sole mail-order carrier, as well as its logistics carrier, bringing UPS's equipment and expertise to the partnership. Such a commitment signals a willingness by each player to modify its existing systems to fit the other, inextricably binding these companies together.

Further, commitment is present in a supply chain relationship when an exchange partner believes that an ongoing relationship with another is so important as to warrant maximum efforts at maintaining it. Commitment implies an importance of the relationship to the partners and the desire to continue the relationship into the future, leading to a positive effect on relationship profitability. According to Anderson and Weitz, commitment comprises three facets: a desire to develop a stable relationship; a willingness to make short-term sacrifices to maintain the relationship; and a confidence in the stability of the relationship.[10]

## Cooperation

Cooperation is defined as the activity that both the customer and supplier are working jointly to achieve mutual and individual goals. Cooperation also involves coordinated activities between supply chain actors aimed at producing desirable results for all firms. Cooperation among supply chain actors often takes three forms: cooperation in development, technical cooperation, and integration of management.[11] The gains experienced by cooperating in the customer–supplier relationship can more than offset the loss of autonomy in a relationship. Moreover, cooperation frequently involves a willingness to develop joint goals and even share resources. Procter & Gamble actually manages Wal-Mart's inventory, and it is P&G's responsibility to decide when Wal-Mart needs shipments. To do this, P&G has complete access to Wal-Mart's inventory. It manages everything and makes decisions on its own shipments. This arrangement is beneficial for both parties; Wal-Mart can charge less because it does not have the cost of tracking or storing inventory, while P&G has a much bigger share of business, and it does not have to compete with other suppliers.

## Dependence

Weinstein and Johnson define dependence as a willingness to invest time and dedicate resources for the purpose of establishing and strengthening a business relationship.[12] The gains realized from increased dependence include a higher level of shared information, streamlined and efficient transactions, cost savings, technological and process innovation, shortened

**Table 6.1   Rankings of Relationship Enablers among Global Hi-Tech Firms**

| Relationship Enabler | Ranking |
|---|---|
| Trust | 1 |
| Commitment | 2 |
| Dependence | 3 |
| Information exchange | 4 |
| Cooperation | 5 |

lead times in product development, logistics management, and other marketing programs such as joint promotions and shortened response times.

For instance, let us examine Gillette's relationship with Advertising Display Company (ADC), a promotional materials supplier. ADC's partner relationship with Gillette initially started when ADC was chosen to help develop a display program for Gillette's new men's toiletry line, The Gillette Series, consisting of shaving preparation products, deodorants, antiperspirants, and aftershave products. ADC's involvement began with the initial display concept, followed by prototyping, engineering, and assembling prepacked displays, which were shipped to Gillette's major distribution centers. ADC acted as an extension of Gillette's manufacturing and marketing by providing coordinated logistics, display development, pack-out, and distribution. ADC committed 54,000 square feet of manufacturing space and over 100 employees to this product launch.

We conducted research with three global high-technology firms, obtaining rankings of these relationship enablers from key marketing informants. We found that earlier thinking on the relative importance of these relationship factors was in fact supported. That is, trust and commitment were consistently ranked higher when marketing personnel from these hi-tech companies were asked to consider what factors were most important in maintaining strong business relationships. Rankings for all five relationship enablers are outlined in Table 6.1.

Clearly, these relationship enablers are important for establishing relational bonds among supply network actors. Technology sharing and process integration will occur to the extent that these relationship bonds are developed and sustained. Using the checklist in Exhibit 6.1, a company can evaluate the "health" of its supply network relationships.

## SUMMARY

New ways to organize and manage supply chains and business relationships, based upon these interaction economics, are being deployed that

Considering your supply chain partners, <u>rate</u> how they perform on each Relationship Enabler using the scale below:

|  | Excellent | Good | Needs Improvement | Unacceptable |
|---|---|---|---|---|
|  | 4 | 3 | 2 | 1 |
| Trust | _____ | _____ | _____ | _____ |
| Commitment | _____ | _____ | _____ | _____ |
| Dependence | _____ | _____ | _____ | _____ |
| Cooperation | _____ | _____ | _____ | _____ |
| Info. exchange | _____ | _____ | _____ | _____ |

The goal of relationship marketing is to achieve some long-term business goal leading to a sustainable competitive advantage. Using the same customer or supplier as before, what is the <u>likelihood</u> that improvements in the business relationship will produce positive business outcomes (i.e., a sustainable competitive advantage)? Using a 7-point scale, where 1 indicates "No Chance" and 7 indicates "Complete Certainty," assess how likely improvements in your relationship with your buyer (supplier) will lead to positive business outcomes:

|  | Probability | | | | | | |
|---|---|---|---|---|---|---|---|
|  | No Chance | | | | | Complete Certainty | |
|  | 1 | 2 | 3 | 4 | 5 | 6 | 7 |
| What is the probability that improvements in this relationship will substantially reduce costs or lead to better asset utilization? | 1 | 2 | 3 | 4 | 5 | 6 | 7 |
| What is the probability that improvements in this relationship will improve customer service as indicated by the customer? | 1 | 2 | 3 | 4 | 5 | 6 | 7 |
| What is the probability that improvements in this relationship will result in higher profitability for both partners? | 1 | 2 | 3 | 4 | 5 | 6 | 7 |

**Exhibit 6.1   Diagnosing the Health of Supply Network Partners**

are drastically changing the competitive landscape. Integrated, interoperating trading partner networks with thousands of independent companies are operating and acting as one. Integration of this sort could lead to a whole new level of business performance opportunities. For example, Yankee Group Research, Inc. reports that, over the next five years, collaborating over the Internet will save companies $223 billion in reduced transaction, production, and inventory costs.

New Web technologies are extending the enterprise to include not just customers but all supply network actors, such as suppliers, complementors, and other third-party suppliers. Similar to the sellers, these players will have the same complete, instantaneous access to the customers' information.

We believe that corporate survival in the networked economy will depend both on the effectiveness of internal processes as well as their integration and alignment with supply chain partners and customers. As we have seen, information exchange and strong personal–interpersonal network bonds enable supply integration to go forward. The relationship enablers, such as trust and commitment, are the "glue" that holds internetwork relationships together. Supply network actors will also rely increasingly on dependence, due to the unbundling of the organization. Organizations in the network economy simply cannot "do it all" as in the past.

Cross-network supply chain management will serve as the coordinating mechanism for process integration among supply chain partners where "fit" forecloses competition. Competitors can match individual processes or activities, but cannot match the integration or fit of these activities within a cohesive network. In order to move forward in building a networked economy business or an e-corporation, however, the network must first commit to becoming business process oriented *across the network*. This commitment is critical since it will guide the hundreds of decisions about jobs.

Chapter 7 presents a framework for classifying and understanding the component parts of a network supply chain.

## REFERENCES

1. Staff. (November 1, 2001). Will the corporation survive? *The Economist.*
2. Hagel, J. and Singer, M. (March/April 1999). Unbundling the corporation, *Harvard Bus. Rev.*
3. Lee, L.H., Padmanabham, V., and Whang, S. (Spring 1997). The bullwhip effect in supply chains, *Sloan Manage. Rev.,* 93–102.
4. Lee, H.L., So, K.C., and Tang, C.S. (May 2000). The value of information sharing in a two-level supply chain, *Manage. Science,* 46, 5, 626–643.
5. Von Hippel, E. (1988). *The Sources of Innovation.* New York: Oxford University Press, 89.

6. Gummesson, E. (2001). Relationship marketing in the new economy, *J. Relationship Mark.*, 1, 1, 53.
7. Zaheer, A., McEvily, B., and Perrone, V. (August 1998). The Strategic Value of Buyer–Supplier Relationships, *Int. J. Purch. Mater. Manage.*, 20–26.
8. Ganesan, S. (April 1994). Determinants of long-term orientation in buyer–seller relationships, *J. Mark.*, 58, 1–19.
9. Noordewier, T.G., John, G., and Newin, J.R. (October 1990). Performance outcomes of purchasing arrangements in industrial buyer–vendor relationships, *J. Mark.*, 54, 80–93.
10. Wilson, D.T. (1995). An integrated model of buyer–seller relationships. *J. Acad. Mark. Science,* 23, 4, 335–345.
11. Smeltzer, L.R. (January 1997). The meaning and origin of trust in buyer–supplier relationships, *Int. J. Purch. Mater. Manage.*, 41.
12. Anderson, E. and Weitz, B. (February 1992). The use of pledges to build and sustain commitment in distribution channels, *J. Mark. Res.*, 29, 18–34.
13. Olsen, R.F. and Ellram, L.M. (1997). A portfolio approach to supplier relationships. *Industrial Mark. Manage.*, 26, 101–113.
14. Weinstein, A. and Johnson, W.C. (1999). *Superior Customer Value: Concepts, Cases, and Application in Services Marketing.* Boca Raton, FL: St. Lucie Press.

# 7

---

# UNBUNDLING
# THE CORPORATION:
# A BLUEPRINT FOR SUPPLY
# CHAIN NETWORKS

## by William T. Walker, CFPIM, CIRM

Chaotic supply chain networks, the result of unbundling the corporation, are defined by the success, or failure, of integrating information flow, physical distribution flow, and cash flow.[1] While the capability of interconnecting companies worldwide over the Internet is unparalleled, the strategy and design behind the formation of a networked supply chain must make good business sense to be viable. At the end of the day, organizations invited to join a particular supply chain as trading partners must add value.

This chapter provides a framework to build and operate supply chain networks that realize the competitive benefits of business process orientation (BPO). The five APICS principles of supply chain management (SCM) are offered as a way to align and design the strategic intent, purpose, and processes of a supply chain network. Using these principles in the design and operation of the value-generating potential of the network, coupled with consistent BPO maturity throughout the network, will achieve superior network business performance and esprit de corps.

## UNDERSTANDING SUPPLY CHAIN NETWORKS

The strategy behind the formation of a supply chain network — the why and how — varies considerably. A network can be formed for the purpose of a cost advantage, a cycle time advantage, a product technology advantage, or some other competitive reason. The diversity and maturity of different organizations brought together to form a network may provide the desired synergy needed or limit the potential performance of the network depending upon the fit and integration. For example, an architect can envision the form, fit, and function resulting from the integration of the building components of glass, brick, wallboard, and steel. Once the building is constructed, however, its occupants may or may not find the results of the integration to be as envisioned. As the supply chain architect assembles the components to construct a supply chain network, the resulting impact can be anywhere from process-oriented and highly competitive to immature and dysfunctional, depending upon the successful integration of the components. Buildings have a blueprint to help in this integration. What is the blueprint for a supply chain network?

## Identifying the Main Thread and Business Strategy Alignment

A supply chain network can best be described by following the *main thread* from the demand side to the supply side. The main thread will vary depending on the purpose of the network, such as delivering a product or a service in the forward direction or the reworking or repair of a product in the reverse direction. In building the blueprint, it is helpful to sketch a picture of the physical flow, as it moves through the network, to understand the main thread. This picture will ask many questions. When is the physical flow a container of products, a pallet of assemblies, or a carton of components? What organizations are involved? Where are these organizations located? Where are the highest dollar value assemblies? What is the time sequence of the flow? Why does the product involve import/export? How does the customer receive the product or service? Figure 7.1 depicts one example of how the overlay of the product structure, the supply chain network, and the geography of the trading partners for an electronic instrument can point out the main thread.

The following starting points can be used to identify and trace the main thread:

- If the network delivers product through the forward supply chain — start with the complete product at the customer and trace the *physical flow backward* to raw material.
- If the network delivers service through the forward supply chain — start with the delivery of customer services and trace the *information flow backward* to the source of the service.
- If the network recovers product through the reverse supply chain — start with the product return at the customer and trace the *physical flow forward* to restock, repair, reuse, or recycle.

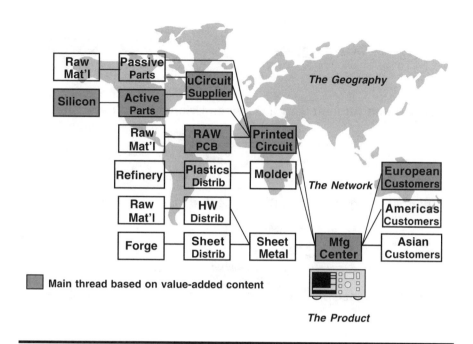

**Figure 7.1   Tracing the Main Thread**

The next step in developing a deeper understanding and clear blueprint of how this network works is to learn where the supply chain network must align with the business strategy.[2] These points of alignment illustrated in Figure 7.2 may occur *upstream, midstream, downstream,* or *reverse stream* in the network.

Alignment *upstream* in the supply chain network, close to the supply base, is essential for a business strategy that focuses on applying new technology to products. This can be a winning strategy because technologically advanced products can provide complete solutions for customer in ways that create competitive advantage.

For example, a supply chain network competing in an ultra-accurate strain gauge instrumentation market might purchase the world's supply of the heat-treated alloy required to make the sensor; it would also want to control the smelt schedules on the forging of new ingots of this alloy. This network blueprint would be carefully drawn to protect and leverage the source of its technology along with the access to associated raw materials and market research.

Alignment *midstream* in the supply chain network is essential for a business strategy that focuses on being the low-cost producer in the market. This can be a winning strategy, particularly in a commodity business, where customers buy on price alone. Such a network may deliver

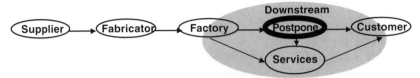

**Downstream Aligned with a Services-Oriented Business Strategy**

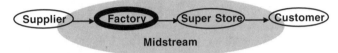

**Midstream Aligned with a Cost-Oriented Business Strategy**

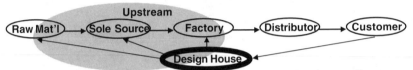

**Upstream Aligned with a Technology-Oriented Business Strategy**

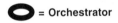 = Orchestrator

**Figure 7.2   Aligning the Network to the Strategy**

products only, without any complementary services, to minimize total cost. Colocation of network members may also reduce costs. For example, the supply chain network for low-cost windows might eliminate a layer of shipping and warehousing by colocating the sash hardware fabricator within the final assembly process of its window factory, thus reducing the overall cost.

Alignment *downstream* in the supply chain network, close to the marketplace, is essential for a business strategy that focuses on delivering services that integrate with the internal processes of the customer. This can be a winning strategy because the customer can outsource a portion of its value-adding process to a business partner having greater competency in a specific process area. After a while, the customer cannot imagine doing business with anyone else. For example, the supply chain network, through its partners, can provide leasing, installation, and application services to a customer or manage a customer's purchased inventory and inbound logistics.

*Reverse stream* alignment in a supply chain network is essential for reverse supply chain networks with business strategies that focus on returns, repair, remanufacturing, or recycling. A competitive reverse stream network is often a required condition to make a products and services business strategy viable in the world market. For example, in the automotive industry, old starter engines, called cores, are pulled from junkyards, remanufactured, and resold in a lucrative automotive parts aftermarket. The raw materials in any cores that are beyond being refurbished are recycled. This network blueprint would be carefully drawn to have a good supply of cores and spare parts, economical recycling, and branded marketing in lower-cost replacement markets.

When the supply chain network design is in serious misalignment with the business strategy, neither expensive information technology systems nor a focus on business process orientation can regain its competitive edge. The network must be reconfigured and aligned to support the business strategy or network business performance will suffer.

## Classifying the Supply Chain Players

By identifying the main thread and examining business strategy alignment, an obvious set of supply chain players will emerge. These will be members of the supply chain network that contribute to the main thread or are key to supporting the business strategy. The next step in the blueprinting process is to classify all the players in the supply chain network into three classifications: trading partners, nominal trading partners, and the orchestrator.

The first class, called *trading partners,* provides an exclusive value-add to the product or service transformation that occurs along the main thread. "A trading partner is an independent organization that plays an integral role within the supply chain network, and whose business fortune depends on the end-to-end success of the supply chain network."[3] Tier one distributors, manufacturing centers, contract manufacturers, and third-party logistics (3PL) service providers are good examples of trading partners. Network throughputs might represent 20%, 33%, even 100% of a trading partner's total revenue, but in each case they would be classified as a trading partner because of their integral roles within the supply chain network.

A second class, called *nominal trading partners,* provides the network "glue" to complete the point-to-point connections for the physical distribution flows, the information flows, and the cash flows that are essential to the operation of the supply chain network. "A nominal trading partner is any independent organization that provides an essential material or service within the supply chain network, but whose financial success is largely independent of the end-to-end financial success of the network."[4] Generic parts suppliers, second-tier distributors, wholesalers, less-than-truckload (LTL) carriers, freight forwarders, customs brokerage services, commercial banks, credit card services, wireless services, and Internet service providers are all examples of nominal trading partners. Network throughputs may represent only 3%, 1%, or 0.02% of a nominal trading partner's total revenue.

The implementation of the business strategy is independent of any nominal trading partner. For this reason, nominal trading partners have the characteristic of being substitutable within the supply chain network, while trading partners are difficult to replace. For example, a number of LTL motor freight carriers service New York City to Philadelphia at about the same transportation cost. A nominal trading partner's product or service may be indistinguishable from similar products or services, but they provide the network glue.

While the main thread of a supply chain network may have only a handful of trading partners, dozens of nominal trading partners may be required to complete the network. For example, the supply chain networks for capital goods with high part counts typically include many nominal trading partners to supply every last-nickel-and dime part required in the bill of materials (BOM). Also, the supply chain networks for consumer goods with high customer counts typically include many nominal trading partners to sell and distribute product to one-time buyers and to remote locations.

In addition to nominal parts suppliers and nominal product distributors, three additional groups of nominal trading partners are found in every supply chain network:

1. Logistics service providers to complete the physical distribution flow
2. Information service providers to complete the information flow
3. Financial service providers to complete the cash flow

These additional nominal trading partners make the supply chain network complete. In this regard, whether they are manufacturing or service, commercial or governmental, or for-profit or not-for-profit, supply chain networks are all the same.

A nominal trading partner may be elevated to trading partner status by providing a strategic value-added service. One example is the 3PL that negotiates successfully to manage all of the network's inbound and outbound freight, regardless of the carrier. This 3PL offers a full set of logistics services and it acts as a virtual organization to manage all the other nominal carriers, freight forwarders, and customs brokers in the network.

A third class of supply chain player is the *orchestrator*. The orchestrator, sometimes called the channel master, is the trading partner that envisions and empowers the supply chain network, gathers the trading partners into a network, leads the development of the network business strategy, and maintains alignment during daily operations. While formation of the supply chain network is voluntary, the orchestrator is able to set the information standard for the network, and often directs the level of information technology investment needed to be a network participant.

The orchestrator is the power broker for a supply chain network. Such power can take many forms, such as having the vision of a new business, having access to strategic customers and markets, having access to proprietary technology, or having the key financial leverage. It is important to understand the basis of the orchestrator's power when analyzing a network because this is the force that drives the network personality and environment. The power aspect of the members of a supply chain network is explored in Chapter 8.

## Tracing the Flows through the Network — Physical, Information, and Cash

A supply chain is the integration of three flows: *physical flow, information flow,* and *cash flow.* Every trading partner, nominal supplier, nominal distributor, and logistics service provider is connected into all three flows at their respective points in the network. On the other hand, information service providers and financial service providers are only connected into the information flow and the cash flow.

Now imagine each player in the supply chain network as three coins stacked vertically one on top of the other. The top coin represents the physical transactions that this player might have with the supply chain network. The middle coin represents the information transactions this player might have with the supply chain network, and the bottom coin represents the cash transactions this player might have with the supply chain network. Now imagine that all the coins for physical transactions in the network are held up by a top tray, or plane; all the coins for information transactions are held up by a middle tray, or plane; and all the coins for cash transactions are held up by a bottom tray, or plane; see Figure 7.3.

A supply chain network accomplishes its work through the proper sequencing and synchronization of these process flows: information ↔ information, information ↔ physical, information ↔ cash, cash ↔ cash, and physical ↔ physical. These different interactions can be categorized in the following way:

- An ***arc*** is the intraplane (within the same plane) movement of physical goods or information or cash from one player, or node, to another.
- A ***loop*** is the value-adding processing of physical material or information or cash that occurs within a plane within the same player, or node.

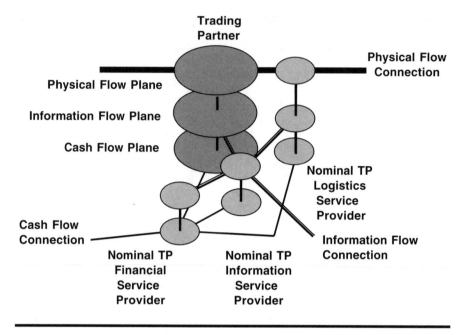

**Figure 7.3   Elements of a Supply Chain Network**

- A *trigger* is an interplane (between two planes) connection that synchronizes a cross-flow process within the same player, or node.

In the most basic process sequence, a product order information flow on the information plane causes a product delivery physical flow on the physical plane. Then, a product invoice information flow on the information plane causes a product payment cash flow on the cash plane. The time sequencing and synchronization of the arc, loop, and trigger connections act together to make the value-adding process work throughout the supply chain network. The main thread can now be described in terms of an exact flow sequence that starts and ends at the same node on the same plane. An example is described in Table 7.1 and illustrated in Figure 7.4. The network flows of the associated nominal trading partners are not normally shown. This simplifies the diagram and adds clarity to the operation of the main thread.

The network blueprint can become very complex. For example, import/export adds an explosion of relationships to the supply chain network. When an international customer places an order with a factory and finances this purchase through a letter of credit, many nominal trading partner nodes are added to the network. The physical flow plane is expanded to include a freight cartage company at the origin and destina-

**Table 7.1   Example Flow Sequence for the Supply Chain Network in Figure 7.4**

| Sequence | Type of Transaction | Process Step |
|---|---|---|
| 1 | Loop | Forecast demand at trading partner. |
| 2 | Arc | Send replenishment order by e-commerce. |
| 3 | Loop | Process replenishment order at supplier. |
| 4 | Trigger | Trigger shipment at supplier. |
| 5 | Loop | Process for shipment at supplier. |
| 6 | Arc | Transport to trading partner. |
| 7 | Trigger | Trigger invoice at supplier (optional). |
| 8 | Arc | Send invoice by e-commerce (optional). |
| 9 | Trigger | Verify material received at trading partner. |
| 10 | Trigger | Trigger payment at trading partner. |
| 11 | Loop | Process payment at trading partner. |
| 12 | Arc | Send payment by e-commerce. |
| 13 | Trigger | Close replenishment order at supplier. |
| 14 | Arc | Capture a customer order by e-commerce. |
| 15 | Loop | Process customer order at trading partner. |
| 16 | Trigger | Trigger shipment at trading partner. |
| 17 | Loop | Process for shipment at trading partner. |
| 18 | Arc | Transport to customer. |
| 19 | Trigger | Trigger invoice at trading partner. |
| 20 | Arc | Send invoice by e-commerce. |
| 21 | Trigger | Verify product received at customer. |
| 22 | Trigger | Trigger payment at customer. |
| 23 | Loop | Process payment at customer. |
| 24 | Arc | Send payment by e-commerce. |
| 25 | Trigger | Close customer order at trading partner. |

tion, a freight forwarder, an airfreight carrier and agent, and a customs bonded warehouse. The information flow plane is expanded to include all the above plus export control and import customs; the cash flow plane is expanded to include all the above plus an issuing bank and an advising bank for the letter of credit.

The most common supply chain network business processes that are connected by the three flows include:

■ A trading partner transforms parts into products.
■ A trading partner transforms information into services.
■ A nominal trading partner (supplier) transforms raw materials into parts.
■ A domestic buyer places an order with a seller, and the purchase is financed through a credit card or procurement card.

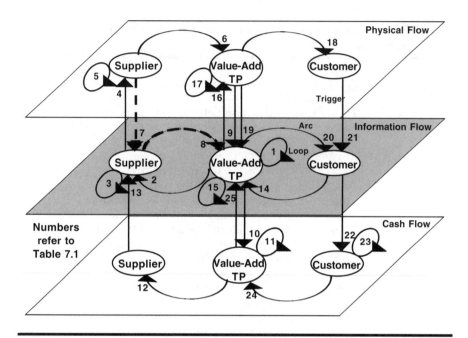

**Figure 7.4 Typical Network Flow Sequences**

■ A product is returned domestically for a refund, and is recycled.
■ An international buyer places an order with a seller, and the purchase is financed through a letter of credit.
■ A product is returned internationally for a replacement.
■ A buyer places an order with a seller based on a forecast of future demand in order to compensate the lead time for the seller's material.
■ A nominal trading partner (logistics service provider) moves physical product, and is paid for the service.
■ A nominal trading partner (information service provider) moves information, and is paid for the service.
■ A nominal trading partner (financial service provider) moves cash in a secure electronic form, and is paid for the service.

## Network Dynamics — Static, Switched, and Chaotic

Not so long ago supply chains consisted of static relationships. A single set of suppliers, factories, wholesalers, and retailers defined a supply chain network that fulfilled orders for customers and created value for shareholders. We call this a *static network*. As product life cycles accelerated, it became commonplace for a new trading partner to be brought into the network, while another was taken out. This dynamic resulted in an

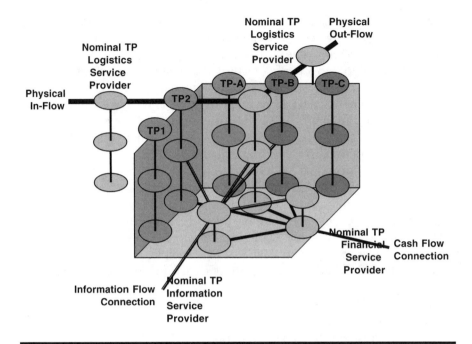

**Figure 7.5    Cross-Section of a Chaotic Supply Chain Network**

adjustment period, as the process interactions and relationships readjusted, until order fulfillment and value creation performance reached previous levels. We call this a *switched network*.

More recently, the word network has come to mean that the set of supply chain players is potentially different for each order fulfilled. We call this a *chaotic network*. Trading exchanges, business-to-business (B2B) e-commerce, and business-to-consumer (B2C) e-commerce over the Internet have made such networks a reality. For every 100 customer orders the static network fulfills orders through a single network configuration, the switched network fulfills orders through two or more different network configurations, and the chaotic network fulfills orders through up to 100 different network configurations. The practicality of dynamically linking and unlinking players to a supply chain network and the interoperability required have been made possible by technological advances in Internet-based hardware and software. Figure 7.5 is a cross-section of one supply chain node in a chaotic network, where arrays of trading partners compete for the next order.

Static networks, switched networks, chaotic networks — how can any sense be made out of such a dynamic in network operations? The answer lies in going back to the competitiveness fundamentals of the static network. Where the static network could afford to spread its return over several customer orders, a chaotic network must make a return on every order-to-cash cycle. Success with a chaotic network is similar to using the technology of a 35mm reflex camera and expecting every frame in the film roll to develop into a perfect picture; this is not likely. Instead, success with a chaotic network should be similar to using the technology of a digital camera, where each bad picture can be quickly deleted and retaken. We believe that building a business-process-oriented network, using the APICS Supply Chain Management Principles as the network blueprint, is the key to competitive network performance.

APICS, the Educational Society for Resource Management, is an international, not-for-profit organization. APICS offers a full range of materials, programs, and certification focused on individual and organizational learning, standards of excellence, and integrated resource management topics. APICS education is available at the local, regional, and society level, and through www.apics.org. The APICS SCM Principles were developed for APICS by the following dedicated team of expert practitioners, consultants, and educators:

- Karen L. Alber, CFPIM — Practitioner
  Vice President, Business Solutions, Quaker Oats
- Cecil Bozarth, Ph.D. — Educator
  Associate Professor of Management, North Carolina State University
- Gary Cokins, CPIM — Consultant
  Director of Industry Relations, ABC Technologies, Inc.
- Steven J. Kahl — Consultant
  Vice President, Global Investment Research, Goldman Sachs
- David L. Rivers, CFPIM, CIRM — Practitioner
  Manager of Ops Systems, DePuy Orthopaedics of Johnson & Johnson
- Gregory L. Schlegel, CPIM, CSP, Jonah — Consultant
  Industry Solutions Executive, IBM Supply Chain Management, IBM
- Sam Tomas, CFPIM, CIRM, C.P.M. — Educator
  Operations and Supply Chain Management Faculty, University of Phoenix
- William T. Walker, CFPIM, CIRM — Practitioner
  Supply Chain Architect, Agilent Technologies

## BUILDING BPO WITHIN A SUPPLY CHAIN NETWORK

Each time trading partners and nominal trading partners come together to form a new supply chain network, the BPO of each must interoperate and align. The following components of BPO in the context of the single firm have been described in earlier chapters: *Process Values and Beliefs,*

*Process View, Process Structure, Process Jobs,* and *Process Management and Measures.* In the next section, the definition of each of the components is expanded into the context of a supply chain network (SCN) that encompasses and integrates multiple players. Here, the BPO components are *SCN Process Values and Beliefs, SCN Process View, SCN Process Structure, SCN Process Jobs,* and *SCN Process Management and Measures.*

## The APICS SCM Principles and BPO

A supply chain network is most competitive when the network achieves a consistently high level of BPO fit and maturity for each of its trading partners. The results, as with a single company, will be high network connectedness with low conflict and a high esprit de corps with high overall network performance. The question is: How do you build the BPO components into a complex, multiorganizational network? Are there strategies, practices, and behaviors that will drive a network toward high levels of BPO maturity when they are applied to a complex network? Are there principles that will operationalize BPO within a network? The APICS SCM Principles are just such a Rosetta stone for unlocking the secrets of how to move a network to high levels of BPO maturity. Figure 7.6 illustrates how the APICS SCM Principles can be used to map the BPO components (the cause) into the BPO impact variables (the effect).

The five principles are based on time-proven, fundamental business truths instead of depending upon a current technological advantage that

| BPO Component | SCM Principles | BPO Impact Variable |
|---|---|---|
| Network Design • SCN Process View • SCN Values & Beliefs | "Build a Competitive Infrastructure" Align with business strategy (nodes) Value-added process velocity Node inventory and process cost | SCN Conflict: Low Inter-plane conflict (nodes) Intra-plane diversity |
| | "Leverage Worldwide Logistics" Transit time variability (arcs) Transit/customs time and delay Pipeline inventory and landed cost | SCN Connectedness: High Intra-plane connects (arcs) Intra-plane connects (loops) Inter-plane connects (triggers) |
| Network Operation • SCN Process Job • SCN Process Structure • SCN Process Management & Measures | "Synchronize Supply with Demand" Drum-system constraint Buffer-protective time Rope-vocalize customer demand The Orchestrator's Role | SCN Esprit de Corps: High Common focus on the customer Everyone pulling together |
| | "Measure Performance Globally" Visualize equivalent throughput Visualize total system inventory The perfect order | SCN Performance: High Customer delight Shareholder value |

**Figure 7.6   Relating BPO Components to BPO Impacts (SCM = Supply Chain Management)**

may decay over time. They provide a common terminology and a rigorous framework from which to optimize return, profit, and positive cash flow within complex networks. At the same time, they are positioned within a context of continuous technological innovation and superior organizational change management leadership. The APICS SCM Principles provide an integrated framework to design and operate new supply chain networks, or to compare the relative competitiveness of an existing supply chain network with a proposed improvement, or to compare the relative merits of the current network against a competitor's network. It should also be noted that these five principles are totally complementary to the Supply Chain Council's "SCOR™" model. Each of the five principles, noted below, is described in detail in the following sections:

- The *Velocity* Principle: **Build a Competitive Infrastructure**[1,4,5]
- The *Variability* Principle: **Leverage Worldwide Logistics**[1,4,5]
- The *Vocalize* Principle: **Synchronize Supply with Demand**[1,4,5]
- The *Visualize* Principle: **Measure Performance Globally**[1,4,5]
- The *Value* Principle: **Supply Chain Creates Net Value**[5]

An auto racing analogy makes it easy to understand how the APICS SCM Principles can help build BPO within a network. The first two APICS SCM Principles, **Build a Competitive Infrastructure** and **Leverage Worldwide Logistics,** are focused on the design aspects of a competitive supply chain network. This is analogous to designing a race car to win a particular class of motor racing. The BPO impact variables, *Connectedness* and *Conflict,* are the goals and hopefully results of such a competitive network design.

The next two APICS SCM Principles, **Synchronize Supply with Demand** and **Measure Performance Globally,** are focused on the operational aspects of a competitive supply chain network. This is analogous to actually driving the race car to victory on a particular racetrack. The BPO impact variables, *Esprit de Corps* and *Performance,* are the results of such a competitive network operation.

The final APICS SCM Principle, **Supply Chain Creates Net Value,** is focused on the value of winning for each of the stakeholders. This is analogous to determining the value of the win to the owner, the sponsor, the driver, and the pit crew. When each network organization is in alignment at the highest level of BPO Maturity, then maximum value is created for all of the stakeholders.

The following sections will help explain how the APICS SCM Principles are used to operationalize BPO and provide the handles and the levers by which one can direct the supply chain network design and operation toward the highest level of BPO Maturity.

## INTEGRATING BPO WITH NETWORK DESIGN

Supply chain network design is the encapsulation of the inputs, processes, and outputs for physical flows, information flows, and cash flows, often involving distributed organizations and vast geographies. The APICS SCM Principles of *Build a Competitive Infrastructure* and *Leverage Worldwide Logistics* drive the blueprint for a competitive network design. Effective supply chain network design, one that is business-process-oriented, must have as one of the key design requirements the components of BPO. In this way, the final network will exhibit the BPO results of low *Conflict* and high *Connectedness* required for superior network *Performance* and *Esprit de Corps.*

### Build a Competitive Infrastructure

This APICS SCM Principle is about designing the node architecture for a supply chain network that aligns with the business strategy and accelerates the value-added process velocity faster than that of the competition. The network nodes set the minimum achievable cost and cycle time for the main thread. It is analogous to designing a race car. The car designer must understand which racing rules and track are to be used. Is this Formula One or NASCAR? Will the most grueling race be at LeMans or Daytona? Then the race car is engineered from a perfectly matched set of components: a powerful engine, fuel injection, a matched transmission, an aerodynamic body, radial tires, etc.

As the supply chain architect examines different scenarios in the chaotic network, the following design questions should be answered:

- What are there fundamental business reasons for each of the value-adding trading partner nodes allowed onto the main thread?
- Is the architecture of the main thread always aligned with a single, focused business strategy?
- Is the role of the orchestrator understood and respected by other players?
- Is the number of nominal trading partner nodes used to reach both domestic and international suppliers kept to a minimum?
- Is the number of nominal trading partner nodes used to reach both domestic and international customer kept to a minimum?
- Can the set of logistics service providers remain constant or be consolidated within the chaotic network?

- Can the set of information service providers remain constant or be consolidated within the chaotic network?
- Can the set of financial service providers remain constant or be consolidated within the chaotic network?
- Is there a competitive node design for the reverse supply chain network?

The BPO-related concept of *Conflict* is a major consideration in the node architecture of a supply chain network. Interplane conflict within a node slows the main thread velocity. This type of conflict occurs between people from different functional areas within the same trading partner, and is driven by differences in local decisions about how to allocate scarce resources. Intraplane conflict also slows the main thread velocity between pairs of trading partner nodes. This type of conflict is evidenced by misunderstanding and miscommunication, and is caused by issues of diversity and the lack of a common language. The people at the different nodes feel separated by time zone and geography, by culture, by language, and by organizational diversity. Even if the network trading partners speak the same general language, they often have their own process terms that have been developed within their individual functional silos over the years. This process language is a dialect so specific to one partner that the other network trading partners do not understand it.

Implementing the BPO component, *SCN Process View*, will address the process language issue. Defining, documenting, and understanding each other's processes, or at least the required interactions, will build a common process language between the nodes, as it has been shown to do between functions. Our research has shown that when people participating in the network view the network as a series of linked, dependent processes — a key aspect of SCN Process View — cooperation increases and conflict is reduced.

It has been demonstrated that *SCN Process Values and Beliefs* improve *Esprit de Corps* and build strong, trusting personal relationships at each interface, be it functional or company-to-company. Common process values and beliefs can greatly reduce conflict. The degree to which customer requirements are heard and met by network processes is a measure of the customer focus of the supply chain community, a critical aspect of SCN Process Values and Beliefs. Other SCN Process Values and Beliefs include continuous improvement as a network philosophy and valuing organizational diversity. Internet technology, while it may reduce interaction costs and friction, is incapable of resolving a personal conflict or a diversity bias. In the auto racing analogy, if a high level of friction occurs in the clearance of the piston heads within the engine cylinders, then wear on the engine parts will limit engine life at the maximum RPM and lose the race. High friction between the nodes in a network will also cause wear and eventual damage.

## Leverage Worldwide Logistics

This APICS SCM Principle is about designing the arc, loop, and trigger architecture for the supply chain network that minimizes process variability better than that of the competition. The network arcs, loops, and triggers set the minimum achievable delay and inventory for the main thread. In the auto racing analogy, flaws in the race car design can result in uneven tire wear and excessive fuel consumption. This variability must be found during the time trials and quickly driven out of the design, or the race will be lost.

Again the BPO components of *SCN Process View* and *SCN Values and Beliefs* are critical here. For example, flows that are delayed due to conflict or poor connectedness accumulate cost and reduce overall competitiveness. Stopped physical flow is material inventory; stopped information flow is database "inventory" and stopped cash flow is capital "inventory." In a supply chain network, the smaller the total number of arcs, loops, and triggers required in the design of the main thread, the shorter the total delay and the lower the total inventory investment.

Each physical distribution arc must be predicable, reliable, and cost effective to be competitive. Here is where one of the SCN Process Values and Beliefs, *Continuous Improvement,* comes into play. Using these principles, specific logistics links that exhibit high variability in transit time or customs clearance time can be identified. Then either a root cause can be identified to fix the problem, or the offending link can be eliminated from the network. The frequent cause of this variability is poor internode communications resulting in time variability to make decisions and to trigger actions. The BPO component, SCN Process View, which builds a process language and mutual understanding, can directly attack this cause thus reducing the variability and improving network performance.

Logistics is not just about material flow. A particular supply chain network can have a good order-to-delivery design, but a poor cash-to-cash design and end up going bankrupt. The best supply chain network will beat the competition in both areas. Order-to-delivery and cash-to-cash concepts are also important in the design of the reverse supply chain network.

Order-to-delivery (and reorder-to-replenishment) cycle time looks upstream from the order originator to the next trading partner in the supply chain network holding physical inventory. In Figure 7.7, this cycle time is the sum of: order transmission time + order processing time + shipment trigger time + cycle time to complete production +

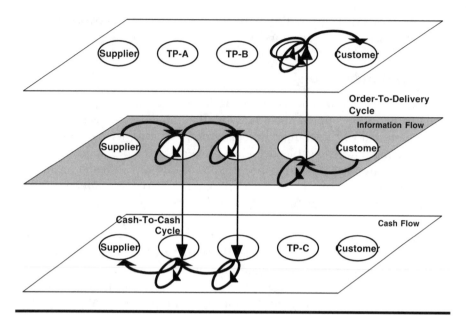

**Figure 7.7  Order-to-Delivery and Cash-to-Cash Cycles**

shipment processing time + transit time + customs clearance time through to delivery.

The lower the order-to-delivery cycle time, the higher is its velocity. Using the SCN Process Value of *Continuous Improvement,* the cycle time elements can be examined to identify opportunities to reduce or eliminate some time through the application of technology. One example is an agreement among the network players to use the open standards of RosettaNet to automate the transmission and capture of electronic purchase orders.

Cash-to-cash cycle time looks downstream from the invoice originator to the next trading partner in the supply chain network that must pay for purchases. This cycle time is the comparison of the supplier-to-trading partner's invoice-to-cash cycle time versus the trading partner-to-customer's invoice-to-cash cycle time. Each of these is the sum of: the invoice transmission time + the delivery receipt processing time + the payment trigger time, plus the payment clearance cycle time, plus the cash transmission time; see Figure 7.7. If the supply chain network can deliver the customer's cash payments faster than specified by the supplier's invoice terms, then the cash-to-cash cycle time is negative. This is very favorable because the customer's cash is being directly used to pay the supplier — this is also the Dell Computer model. If the supply chain network takes longer to deliver the customer's cash payments than specified by the supplier's invoice terms, then the cash-to-cash cycle time is positive. This is unfavorable because the cash of one of the trading partners is being used to pay the supplier. Using the SCN Process Value of continuous improvement, the cycle time elements can be examined to identify opportunities to reduce or eliminate some time through the application of technology. One example is an agreement among the network players to eliminate the paper invoice by using the receipt of material to trigger the payment.

As the supply chain architect examines different scenarios in the chaotic network, the following logistics questions should be answered concerning arcs, loops, and triggers:

- Where is the variability in the physical arc connections?
- Which nodes contain physical transformation process loops?
- Where is the variability in the information arc connections?
- Which nodes contain information transformation process loops?
- Where is the variability in the cash arc connections?
- Which nodes contain cash transformation process loops?
- Are roles and responsibilities for each inter-plane trigger connection defined with a primary and backup person named and a response time established?
- Has the total number of arcs, loops, and triggers for the end-to-end main thread been minimized?
- Is the arc, loop, and trigger design for the reverse supply chain network competitive?

The BPO components of SCN Process View and SCN Process Values and Beliefs and the resulting BPO impact variables of *Connectedness* and reduced *Conflict* are critical to the arc, loop, and trigger architecture of a supply chain network. Intraplane connectedness advances the value-added process flow between nodes through the arcs and within nodes on the same plane through the loops. Interplane connectedness advances the value-added process flow by switching planes within a node through the triggers. Internet technology has effectively made the seconds of transmission time for the information flows and cash flows effectively equal to zero relative to the days of transit time and customs clearance times for the physical flows. This time advantage can be quickly lost, however, when a trigger connection is delayed waiting for a specific decision maker due to a miscommunication or a poor process fit. In the auto racing analogy, if the car's owner allows a sponsor to insist on its brand of fuel injectors, racing cam, or transmission that mismatches the engine's requirements, then the competitiveness of the drivetrain connection will be compromised.

# INTEGRATING BPO WITH NETWORK OPERATIONS

An effective supply chain network operation involves teamwork across the network that is focused on the customer. Clear operational responsibility and authority exists, even though the network is distributed across cultures, organizations, time zones, and geography. Trust is developed among equals with high levels of collaboration and shared information as well as ownership and disciplined management and control.

The APICS SCM Principles, *Synchronize Supply with Demand* and *Measure Performance Globally*, drive the blueprint for competitive network operations. Competitive network operations are also business-process-oriented involving SCN Process Structure, SCN Process Jobs, and SCN Process Management and Measures components of BPO. They provide the handles and the levers by which to optimize the supply chain network operations toward the highest level of BPO Maturity. In this way, the final network will exhibit the BPO results of low *Conflict,* high *Connectedness,* superior network *Performance*, and high *Esprit de Corps.*

The following sections explain how the APICS SCM Principles, *Synchronize Supply with Demand* and *Measure Performance Globally*, along with the role of the orchestrator, can be used to implement the BPO components of SCN Process Structure, SCN Process Jobs, and SCN Process Management and Measures.

## Synchronize Supply with Demand

Once the architecture of the supply chain network has been determined, the focus shifts to optimizing network operations. All the nodes and the proper sequence of connections have been defined. Now, additional principles are needed to understand how best to use the supply chain network. This is analogous to driving the race car. The car must be driven at a very high speed throughout the duration of the race. Unless the driver practices matching the car with the racetrack, learns the reaction of the car to various driving conditions, and learns to trust the pit crew, some other competitor may win.

A product must be driven at a very high speed throughout the network. Unless the trading partners practice matching the supply chain network with the market demand, learn the reaction of the network to changes in inventory and capacity, and learn to trust one another, some other competing supply chain network may win. This APICS SCM Principle is about managing the system constraint, placing the inventory buffers, and vocalizing the customer demand in a way that optimizes end-to-end network throughput. This principle applies the "Theory Of Constraint" production ideas from Eli Goldratt to the supply chain network as a whole. Refer to Figure 7.8 to better understand the description that follows.

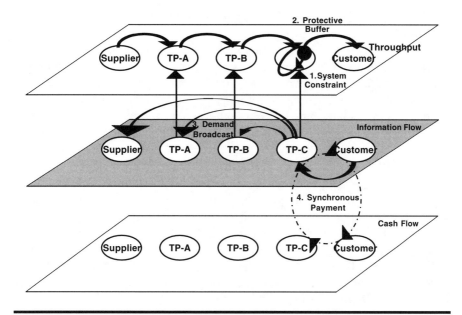

**Figure 7.8  Synchronizing Supply Chain Network Throughput**

One of the trading partners along the main thread effectively constrains the end-to-end throughput for the entire network.[6] This trading partner is the system constraint. In a chaotic network, the system constraint may move from one trading partner on one order to a different trading partner on the next order.

A second effect that limits throughput in a serial network is the statistical fluctuation in the outputs of one node to the next.[6] This can be overcome by placing a protective inventory buffer just ahead of the constraint. Now the constraint will always have enough input to keep working in spite of any statistical fluctuations upstream. In a chaotic network the protective buffer and the system constraint must be kept together within the same trading partner.

Third, throughput is limited by a mismatch of the constraint with the market or by a mismatch of the raw material input with the constraint.[6] This can be corrected by synchronizing the constraint to the rate of actual market demand and by synchronizing the release of new work to actual throughput at the constraint. In a chaotic network, the market demand is simultaneously broadcast to all trading partners, and the trading partner who is the system constraint for that order simultaneously broadcasts a synchronization signal to the rest of the network. Serial communication going upstream with logistics delays coming downstream can cause the bullwhip effect; but the vocalization of demand, the collaboration of effort, and the synchronization of supply will defeat the bullwhip effect normally seen in long supply chains. The trigger for the customer's cash payment may also be synchronized to system constraint throughput.

The practicality of synchronizing supply with demand in a chaotic supply chain network depends upon the capabilities of the Internet-enabled application software. Broadly accepted classes of application software include the virtual shopping cart metaphor downstream, Enterprise Resource Planning (ERP) together with Advanced Planning and Scheduling (APS) midstream, and the trading exchange metaphor upstream. While virtual shopping cart software clearly embraces a chaotic network model on the information and cash (credit card or procurement card) planes, the physical plane is generally not part of this software solution. Early implementations of ERP and APS software applications were able to accommodate switched networks, as long as all possible trading partners had been defined in the database. Later implementations of ERP and APS software applications are pushing the envelope from switched networks toward chaotic networks, as "plug-and-play" interfacing becomes a reality. Trading exchange software fully supports chaotic networks on the information plane, but often takes both the physical plane and cash plane transactions offline.

As the supply chain network is being operated in a chaotic mode, the following competitive practices should be followed for each customer order:

- Which trading partner is the system constraint?
- Does the physical plane, information plane, and the cash plane fully support the movement of the system constraint?
- Is the protective buffer kept in the same node with the system constraint?
- Is daily point-of-sale information sent directly to all trading partners and the system constraint?
- Is the system constraint's synchronization information broadcast to all trading partners in the network?
- How are cash payments synchronized to the system constraint?
- Has the operation of the reverse supply chain network been reviewed for synchronization?

Successful synchronization requires that the main thread nodes, and the people in the network-oriented jobs, understand both the customer need and the business strategy. Successful synchronization requires that people in the trading partner nodes and nominal trading partner nodes alike pull together to satisfy the market. Successful synchronization also requires that each of the trading partners is ready, willing, and able to pitch in and adjust as the dynamics of the business environment shifts the system constraint around.

This is *Esprit de Corps*. A strong winning spirit and sense of teamwork can drive synergistic results to exceed the capability of any one trading partner. In the racing analogy, the esprit de corps of the pit crew can shave seconds off a tire change keeping the completion of an unplanned pit stop synchronized with the yellow caution flag. A well-trained, highly motivated pit crew can change a tire in 14 seconds, while one individual would struggle to change a tire in 14 minutes.

In our research, this esprit de corps is a key result of BPO. SCN Process Jobs and SCN Process Structures specifically relate to the APICS SCM Principle of synchronization. Collaborative teaming structures and process-oriented jobs, a critical dimension of BPO, are the things that enable people to achieve high performance in a chaotic environment.

## Measure Performance Globally

This APICS SCM Principle is about defining a set of operational measures that enable each trading partner to visualize the impact of its daily operational decisions. Unfortunately, traditional financial measures are not timely enough for operations, and the end-to-end supply chain global optimum is not just the sum of the individual trading partner's local optima.[6] Some trading partners will have to defocus their individual operations in order to fully align with the end-to-end supply chain network. There should be an absolute measure for the end customer and a few relative measures for the trading partners operating along the main thread. In the auto racing analogy a key question becomes: What set of performance measures will enable the driver to visualize winning the race? The absolute measure of winning is crossing the finish line with the checkered flag; but the optimal operation of the race car involves maintaining the maximum revolutions per minute (RPM) the track conditions will allow without consuming too much fuel or wearing the tires causing the driver to be called in for an unscheduled pit stop. The driver must watch the dashboard instruments, such as the tachometer and fuel gauge. The driver is in continuous radio communication with the pit crew regarding the number of laps to go and the competing car to be beat.

Every customer wants to experience the equivalent of the checkered flag, or the perfect order. The perfect order is the customer-oriented absolute measure that the right product set is delivered to the right customer location at the right time with no defects and no need for return; it is invoiced perfectly. The perfect order requires the entire supply chain network to stay aligned with the business strategy, while pulling together in daily operations. "Equivalent Throughput" and "Total System Inventory"[7] are two relative measures that give the trading partners operational visibility. The system constraint node tries to match throughput with the market demand and uses its broadcast signal to keep all trading partner nodes synchronized. "The supply chain network is synchronized when the daily equivalent throughput at one trading partner is equal to the daily equivalent throughput at every trading partner." Equivalency means that the BOM is used to relate the quantity of lower level materials at an upstream node relative to the quantity of fully assembled products at a downstream node. In the chaotic network the context for equivalent throughput becomes each single customer order. When the race car is pacing the lead car — the market demand — its engine RPM, gearbox RPM, rear axle RPM, and left/right rear wheel RPM are perfectly matched at equivalent speeds.

While the race car is maintaining its speed — throughput — just behind the lead car, it must not be consuming fuel — system inventory — too quickly. At the start of the race, exactly the right weight of fuel is pumped into the race car's fuel tank. As the race progresses, some of the fuel remains in the tank, while the engine burns some of the fuel. In a perfectly driven race, the race car will cross the finish line with no fuel left in the tank. The total system inventory is the size of the fuel tank times the number of times the tank is refilled. Similarly, a supply chain network operations are started by preloading inventory into the network nodes. One inventory location, called the push/pull boundary, is the point at which upstream inventory is controlled by pushing from a demand forecast, and downstream inventory is controlled by pulling to a customer order. As throughput increases, inventory shifts out of the nodes and into the pipelines. The total system inventory is the sum of all inventories in the nodes and in the pipelines. Practically speaking, inventory visibility gets fuzzy upstream of the push/pull boundary. This is because in a push system, such as "Manufacturing Resource Planning" (MRP II), purchasing will be buying lower-level parts in quantity lots to optimize material cost, and logistics will be consolidating inbound material shipments to optimize logistics costs. In the chaotic network, the context for total system inventory becomes each single customer order.

As the supply chain network is being operated in a chaotic mode, the following competitive practices should be followed on each customer order:

■ How can the supply chain network deliver a perfect order to the customer?
■ Does every downstream, synchronized trading partner have visibility to equivalent throughput by customer order?
■ Does every trading partner have visibility to total system inventory?
■ Are the trading partners practicing collaborative planning, forecasting, and replenishment (CPFR) to drive their planning systems?

- Have global performance measures been established for the operation of the reverse supply chain network?

This APICS SCM Principle is totally aligned with SCN Process Management and Measurement systems. Supply chain network members need process-oriented operational measures to make good decisions, to resolve issues as they occur, and to stay aligned and focused. Network process-oriented measures drive the end-to-end network to a global optimum. The critical BPO process management concept of allocating resources based upon business process also helps trading partners focus investments on improving network performance and avoiding suboptimization of resources. Having network process goals in place, another critical BPO concept, will provide a common improvement direction to people in the network resulting in everyone rowing in the same direction.

An understanding of the business performance is no longer the purview of just one trading partner, but now becomes a continuous conversation among all the trading partners. Know when the team wins, and celebrate the win; then agree to raise the bar, and do it again. Finally, in the racing analogy, it is the combination of flags, dashboard instrumentation, and race management updates by radio that keeps the driver focused in real time on the essentials needed to win the race.

## DRIVING VALUE THROUGH HIGH BPO MATURITY

Static networks, switched networks, and chaotic networks get to stay in business only if they can sustain both profit and growth. Profit and growth are the rewards for exceptional customer satisfaction. Profit and growth are the twin engines driving shareholder value. The final APICS SCM Principle, *Supply Chain Creates Net Value*, is about creating customer delight and shareholder value through coordinated improvements to profit and growth. This principle aligns closely with the overall concept of BPO Maturity. A focus on the income statement can improve profit, while a focus on the balance sheet can improve growth. SCM facilitates profit improvement by using country of origin selection to minimize labor, material, and tax costs; by managing logistics costs along with import/export risks; and by eliminating inventory write-offs. SCM facilitates growth improvement by maximizing return on invested capital and freeing cash flow for new investment. Only when customers are genuinely delighted, when supply is synchronized with demand, when information is substituted for inventory, and when all the trading partners focus on velocity, accounts receivable, accounts payable, and inventory investment, can each be improved. Shareholders are rewarded because profitable revenue growth built on a shrinking asset base means more working capital for investment or dividends, which can result in a higher stock price.

Value-creation goals have at least four dimensions in a supply chain network:

- The end customer expects the value of a total solution as represented by the delivery of product(s) and service(s) in the context of a perfect order experience.
- The trading partner(s) expect(s) the network throughput to generate shareholder value in earnings per share.
- The nominal trading partner(s) expect high velocity transactions that add revenue to their business without the friction cost of disproportionate expense.
- The supply chain network orchestrator expects the network relationships to create the most optimal opportunity to balance net profit and return on invested capital, while keeping a positive free cash flow.

The highest level of value creation is achieved at the highest level of BPO Maturity. The network level of BPO Maturity is the least common denominator level of the BPO Maturity for each of the trading partners. The degree of value created for the customer, the trading partners, the nominal trading partners, and the orchestrator is therefore also a measure of the degree to which the entire supply chain network has reached alignment in BPO Maturity.

## SUMMARY

Chaotic supply chain networks are the result of unbundling the corporation. These new organizations are defined through the successful integration of their information flow, physical distribution flow, and cash flow. In this chapter we have provided a way to define, design, and operate a business-process-oriented networked supply chain.

This chapter also details a blueprint for building and operating networks that realize the competitive benefits of BPO. The five APICS SCM Principles, explained in this chapter, are a way to align and design the strategic intent, purpose, and processes of a supply chain network. BPO has been shown to be a critical aspect of each of these principles and a key ingredient for competitive supply chain networks. Using the concepts of BPO and the APICS SCM Principles in the design and operation of network, coupled with consistent BPO Maturity throughout the network, will achieve superior network business performance and esprit de corps.

# REFERENCES

1. Alber, K.L. and Walker, W.T. (1998). *Supply Chain Management Principles and Techniques for the Practitioner.* Alexandria, VA: APICS Educational & Research Foundation, APICS Stock #07015.
2. Treacy, M. and Wiersema, F. (1995). *Discipline of Market Leaders: Choose Your Customers, Narrow Your Focus, Dominate Your Market.* Reading, MA: Addison-Wesley Publishing Company, 29.
3. Walker, W.T. and Alber, K.L. (January 1999). "Understanding Supply Chain Management," *APICS The Performance Advantage,* 38–43.
4. Walker, W.T. (2000). "Defining Supply Chain Management," reprinted from the APICS Educational & Research Foundation 1999 Summer Academic/Practitioner Workshop Proceedings, *APICS Advanced Supply Chain Management Reprints,* Alexandria, VA: APICS, 3–11, APICS Stock #05017.
5. APICS. (2000). *Advance Supply Chain Management Courseware,* APICS CD/ROM Stock #01640.
6. Goldratt, E.M. and Cox, J. (1984). *The Goal: Excellence In Manufacturing,* Croton-on-Hudson, NY: North River Press, 114–117.
7. Walker, W.T. (1999). Use Global Performance Measures to Align the Enterprise Trading Partners, *Achieving Supply Chain Excellence through Technology, Volume 1,* San Francisco, CA: Montgomery Research, 316–320, www.ascet.com.
8. Walker, W.T. (2000). "Synchronizing Supply Chain Operations," *2000 APICS International Conference Proceedings,* Alexandria, VA: APICS, 13, APICS Stock #04014.

# 8

## THE CHALLENGES OF BUILDING A NETWORKED SUPPLY CHAIN

Michael Dell, in his book *Direct from Dell*, observed, "The real payoff of the Internet is in its enabling of business collaboration — the sort of three-way 'information partnerships' among manufacturers, business partners and customers."[1] He goes on to say that the Internet, as a sales channel, represents only a fraction of the Internet's value to business. We agree with Dell that the real value of the Internet lies in its ability to transform relationships in the traditional supply chain (SC) network, a subject we discussed at length in Chapter 6.

One of the biggest changes in how businesses operate today is how companies view their supply chains — not in a sequential location-by-location fashion, but instead holistically, to better understand events occurring both inside and outside their four walls. This, in turn, is spawning a much greater emphasis on collaboration and supply chain process integration.

Yet, building a successful SC network is very challenging and many factors can influence success. Under what environmental, market, and business relationship conditions will an SC network work best? Do factors such as market turbulence, supply chain power, and network business strategy influence or modify the practical implementation of this new interfirm organization? Based upon preliminary business process orientation (BPO)-related research, we believe that SC network performance is significantly influenced by these factors. This chapter offers a testable, prescriptive approach for identifying the factors that can significantly affect the success of a network and suggests approaches to dealing with their influence.

# INTRODUCTION

In earlier chapters, we examined the forces affecting supply chain structures and relationships. We have shown that, with the Internet serving as a catalyst, SC networks are being established based on powerful, new interfirm organizations-based connections. A framework for SC network design was also offered in Chapter 7 consisting of different classifications of trading partners, material flows, information flows, and cash flows. Through our research presented earlier in this book, we have also shown that BPO is an important component of a successful SC network design and can significantly influence network performance and esprit de corps, the competitive "glue" that holds the network together.

Does this framework and "tool kit" fit every situation? If not, what are the factors affecting the successful use of this framework in building SC networks? How do situational variables such as network participants and relationship type, network strategy, environmental factors (market turbulence, etc.), and supply chain power relationships influence the success or failure of the framework offered in this book?

Due to the newness and early adoption of SC networks, these questions have not yet been definitively answered; however, we have conducted preliminary research that suggests that situational factors, such as market conditions, business purpose of the network, technological dynamics, and relationship dynamics, determine the success of a network. In this chapter, we offer a definition, classification, and understanding of these factors that can significantly impact the successful implementation of an SC network. We also offer ideas for mitigating their influence.

# THE SC NETWORK MODEL

In order to help understand and identify the situational factors that could influence the successful implementation of a network, we had to build a model of the SC network best practices. The overall model that we constructed and used in our research is illustrated in Figure 8.1. We incorporated a BPO framework used in our earlier research on SCM to identify, define, and describe the SC network management concepts and components. BPO improves interfunctional interactions within an organization, therefore, we proposed that a similar effect will result concerning the intercompany interactions within an SC network. We also carry through the relationships to the BPO outcomes of business performance and esprit de corps but from a network perspective. You will notice that we further identified major internal SC network factors and external network factors (environmental) that influence the relationship between network BPO and network performance, as well as esprit de corps. These internal factors are the "personality" of the network such as the business reasons for its

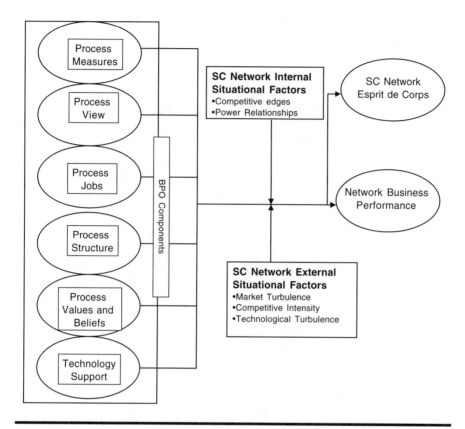

**Figure 8.1    Proposed SC Network Model with Situational Factors (NTP = Nominal Trading Partner).**

creation (e.g., competitive edges) and the power relationships within the network. The external or environmental factors represent market forces that influence the speed and nature of supply chain network development, such as market and technological turbulence and competitive intensity.

SC networks are complex, thus we suggest using the framework in Figure 8.1 when building or improving SC networks. The framework will also help in preparing contingency strategies to reduce the potential negative impacts of the situational factors. The framework can be used to address the following questions:

1. What are the *internal* supply chain network factors that will potentially impact overall supply chain network performance and esprit de corps?

2. What are the *external* supply chain network factors that will potentially impact overall supply chain network performance and esprit de corps?

3. Which components of the network (process jobs, structures, etc.) will be impacted by the situational factors identified?
4. What are the potential strategies needed to mitigate the impact of major situational factors?

# BUILDING THE MODEL

## Concepts and Components

In order to effectively identify and define supply chain management (SCM) best practices to be used in our SC network model, several groups of intercompany SCM activities were identified from focus groups, interviews, and a literature review. These groupings were proposed as best practice SC network management strategies that will lead to superior network performance.

Eight preliminary supply chain network management concepts identified and used as a basis for developing the model are listed next:

1. Supply chain visibility
2. B2B available-to-promise or capable-to-promise
3. Supply chain event management
4. Supply chain partnership management
5. Supply chain configuration and rapid reconfiguration
6. Supply chain "outsourcing" management
7. Supply chain collaborative planning and forecasting
8. Supply chain auto-replenishment

These concepts were then examined in detail through an additional literature review, expert interviews, and focus groups consisting of manufacturers, suppliers, software firms, and service firms. Based on this data gathering, the previous list was reduced to two major concepts that appear to capture the essence of SC network management best practices:

1. *Supply Chain **Event** Management* — the process of simulating, responding to, and controlling exceptions to planned and unplanned events in the supply chain.
2. *Supply Chain **Partnership** Management* — the process of developing, monitoring, managing, and maintaining strategic alliances between supply chain members that complement and support the business goals and objectives of each trading partner.

Once we had identified these concepts we then merged SC event management and partnership management into the single concept of supply chain network management. Then we used the BPO framework used in the earlier SCM research to define the individual components and build a testable model. The details of each component in the model are included in Appendix D. The following is a review of the BPO framework used to build the components of the model:

1. A **process view** of how the supply chain network works — not just a picture but understanding and agreement of this view by all participating partners
2. A **structure** that enables the network interactions to work — a simple example would be a supplier–customer partnership agreement that creates a working relationship that reduces friction. Joint venture or distribution agreements are both examples of structure types, but the network trend is creating new forms. How they are managed is important. Are they transactional or collaborative in nature? Are they cooperative or conflict-oriented? Shared investments and dedicated resources are also critical to the structure.
3. **Jobs** that operate in this network structure that have authority and responsibility to take actions — these are new job types that span companies in the network.
4. **Shared measures** that align the actions of network partners toward common goals — shared measures represent measures and goals that operate across the network of partners.
5. **Aligned values and beliefs** that guide the actions of the partners as they interact — opportunistic behaviors that take advantage of another partner will definitely add friction in this area. Rules that handle this are an important part of making an SC network successful.
6. Finally, technology serves as the **nervous system** for the network by providing the connections to the various nodes. For example, the Internet as well as the interaction and common data standards (i.e., RosettaNet and extensible markup language (XML)) used are primary enablers of SC network management.

Based upon our earlier research, this business-process-oriented approach to operationalizing the SC network management concepts and organizing the measures produces a more complete and robust model. Because this approach also groups the measures into higher level concepts, this has been shown to aid in the transfer of knowledge across industries and improve the effectiveness of the concept application.[2]

## Measuring SC Network Performance

Measuring the performance of an SC network in a straightforward way is a challenge, especially when measuring attitudes of the participants about the network. As changes and improvements are made in the network, tracking impacts on performance over time becomes very important to building a network. "Where are you?" and "How far have you come?" are key questions for the network development team.

In general, our model applies the BPO concepts and relationships of our earlier research to the SC network, not just one organization but an organization of partners, and proposes that business-process-oriented components will have a similar impact on overall network business performance and network esprit de corps. Therefore, the outcomes shown in Figure 8.1 are *overall network business performance* and *network esprit de corps*. The detailed measures of these are given in Appendix D.

Business performance is said to be in the eye of the beholder. The constant argument between short-term, long-term, customer perception, and financial measures make the concept difficult to quantify.

In our model, we use the SC network participant's self-evaluation to capture the level of business performance. This is the same measure of performance used in our earlier BPO model, except that it is network performance that is assessed instead of individual company performance. Two questions are answered by respondents in order to assess their network's overall performance and their performance relative to major competitor networks on a scale of 1 through 5 (poor to excellent, respectively).

As we have discussed earlier in the book, esprit de corps within an organization is a well-known indicator of organizational health and a predicator of superior business performance. It has been said to be the "glue" that holds a group together.

The term esprit de corps means:

*a set of enthusiastically shared feelings, beliefs, and values about group membership and performance.*[3]

Esprit de corps manifests itself as a strong desire to achieve a common goal even in the face of hostility. At the work group level, esprit de corps is said to exist when individuals in the same department or team enthusiastically share values and goals. We believe that this concept, already shown to have a strong relationship to BPO within an organization, can be extended to an SC network as a powerful alignment mechanism strengthening the SC network. To measure esprit de corps in our model, we used a modified version of the esprit de corps measures used in our earlier research (Appendix D). This measure is versatile enough to measure esprit de corps in a network's current state as well as after changes are made.

## Situational Factors

The situational factors identified and used in our SC network model are also shown in Figure 8.1. These factors will potentially influence the success or failure of an SC network or significantly force the modification of one or more of the components. For example, an imbalance in the power relationship between the network partners and the overuse of negative power might destabilize the structure of the network process in such a way as to render a key best practice, such as collaboration in developing a network sales plan, ineffective. SC network management requires a high degree of trust and a win–win relationship in order to operate successfully. If this were not possible in a particular power relationship situation, then the success or effectiveness of SC network management approaches would be significantly at risk.

The situational factors in the model are divided into internal and external perspectives:

1. SC Network Situational Factors — Internal
   ■ Network business objectives or "competitive edges"
   ■ Network power relationships
2. SC Network Situational Factors — External (Environmental)
   ■ Market Turbulence
   ■ Competitive Intensity
   ■ Technological Turbulence

### *SC Network Situational Factors — Internal*

When building an SC network, it is critical to define the purpose and get agreement from all participants. Lockamy and Cox,[4] leading researchers in field of operations management, argue that firms, and we believe networks, must develop core competencies on the "competitive edges" upon which they compete in the marketplace. These competitive edges are product or service characteristics. Improvement of these characteristics leads to a strategic advantage in a specific market or market segment.

Networks can compete on nine competitive edges:

1. Price
2. Quality
3. Lead time
4. Due date performance
5. Product flexibility
6. Process flexibility
7. Field service

8. Innovation
9. Product introduction responsiveness

The *price* on which a network can compete is based on market factors such as turbulence and competitive intensity. Superior product and service attributes, based on actual market requirements or needs, must be established in order to develop a competitive edge in the area of *quality*.

A competitive edge of *lead time* refers to the time between recognition of the need for an order and the receipt of goods by the customer. Networks competing on lead time must continually maintain (or reduce) their order cycles in order to get and keep customers and make superior margins.

To compete on *due date performance*, networks must consistently deliver goods based on promise dates determined by the customer.

*Product* and *process flexibility* refer to a network's ability to configure and adapt its products and corresponding processes to conform to changing customer requirements.

*Field service* organizations can provide a competitive edge through their ability to respond to post-sale problems encountered by the customer.

*Innovation* refers to a network's ability to offer creative solutions to its customers that lead to a distinct market advantage.

Finally, networks that can rapidly respond to customer needs by introducing new products can exploit first-mover advantages via the competitive edge of *product introduction responsiveness*. (*Note:* We have created a measurement tool, located in Appendix D, which can be used to assess a network and determine the levels of emphasis and agreement around these network purposes.)

Why are these competitive dimensions important? In a given market, the order-qualifying criteria for a product allows firms, and in this case networks, to be considered as a potential supplier of the product. This is usually the minimum cost of entry into the market. Order-winning criteria, on the other hand, provides a competitive advantage. Improvements above a threshold level in the order-qualifying criteria will not win orders, but these improvements prevent firms from losing orders to competitors. Thus, to create and maintain competitive market advantages, firms must develop methodologies for identifying and continually improving order-winning criteria. Order-qualifying criteria must also be met and maintained because they are necessary conditions for competition.

With SC networks as the form of industrial competition, supply chains will replace individual firms as the economic engine for creating value, and will compete among themselves for the loyalty of end users. With this in mind, SC networks must agree upon and develop distinctive competencies, built upon their defined competitive edges, establish ways to improve on order-winning and order-qualifying criteria, and integrate core value-creating processes among trading partners.

SC networks can achieve competitive advantage through the cooperative development of distinctive network competencies as defined by these competitive edges. Our research indicates that SC networks are formed around specific competitive edges, or network objectives. Each competitive edge, or combination of edges, dictates the personality of the SC network and can influence the implementation of a BPO component or the influence of the BPO component on SC network performance or esprit de corps.

*Power* is going to play a key role in network formation and function as well. In our model, we define interfirm supply chain power as the ability of one firm (the source) to influence the intentions and actions of another firm (the target). This concept was defined and investigated in the automotive industry and found to significantly influence, both in the positive and negative, network relationships.[5] Supply chain power was also found to be related to supply chain performance. The following six supply chain power types are defined and used in our network model (a detailed measurement instrument of these power types is contained in Appendix D):

1. *Reward* — the ability of the source to mediated dividends to the target
2. *Coercion* — the ability of the source to mediated punishments to the target
3. *Expert* — the perception that one firm holds information or expertise that is valued by another firm
4. *Referent* — one form desires identification with another for recognition by association
5. *Legitimate* — the target believes in the *inherent* right of the source to wield influence
6. *Legal Legitimate* — the target believes in the *legal* right of the source to wield influence

What role does *power* play in building an SC network? We believe that the use of negative power in the network, defined in this earlier study as coercion, legal legitimate, and sometimes reward power, can and will dampen the successful performance of the network. It is also apparent that it will affect network esprit de corps. We believe that even with the best design and implementation of a BPO network model, the type of network power use can have a dramatic affect, both positive and negative. The identification, measurement, and adjustment of the types of network power being deployed is critical to the relationships and survival of the network. We believe, and are continuing to investigate, how network power influences network performance and, at times, prevent a network from operating.

### SC Network Situational Factors — External (Environmental)

*External* or environmental factors are also likely to affect network performance. In our model, we propose situational measures (see Appendix D) that are commonly cited in the marketing literature.[6] These external factors are:

1. *Market Turbulence* — the rate of change in the composition of customers and their preferences
2. *Competitive Intensity* — the behavior, resources, and ability of competitors to differentiate
3. *Technological Turbulence* — the rate of technological change

Who can argue that markets today are difficult to predict? Turbulent markets require flexibility and responsiveness in a supply chain. In this market situation, the changing demand, mix, price, and configurations require timely detections and effective responses. The reconfiguration of the SC network, one of the network management best practices in our model, is a key factor in this response. Collaborative planning and forecasting can also be a key SC network best practice in this type of market situation. In fact, it appears that a turbulent market environment will require effective cross-network implementation of most, if not all, of the best practices in our SC network management model. For this reason, we believe this is a critical factor and could significantly influence the success or failure of a SC network design.

Markets are not only changing but also becoming more competitively intense. Someone recently observed that "today's markets are wicked." We could not agree more. Competitive intensity, or the ability for competitors to differentiate, is also an important factor in our model. Responsiveness and flexibility of a network are important in any market. This is even more the case in intensely competitive markets lacking strong product differentiation, where unique SC network configurations serve as the primary competitive advantage.

For example, developing a unique series of agreements and integrated processes across a SC network will significantly reduce the cycle time of a build-to-order product, while leading to improved margins and overall business performance. This would particularly apply in highly competitive markets, characterized by a lack of differentiation between product or service offerings. Dell Computer's network serves as a good example. Dell's unique personal computer SC network is said to have a 30-hour cycle time (from order to delivery) and generates, not consumes, working capital. This has given Dell a significant competitive and financial advantage in an intensely competitive market. Conversely, a price increase might be difficult to push through in a highly competitive market, cycle time improvements notwithstanding, thus dampening the impact of the practices on business performance.

Finally, changes in technology often blindside companies, catching them flat-footed. Christiansen discussed the role of "disruptive technologies" that bring to a market a very different value proposition that had been previously available.[7] Technological turbulence is the final situational factor used in the model. As with some of the other situational forces, flexibly and responsiveness are key to the SC network's ability to rapidly retool for the next technology and not get caught with the old technology in stock. We anticipate that this factor will raise the importance of cross-network best practices. Shifts in technology will necessitate reconfiguring the SC network to minimize inventory and respond to downstream demand signals, effectively managing supply chain network partnerships and responding to events on the network.

## APPLYING THE MODEL TO AN SC NETWORK

### The Focus of the Model

The focus when applying our model is not on a single firm but the SC network illustrated in Figure 8.2. This new form of organizing SC or trading partner networks, discussed earlier in this book, can be defined as:

> *a block of interdependent companies operating within a given industry to achieve a stated business goal or provide a specific end product*

In our framework for organizing and classifying SC networks presented in Chapter 7, these networks of companies are formed and lead by network *orchestrators*. These are the dominant companies within the network and usually the ones close to the demand or the customer. The orchestrator takes the lead in organizing the network, usually because it needs to gain a specific capability or competency (competitive edge) that will lead to broadening or deepening their final offering to their customers, leading to increased profitability or market share. The orchestrator selects and recruits members of the network based upon this need. This orchestrator and its associated network can be represented by different tiers of the overall supply chain and not necessarily always at the final end customer

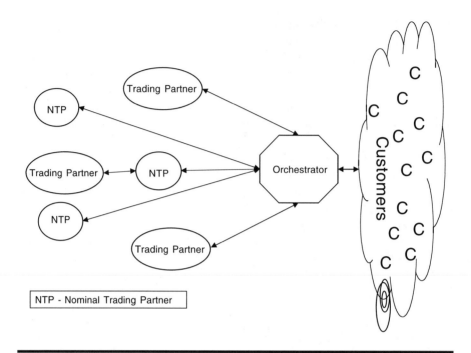

**Figure 8.2 An SC Network**

level. For example, several manufacturers of automotive and aerospace subassemblies are playing the orchestrator role. Several contract electronic manufacturing firms, including Solectron and SCI, are also functioning in this role.

As presented earlier, network members can be classified into two types, trading partners and nominal trading partners. *Strategic trading partners* offer a unique competitive advantage to the network and are often the sole suppliers of a specific good or service deemed critical to the network end product and business objectives. Nominal *trading partners* are recruited to provide a specific good or service due to nonstrategic factors such as location, cost, capacity, or reliability. Often, more than one nominal trading partner is available for this product or service. Each type of trading partner would participate, at the direction of the orchestrator, in applying our model to evaluate and diagnose its network.

## Using the Model to Create Alignment within the SC Network

Alignment between the members of the network is an important factor in successful implementation of the network model. This alignment takes four forms: strategic, rewards, information standards, and interaction platforms and processes.

*Strategic* alignment means that the involved trading partners agree upon and act upon the competitive edges selected by the orchestrator. These are embodied in network and trading partner measures, goals, objectives, and rewards. Using our competitive edges survey contained in Appendix D, the orchestrator can assess the trading partners involved in the SC network and can assess this alignment. In the model, we ask the leadership of each trading partner to rank the nine competitive edges in order of importance. This provides a quick picture of network strategic alignment. Adjustments can then be made based upon this snapshot. After the network is aligned around the agreed-upon competitive edges, measures, goals, and rewards system can be out in place by the orchestrator.

Alignment of *rewards* is accomplished when the orchestrator establishes rigorous performance standards, based upon end customer evaluations and process performance requirements. Incentives are also included that reward trading partner performance and conformance. In our research, we found that the orchestrator establishes the rules and rewards of membership and enforces them. Noncompliance or performance results in strong actions by the orchestrator. The orchestrator also ensures distribution of network benefits to trading partners. These networks are not "networks of equals" but organizations with power, authority, and status with the rewards distributed accordingly. Balance and perceived justice is a key factor for network health, performance, and long term survival. Using the model to assess the implementation of the supply chain network management (SCNM) best practices, power relationships, and levels of esprit de corps within the network can help gauge this alignment and identify opportunities for improvement.

For a network to operate successfully, we found that the network orchestrator must also set the *information standards* and *interaction platforms* that enable efficient interactions within the network. This is a key to network effectiveness and is not optional. It is a requirement of membership in the network and each trading partner must agree to conform. Cross-holdings of debt or equity no longer hold these networks together, but an information standard that confers significant efficiencies and benefits to network participants can. The technology support section of the model can be used to assess this alignment in the network and point to the issues (or partners) needing attention. This model, contained in Appendix D, measures the level of technology support in the network for the critical processes of supply chain network management from the end user perspective. It can identify the weakest technology link in the network before it breaks.

In a successful network, key business *processes* are interconnected and aligned within the network. Interoperability is enabled by process standardization and information exchange standards such as electronic data interchange (EDI) and Internet-based standards such as RosettaNet. Here, BPO also comes into play. Alignment is not just between information systems and process activities. The BPO components of process jobs, structures, measures, and values and beliefs need to be aligned between network members as well. In our earlier research, this alignment between functions within a company has been shown to lead to improvements in interfunctional cooperation, company performance, and esprit de corps; we believe that this will have the same effect within the network.

For this reason, we propose that BPO alignment within the network is a key factor in the success of the network. If the SCM maturity, as defined earlier in this book, of the orchestrator is at the "extended" level — the most mature and network ready level — and several trading partners are at the "ad hoc" level — the lowest level — serious problems will result when linking the processes. The high variability generated by the ad hoc processes will feed into and disrupt the mature processes of the orchestrator, eventually bring the process down to a lower maturity level. Using the model and assessment survey to identify each partner's level of BPO maturity can help the orchestrator detect problem areas in the network and focus efforts to improve the BPO maturity of individual partners and the network as a whole.

## CONCLUSIONS

This chapter proposed the use of BPO for creating a practical SC network management assessment model. In doing this, we feel that we have expanded the understanding and application of supply chain network management practices by defining key concepts, measures and influencers. In addition, we identified those concepts that significantly influence network business performance and esprit de corps — critical metrics of network success.

By using this model, the classification framework from Chapter 7 and the understanding gained from the rest of the book of how to apply BPO in an interfirm supply chain, most supply chain leaders will have a better chance at building a successful SC network. To aid in this learning, we have included several case studies in the remaining portion of this book. These case studies, "Herding Cats in the Supply Chain" and "Envera™" provide lessons learned from real attempts to build a network.

Finally, this book has endeavored to provide useful strategies, tactics, and methods to help companies prosper in the network economy as well as build upon the foundation of our first book on BPO. The vision we have presented here is one of "connected communities" with a common purpose and high levels of esprit de corps, working together on activities of value, and sharing in the knowledge and rewards of this community. We anticipate a very exciting future!

## REFERENCES

1. Dell, M. and Fredman, C. (2000). *Direct from Dell*.
2. Santos, A., Powell, J., and Hinks, J. (2001). Using pattern matching for the international benchmarking of production practices. *Benchmarking: An Int. J.,* 8, 1, 35–47.
3. Boyt, T.E., Lusch, R.F., and Schuler, D.K. (Spring 1997). Fostering esprit de corps in marketing, *Mark. Manage.,* 6, 1.
4. Lockamy, A. and Cox, J.F. (1994). *Reengineering Performance Measurement: How to Align Systems to Improve Processes, Products, and Profits*. Burr Ridge, IL: Irwin.
5. Maloni, M. and Benton, W.C. (2000). Power influences in the supply chain, *J. Bus. Logistics,* 21, 1.
6. Kohli, A.K. and Jaworski, B.J. (July 1993). Market orientation: Antecedents and consequences, *J. Mark.,* 57.
7. Christiansen, C. (1997). *The Innovator's Dilemma*. New York: HarperCollins Publishers.

# Case 1

## HERDING CATS ACROSS THE SUPPLY CHAIN[1]

*Ram Reddy and William C. Johnson*

*Case prepared by Richard Chvala, former Director of Global Marketing and eBusiness of Envera™ and William C. Johnson, Professor of Marketing, the Huizenga Graduate School of Business & Entrepreneurship, Nova Southeastern University.*

Customer relationship management (CRM) is a set of business strategies to obtain new customers, keep existing customers, and provide additional value-added products/services to current customers. A major objective of CRM programs is to provide customized products and services at a cost that customers are willing to pay. The premise of CRM processes and supporting systems is that interactions — all interactions, not just sales interactions — with customers should be consciously managed to optimize the value of relationships with customers. Further, CRM should provide a "360-degree view" of the customer in terms of frequency of interactions and how favorably customers view those interactions. The CRM system challenge is that this requires a realignment of business processes — both within the original equipment manufacturer (OEM) and across its supply chain — around the customer. The following is a case study from the automotive sector that is loosely based on actual events. This case highlights the difficulty in designing and implementing the necessary business process changes within the firm and across its supply chain in support of realizing CRM objectives.

### BACKGROUND

A large OEM supplier (we will call it "ACME") makes and supplies customized car seats to multiple automobile manufacturers. The manufacturing requirements for ACME's customized car seat components changes frequently, based on user satisfaction surveys and quality-related warranty work. For example, if a significant number of customers express dissatisfaction with a particular feature of a car seat, ACME will change its engineering and manufacturing specifications to remove the irritant. Thus, the primary objective of the ACME's CRM initiative was to implement processes and supporting systems that could sense and respond rapidly to changes in customer (and hence manufacturing) requirements.

Before the project, it would take two to three months for a change in customer requirements to "trickle down" to all participants in the supply chain. Because of this "time-lapse" view of customer requirements, every participant in the supply chain had a different view of what the requirements were, at any given time. This time-lapse view forced participant companies to stock up on various combinations of components to meet current and future requirements of ACME. Not having a current real-time view of the requirements resulted in the supply chain participants incurring unnecessary costs. These costs ranged from inventory holding costs to excessive working capital requirements.

In this supply chain environment, implementing a CRM solution focused on delivering customized solutions, at an affordable price and with reduced cycle time, was like trying to put out a fire with gasoline. Runaway inventory holding and working capital costs inflated the cost of customized products, turning customers off. The customers of ACME in this case were automobile manufacturers, and that enforced a cap on what they would pay for a car seat.

The project goal, therefore, was to realign business processes and supporting systems across the supply chain to enable cost-effective CRM systems. The project team was constantly pulled in different directions by various functional groups within the OEM and its suppliers throughout the five-month reengineering effort; however, the focus on customer requirements, the creation of a business process realignment team charter (derived from an actionable definition of the business problem), and executive sponsorship helped overcome these problems.

## DEFINING THE PROBLEM

The business problem needed to be clearly defined before processes and systems could be realigned to support the CRM initiative. This task proved to be quite challenging. The first attempt at getting a clear definition of the business problem resulted in a simple "We need a CRM system!" This goal was obviously too vague to be actionable, so key personnel from the OEM and its supply chain partner were interviewed to get a clear definition of the problem.

Interviewees were asked to describe the problems they faced in their particular operational area, without any thought to upstream or downstream processes. Interestingly, although all of them emphasized the need to increase the internal efficiencies of their particular functional group, none of them described the problem in terms of the customer. Instead, the business problems they described were inward-facing and involved streamlining existing processes. Eventually the executive sponsor from the OEM (the vice president of manufacturing operations) became disappointed about the disjointed problem definitions arising out of the one-on-one interviews.

Consequently, all the key stakeholders — such as the vice presidents of sales, comptrollers, and directors of purchasing from the OEM and across the supply chain — were invited to a one-day "visioning session." The objective was to collectively define the problem from a customer standpoint and use it as the basis for developing our CRM system. During this session, two main business problems were identified:

- Reduce cycle time for communicating customer requirements across the supply chain
- Reduce costs, including working capital requirements, inventory holding, and unplanned shipping costs across the supply chain to make the product more affordable for customers

Now, with the business problem clearly defined, the suggestions for solutions arrived fast and furious. The OEM executives wanted to implement an ERP (enterprise resource planning) system across the supply chain, but they were reminded of the difficulty that they were already having realigning internal processes in an ongoing internal ERP implementation. That experience highlighted the enormous difficulty of implementing a complex integrated ERP-type solution within a single firm, let alone across multiple firms.

Furthermore, the OEM's infrastructure consisted of a hodgepodge of legacy and client–server systems across which various pieces of customer information were distributed. These systems were unable to store and communicate customer requirements reliably within the firm or across the supply chain. Multiple systems of record contained customer requirements and changes; no single system could access customer information inside the OEM or from supply chain partners. Unfortunately, this situation is all too common. Data warehouses and data marts may aggregate information from various systems of record, but by definition they do not support the level of customer detail needed for CRM efforts.

## PROPOSED SOLUTION

The stakeholders who had articulated the business problem were asked to define a high-level solution. This experience turned out to be very educational. The stakeholders had no problem defining a high-level process flow that addressed communication issues across the supply chain.

The challenge in implementing the solution became evident as each individual component of the solution was examined in greater detail. At first glance, each item seemed relatively easy to implement. However, the domino effect on the entire supply chain would be substantial. For example, real-time changes in customer requirements for an existing order would lead to a lengthy analysis on the disposition of work-in-process inventories, intermediate goods in shipment between suppliers, and so on.

The OEM had brushed aside previous discussions on these details and deemed them "a supplier problem." These details could no longer be overlooked, however, and the company was forced to consider implementing a channel partner relationship management system. Selecting and implementing partner relationship management would require many infrastructure changes across the supply chain. Thus, the OEM decided to pilot the business process changes initially with a Web-based workflow system before considering a partner relationship management system.

Next, the complex task of implementing all facets of CRM — product and service information, field service management, and so on — forced the stakeholders to prioritize different areas of functionality for implementation. They based this prioritization on the business benefits and operational feasibility of each CRM deliverable. For example, although the proposed CRM solution covered areas such as marketing automation, sales, product and service information, and product and service configuration, the stakeholders drilled down and defined only small pieces of functionality that addressed the most pressing business problems. This task became relatively painless, given that the same group of stakeholders had defined the common business problems to begin with. Eventually each process and system deliverable was allotted a two- to four-month cycle time from the visioning session to implementation.

## THE 800-POUND GORILLA APPROACH — ROLE OF THE CHANNEL MASTER

The business process alignment and functional specifications for the CRM effort nearly became victims to the 800-pound gorilla, the "channel master." When the channel master (in this instance ACME) for the supply chain began to develop the processes and systems for the solution, it assigned groups from different functional areas of the company that were not represented in the initial visioning and prioritization sessions to help define the solution. These assigned groups from ACME did not share the same vision as the original stakeholders; instead, they focused on addressing their immediate operational needs.

As it turned out, these groups wanted to arbitrarily change the system functionality and process alignment specifications. For example, the more powerful functional areas pushed changes in processes out of their areas to less powerful ones, ensuring that the status quo was maintained for their respective parent departments. They also asked for automated system workarounds instead of changing their processes to support CRM objectives. For example, the customer service department opposed any change in the way they recorded information about warranty work authorizations. The customer service manager was reluctant to add any additional data capture tasks to his staff and wanted an automated workaround instead.

When these functional areas then began to push the majority of the changes out to the suppliers, that was the last straw: The resulting "business process realignment" and system specifications became disjointed and unattainable. Furthermore, the less powerful departments within the OEM and the supply chain partners were alienated from the project and did not believe the solution would truly address their business problems.

Fortunately, the original stakeholders had to review and sign off on the proposed solution. During this review, it became clear that the group's vision was not reflected in the proposed solution. Stakeholders from less powerful departments and the supply chain were very vocal about the lopsided nature of the business process alignment and system changes. It was evident that attaining the project objectives required the willing participation of the entire supply chain and all OEM departments. If some of these groups did not participate in the process design and "take ownership" of the solution, the CRM implementation would never fulfill its business objectives. As a result, the stakeholders decided to build a team that could define a solution acceptable to the entire supply chain.

## COLLABORATIVE TEAM APPROACH — A WIN–WIN FOCUS

The initial attempt at process alignment was unanimously characterized as trying to "herd cats." Fortunately, a new team was formed which was committed to getting the right membership, charter, and executive access for success.

First of all, the team leader came from outside the OEM. This element was critical in gaining the trust of the supply chain partners. Furthermore, team members who were nominated from across the supply chain had operational knowledge of the processes to be realigned. They were also empowered to make process decisions — a critical step, in that they were expected to sell the redesigned processes to their respective organizations. In contrast, in the initial failed effort, the most expendable people with minimal operational knowledge were assigned to participate on the design team.

The time allotted for process design and developing functional specifications was a single, focused, two-day work session. Each prioritized deliverable's cycle time was 3 months on average, therefore, the solution was not very hard to design.

Given the previous resistance to process change across the supply chain, the team members were expected to deliver a CRM solution acceptable to the entire supply chain. Thus, they were chartered to use the agreed-upon business problem definitions to guide their process redesign efforts. They were also empowered to evaluate whether a process change or functional specification contributed to solving the business problem; for example, they considered and discarded many functional specification requests that were cosmetic in nature and found to be lacking in any real business value.

All proposed changes to process or functional specifications were subject to a change–control process managed by the team. This approach helped protect the credibility of the team members in selling the process redesign and solution to their respective firms.

## WHAT HAPPENED?

A rather surprising fate awaited the newly chartered team as it embarked on its mission. ACME's various departments found innovative ways to define hitherto non-CRM functions and features as critical to the project's success. An imaginative sales manager insisted that this project could not succeed without upgrading ACME's contact management software. Closer examination revealed that the proposed changes did not directly interact with any component of the contact management process.

Seeing the trend, the supply chain partners wanted to get some of their stalled projects implemented under this initiative. Suddenly, the information technology (IT) departments from the OEM and supply chain partners needed new hardware and software upgrades. In essence, sensing that the team would successfully develop and implement a solution, the whole supply chain tried to add "pork" to it.

Ultimately, the team overcame these "distractions" and completed its mission successfully. Clear definition of the CRM problem in measurable and actionable terms acted as a filter in keeping the pork barrel projects at bay. Success was also due, in no small part, to access to executive leadership within the OEM and across the supply chain.

## THE LESSONS LEARNED

Based on this experience, it is clear that executive sponsorship and access are mandatory for implementing solutions that cut across the OEM and supply chain. This access is the most important element in implementing process redesign solution deployment. The team leader has to insist on weekly face-to-face meetings with key executives, especially those at ACME. This weekly "face time" helps keep "scope creep" in check.

For example, the project team's attempts to explain impending process changes can be preempted by direct reports from managers who have regular operational contact with the executives. Often these reports do not present proposed process changes in the best possible light. Without regular face time with the team leader to discuss impending changes in an objective way, the executives can and do become alienated from the team's objectives.

Moreover, the team leader should also have direct access to the executive sponsors, not to some intermediary acting on the team's behalf. Perception turns out to be more important than reality when successfully selling process changes to the executives of each supply chain partner.

The team leader also needs immediate access to executives on an as-needed basis to address sudden showstoppers. Most showstoppers come from the operations area during process redesign. In such situations, people who are good at operations tend to overanalyze and fail to make decisions quickly.

In contrast, executives usually evaluate problems from a big picture standpoint, take decisive action, and then communicate with their respective organizations. Similarly, the executive sponsors have to communicate project status, features, and functionality to their respective organizations with staff support from the team. This makes the final executive sign-off on the CRM solution easy and predictable.

Succeeding and surviving the implementation of such process changes requires deft maneuvering. It is all too easy to become dazzled by technology and ignore the organizational changes that come along with its implementation. If you manage people and perceptions effectively during process realignment, the process and technology components will be relatively easy to implement.

First, the team leader has to learn and work within the organizational culture of the firm. A team leader may be brilliant technically, but a lack of sensitivity to organizational culture can stall the process changes associated with CRM. Instead, the leader has to possess a sense of empathy and understanding of challenges facing a group before asking them to change their processes.

Second, the process redesign team should constantly remind themselves that people dislike change, not the team or its leader. Getting defensive or confrontational is a natural response to change; you have to listen patiently to people who do so. If you agree that they have legitimate concerns and then shift their focus to the long-term benefits involved, more often than not, their resistance to change will decline. In fact, on a couple of occasions, dissenting voices raised legitimate concerns that were not evident during the process design. The dissenters then became advocates for the proposed process and solution within their respective departments. These advocated helped ACME gain credibility for the proposed solution and organizational buy-in across the supply chain.

Third, ensure that non-IT executive sponsors and stakeholders get credit for defining and deploying the solution. It is the team's job to ensure that the day-to-day operations staff who will work with the CRM solution take ownership of the realigned processes. CRM across the supply chain requires multiple individuals across different organizations to work in unison to support a customer they do not directly interact with. An incentive structure for key operatives within the ACME's organization and across the supply chain to use the solution has to be instituted to ensure the success of the realigned processes.

Finally, implementing CRM across the supply chain requires a fundamental shift in the way the dominant channel partner interacts with its supply chain. Implementing limited process realignment across the supply chain lays the foundation for this new relationship, or supply chain community. In such a community, everyone works together as peers despite the presence of a dominant OEM, collaboratively squeezing waste out of the chain, optimizing processes, and sharing the gains equitably among all members. Without this change in mindset, supporting CRM across the supply chain will be impossible. The traditional "arm's-length" relationship between suppliers and the dominant channel partner cannot support the processes to sense and respond to the customer with products and services at an affordable price.

## CASE QUESTIONS

1. Explain how CRM (customer relationship management) should *ideally* function.
2. What are some of the challenges highlighted in the case — and typical to many companies considering a CRM system — to implementing an effective CRM system?
3. Discuss the pros and cons of the "channel master" taking the lead in building supply chain integration.
4. Discuss the "human element," particularly the role that trust plays in process alignment across the supply chain network.
5. What are the "key success factors" for successful supply network integration?

# REFERENCES

1. Reddy, R. (September 8, 2000). *Intelligent Enterprise,* 3, 14, 44–48.

# Case 2

ENVERA™:
# CREATING VALUE THROUGH SUPPLY CHAIN OPTIMIZATION IN THE CHEMICAL INDUSTRY

*Richard Chvala and William C. Johnson*

*Case prepared by Ram Reddy, President of Tactica, a technology and business strategy consulting firm (www.tactica-group.com) and William C. Johnson, Professor of Marketing of the Wayne Huizenga Graduate School of Business, Nova Southeastern University.*

## HISTORY

In 1999, as many global companies were gearing up for the Y2K computer and Internet issues, three information technology (IT) and marketing executives from a long-standing chemical firm embarked on a mission to create a value chain enhancement for supply chain connected firms via the Internet. This case study encompasses the value creation process utilized by this new offering, Envera, as well as other concepts and eBusiness issues that beset the chemical industry during the early years of the Internet revolution.

Rich Chvala, director of global marketing and eBusiness, Mike Giesler, vice president of IT, and Mason Moore, director of IT systems were employees of Ethyl Corporation in 1999. Ethyl Corporation, a Richmond, Virginia-based company, provides additive chemistry solutions to enhance the performance of petroleum products. Ethyl develops, manufactures, blends, and delivers chemical additives for fuels and lubricants around the world.

## ENVERA'S VALUE DEVELOPMENT AND DEPLOYMENT

Many aspects of the value of Internet communication and data transmission were being examined and tested in the late 1990s. For the most part and in most industries, however, these efforts were devoted to one-to-one links between a company and its customer or supplier. The aerospace and defense industries were the first to develop an Internet connected multiple company supply chain link. They developed this link as a method to distribute data and planning systems for the government F-22 world-class jet fighter project. This Internet supply chain consortia was called Exostar.

The chemical industry was an early adopter of enterprise-wide resource planning systems (ERP). Although many firms had adopted ERP, most of the systems were a mixed bag of software offerings that enabled internal management of the manufacturing and finance accounting operations for a company. A major issue facing the chemical industry in the late 1990s was creating an effective order handling process, as, with the chemical industry, simply placing an order for chemicals would often involve 12 to 16 different steps and document transfers (see Figure CS 2.1)

### Explanation of Value Chain Economics

The value chain most beneficial to all parties with Envera was the impact on the order/delivery process engaged within the chemical industry. When one orders or purchases a retail gift or item, the process is a two- or three-step event:

Select item > purchase > receive item

In the chemical industry, due to the impact of the regulatory measures, supplier sourcing initiatives, global handling issues, and the multipoint handling of chemicals within a company, the order to fulfillment transaction includes many document transfers and related communications. Typically, a chemical-to-chemical company "sale" involves 12 to 16 communications. Many of these communications or transactions require personnel to manage the system to reduce order entry and related data input time. Unfortunately, studies demonstrate that the costs associated with the personnel and data entries involved reach over thousands of dollars per transaction, causing many companies to raise prices or eliminate services to smaller purchasers.

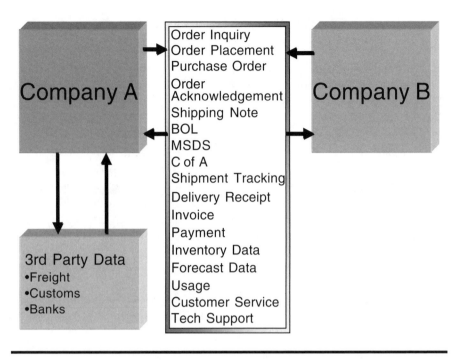

**Figure CS 2.1 and CS 2.2    Steps in document transfer.**

The chemical industry is well known for having some of the highest transaction costs in manufacturing, ranging from the low hundred's to several thousands per transaction, resultant from the many costs associated with the process and people involved in the completion of the sales transaction. These costs include sales contact, contract negotiation, safety and material handling, document preparation and communication, as well as logistical management of the product. Although some companies were improving supply chain management costs, the average industry spend on supply chain management in the chemical and related pharmaceutical industry was 9.8% of revenue. Best in class performers were significantly better at 4% of revenue, resultant from a focus on improving communications and information flow throughout the supply chain.

Another fairly unique feature of the chemical industry is its very incestuous nature. Because there are many modifications made in chemical processes, companies will often sell products to another chemical firm that will further modify the product and sell it back to them. So, in many cases, companies sell to their competitors. Therefore, while the chemical industry was a leader in ERP systems internally, their concern for secrecy and security was tantamount in providing any communications between firms.

## ORIGIN OF THE ENVERA™
## BUSINESS-TO-BUSINESS (B2B) EXCHANGE

The original software system that gave birth to Envera was a new offering to further build the relationship between lubricant additive customers and Ethyl Corporation. This link was trademarked as the "Customer-Connection™," allowing top-tier customers, via an Internet link, to explore their secure order and production records through Ethyl's ERP system. A great value-added feature, but the customers wanted more.

One executive vice president of a large, multi-billion dollar global oil producer asked, "Wouldn't it be great if we could access this type of system for all of our suppliers, to be able to place orders and receive transaction documents over the Web?" That encouragement set the small "skunk-works" team to begin exploring the technology and intercompany Internet links to create that opportunity.

The goals were clear:

1. Change the process of conducting business between chemical companies and their supply chains from paper and phone calls to the speed and clarity of the Internet.
2. Connect the companies not only to their product suppliers, but also to their service providers (i.e., logistics, transportation, regulatory, banks, and related areas of service).
3. Provide these services at a cost significantly lower than current transaction support spends.

Once the goals were clearly defined, a vision was developed to help sharpen the focus on pursuing the process necessary for success. Envera's vision follows:

> To fundamentally change Business-to-Business integration to Business-FOR-Business by combining point-to-point integration into a value-added clearinghouse network of systems and services.

Figures CS 2.2 and CS 2.3 depict the transformation from one-to-one links of normal supply chain information flows to the Internet hub concept of Envera. Figures CS 2.4 and 2.5 illustrate the enhancement of data flow resultant from the Internet data language (extensible markup language or XML, used by the Internet hubs to transmit supply chain data safely and securely through to a company's supply chain partners).

The typical transaction categories used by chemical companies to complete a "sale" include the following items as depicted in this graphic.

These document transactions were often handled via the accepted but antiquated "pre-Internet" channels of communication:

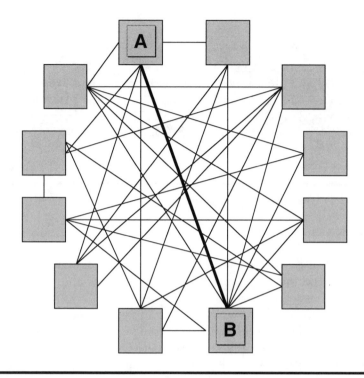

**Figure CS 2.3  One-to-one links in the chemical supply chain.**

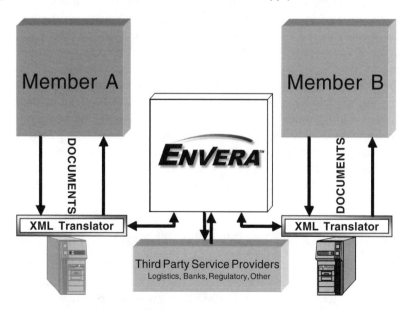

**Figure CS 2.4  Envera document handling.**

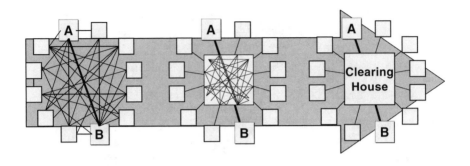

**Figure CS 2.5   The Envera clearinghouse.**

- Telephone
- Fax
- Postal mail systems ("snail mail")
- EDI (electronic data interchange)
- E-mail attachments

With the Envera concept, companies would use XML to send and retrieve data from any of their supply chain partners (customers and suppliers).

Member company A, as depicted in Figure CS 2.4, would send the document upon order through Envera. Envera would route the document to the proper receivers, including Member company B "supplier," shipping company, regulatory agency, banks, and related support enablers. Envera would also store the data transaction as a secure record document and serve as a third-party "objective" review board in case of any order discrepancies.

The concept was to create a "frictionless" exchange network by eliminating the direct buyer-supplier exchange relationships in favor of an industry "clearing house" concept (see Figure CS 2.5). Here, Envera served as the hub, facilitating exchange among multiple buyers and sellers.

Prior to Envera coming on the scene, the industry was characterized by a myriad of discreet and redundant process flows between various industry actors. Envera reconciled these inefficiencies by consolidating the process flows through a single, rather than multiple, redundant sources.

## DEVELOPING AND LAUNCHING ENVERA — FIRST STEPS

The first initiative was to create a suitable brand name and brand image to assist the presentation of value into the selected markets. Envera, loosely translated Latin meaning "in truth" was selected as a name for three primary reasons:

- Companies were concerned about their confidential data being communicated via a consortia link over the Internet.
- Many dot.coms were viewed as "outsiders" from the old line manufacturing companies and seen as competitors
- Most of the English language was "used up" in other dot.com registrations

The three Ethyl executives promoted their concept to Ethyl's board and gained a $5 million equity infusion along with an estimated $5 million "investment in kind" of travel, development, and office support. By early 2000, the three teamed up to take Envera's story on the road, developing a value proposition promotional presentation, contacting a list of chemical industry executives, and establishing meeting dates to review the Envera value proposition. In many cases, premeeting reviews were scheduled via teleconference and viewing an animated Powerpoint™ presentation.

In March of 2000, a meeting was held in Atlanta to firm up the interested chemical companies and create a limited liability company to support the Envera concept as a separate company. Several chemical companies immediately saw the "cost savings" and quality initiatives imbedded within the Envera technical architecture, as well as a method to demonstrate strategic competencies above their direct competitors. When the financing was completed, 10 chemical companies had invested over $30 million in the creation of Envera. These firms included Albemarle Corporation, Borden Chemicals, Inc., Ethyl Corporation, Equistar, Lubrizol, Lyondell, Mays Chemical, Oxychem, PhenolChemie, and Solutia.

Following Envera's move, another group of larger chemical companies were not content to share the power of an industry consortia with Envera's mid-sized chemical companies. Citing a parallel value proposition to speed the process and add efficiency to supply chain management, Dow Chemical, DuPont, BASF, Ciba, Rohm and Haas, and others formed Elemica. Industry analysts saw the copycat move as a defensive measure to maintain a power structure in the chemical industry as other industry Internet consortia approaches displayed more equality and unity in their activities.

Nonetheless, the overall goal for the chemical industry's advancement into Internet-linked consortia hubs was to provide easier access to the soon-to-be established hubs serving other industries (see Figure CS 2.6).

## TRANSFORMING CHEMICAL INDUSTRY SUPPLY CHAINS

As mentioned previously, after the Y2K technology issue was addressed in 1999, companies involved in raw material and chemical manufacturing began to study the value and benefits of integrating supply chain activities via emerging technologies. Overall, the chemical industry had become an

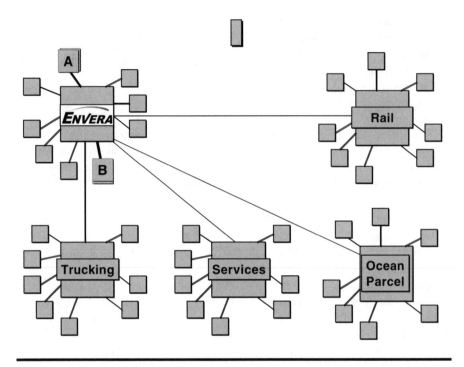

**Figure CS 2.6  The Envera hub concept.**

early front-runner in technology applications, resulting from the use of ERP systems and the computer as a process management tool in the complex manufacture of chemicals.

Early interventions in supply chain management associated one strategic supplier with a top-tier customer. Then, as technologies and interest developed, more companies saw the value of integrating as many links of their supply chain as possible. Two key driving forces emerged as value propositions; collaborative forecasting, and reducing the overall cost to serve.

Due to the fragmented nature of the chemical industry and its customers, companies have very close and extensive trading relationships with each other. In fact, many companies in these industries may compete in certain products yet be trading partners in others. The nature of these relationships lends itself to a Web-enabled B2B network.

## FORCES OF CHANGE

The chemical industry is under considerable financial pressures. Increased raw material and energy costs have resulted in reduced margins. A weaker stock market and falling consumer confidence have resulted in increased borrowing costs and higher inventory and receivable levels.

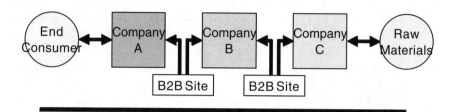

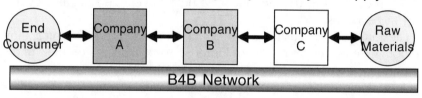

**Figure CS 2.7    B2B emerging approaches.**

These factors are driving companies to focus on cutting costs, strengthening their balance sheet and focusing on customer success, not just customer satisfaction. It is apparent that competition today is not company to company, but supply chain to supply chain. Technology is the driver and the Internet is the facilitator helping companies apply eBusiness to the basics of business.

Although the chemical and petroleum industries, especially the chemical industry, have been the focus of several eBusiness ventures, the initial eBusiness ventures consisted of mostly informational web sites showing company catalogs. The web site-evolved order sites began as companies assessed their Internet marketplace opportunities. In the late 1990s, several chemical auction sites emerged offering an "eBay-like" trading exchange for bulk commodity chemicals. Examples of chemical industry auction sites include ChemConnect and CheMatch. Early users saw this as a trendy method to off-load oversupply or lower quality production runs, however as time continued, many chemical companies began to use this method to increase their customer base. Alongside that motive, other chemical firms looked for methods and systems to communicate more efficiently between buyer and seller (see Figure CS 2.7).

Emerging almost concurrent with these auction sites were on-line trading exchanges that allowed companies to conduct their normal, non-auctionable business transactions. Covalex, e-Chemicals, and OneChem began as examples of these forms of exchanges; however, industry concern over transaction fees, liquidity, and technology requirements have caused many exchanges like these to revisit their business models and either significantly alter their offerings or remove themselves from the market, as did Covalex and e-Chemicals. The e-Marketplace, which was the term used to describe the overall services of a network hub consortia, soon became the favored entity for supply chain activities. Envera gained recognition as one of the best B2B web sites by Forbes Magazine in July 2000.

The industry was exploring methods to better integrate suppliers with their customers, thus strengthening existing relationships. The concept to Web-enable the core B2B transactions and to provide value-added services is known as a consortia network hub. Both Envera and Elemica evolved from those needs.

The automobile industry has fewer than 20 manufacturers, which allows the dominant players to create and impose Web standards on their trading partners. In early 2000, Ford, GM, and DaimlerChrysler agreed to jointly create a single marketplace for the industry named Covisint. The global automobile industry will probably end up with one common marketplace with one set of standards for B2B transactions.

Due to the fact that the chemical and petroleum industries have many more players than the automobile industry, the impetus for coordination and cooperation on Web standards for chemical and petroleum companies should come from a broad consortium of global companies. Envera and Elemica took a leadership role with Chemical Industry Data Exchange (CIDX) and the e-standards committee in setting the standards for B2B transactions. As stated on the CIDX Web site, "Chem eStandards™" are the uniform standards of data exchange developed specifically for the buying, selling, and delivery of chemicals. They are based on the universally recognized "gold standard" for electronic data exchange, XML. As of the first quarter of 2001, standards have been established for 47 documents used to conduct business in the chemical industry. The standards are identified as CIDXml or simply Chemical XML. The value of an industry standard, especially for the over 12,000 companies making up the chemical and petroleum industry worldwide, was a key driver in early implementation of Internet communications for supply chain management.

## BENEFITS OF SUPPLY CHAIN TRANSFORMATION

Early adopters of the consortia network hub design and users of XML document communications via the Internet were discovering efficiencies and cost benefits specifically in the management of their supply chains. Key savings were achieved in the following areas:

**Table CS 2.1   Supply Chain Improvement Benefits**

| | |
|---|---|
| Delivery performance | 16–28% improvement |
| Inventory reduction | 25–60% improvement |
| Fulfillment cycle time | 30–50% improvement |
| Forecast accuracy | 25–80% improvement |
| Overall productivity | 10–16% improvement |
| Lower supply chain costs | 25–50% improvement |
| Fill rates | 20–30% improvement |
| Improved capacity realization | 10–20% improvement |

- Reduction in purchase order errors
- Reduction in errors in data delivery and receiving
- On-time delivery performance
- Suppliers offering vendor-managed inventory (VMI) were able to reduce inventory volumes at customer sites
- Sales and manufacturing forecasts were improving on compatibility
- Cash-to-cash cycle times were greatly reduced

Integrating with supply chain partners, customers and suppliers can produce immediate and positive cost savings. The additional benefit a consortia hub brings to the Internet link "table" is that by creating one link to the hub — a member company will be automatically linked to the other consortia member companies. The average reduction in transaction costs accruing to a typical chemical industry member of Envera ($1 billion in annual sales) was nearly $6 billion. The Supply Chain Council has also reported impressive gains from supply chain integration (see Table CS 2.1).

## THE CHALLENGES AND COMPETITIVE RESPONSES

Three major competitive groups saw Envera as a threat, which provided various responses:

- Software providers and technology companies (the dot.coms) were concerned that a consortium would reduce the revenue opportunities as firms "pooled" their needs via the consortia approach.
- Large chemical companies that did not desire participation in a consortia, as they saw the "team efforts" as a way to reduce their "power" within the industry.
- Consultant firms, such as the "Big 5," saw the consortia approach as a threat to their revenue base in reducing the number of companies that needed their services.

The greatest competitive response to Envera came in the form of an internal competitive move by the larger chemical firms that made up Elemica. Although Envera invited these chemical giants to join and become initial investors in Envera, the members of Elemica decided not to dilute their collective power by sharing the consortia with the smaller, mid-sized Envera trading members.

As Envera grew, it followed its vision of "one link — global reach" by aligning through hub-to-hub connectivity with other industry consortia's, including the forest and paper products, rubber industry, auto, plastics, and related industry hubs.

Unfortunately, continued "connectivity" discussions with Elemica, the other chemical industry network hub, proved fruitless. It was obvious that Elemica was using a delay and deny tactic to reduce Envera's value and viability. Strategically, if Envera connected its members to Elemica, then there was no need to join Elemica.

## CASE STUDY QUESTIONS

1. What were the "value gaps" filled by consortia marketplace hubs like Envera and Elemica while serving the chemical industry?
2. What were the incentives for member firms to join these consortia marketplace hubs?
3. Why do you suppose the major players in the chemical industry, i.e., DuPont, Dow, BASF, resisted participating in the Envera exchange?
4. Describe Envera's Value Proposition. (Hint: The purpose of a value proposition is to create a shared understanding between a firm and its customers; it should be clear, concise, and not easily imitated, while clearly defining why a company's offer should be preferred over that of a competitor.)
5. Did Envera select the best merger partner in ChemConnect, or would the industry be better served by merging with Elemica?
6. How does an Internet marketplace consortia hub (or network) add value to a company's value chain?

# Appendix A

## FINAL SURVEY QUESTIONS

### EXHIBIT A.1 BPO SURVEY QUESTIONNAIRE

The purpose of the attached survey is to gather data for a study investigating the relationship between Business Process Orientation and organizational performance.

Thank you for your participation in this survey.

Please return all completed questionnaires to:

Kevin McCormack
2232 Baneberry Dr.
Birmingham, AL 35244
Tel. 205–733–2096
Fax 205–733–2094
kmccorm241@aol.com

The following questions ask you to comment on your organization. What we wish to know is how you perceive your organization as to the way the organization is structured toward getting work done. Each question will ask you to agree or disagree with the question on the following scale.

### (PLEASE CIRCLE <u>ONLY ONE</u> NUMBER FOR EACH QUESTION)

| Completely Disagree | Mostly Disagree | Neither Agree Nor Disagree | Mostly Agree | Completely Agree | Cannot Judge |
|---|---|---|---|---|---|
| 1 | 2 | 3 | 4 | 5 | 8 |

## Process View (PV)

### (PLEASE CIRCLE <u>ONLY ONE</u> NUMBER FOR EACH QUESTION)

| Completely Disagree 1 | Mostly Disagree 2 | Neither Agree Nor Disagree 3 | Mostly Agree 4 | Completely Agree 5 | Cannot Judge 8 |
|---|---|---|---|---|---|

1. The average employee views the business as a series of linked processes.  1 2 3 4 5 8

2. Process terms such as input, output, process, and process owners are used in conversation in the organization.  1 2 3 4 5 8

3. Processes within our organization are defined and documented using inputs and outputs to and from our customers.  1 2 3 4 5 8

4. The business processes are sufficiently defined so that most people in the organization know how they work.  1 2 3 4 5 8

## Process Jobs (PJ)

1. Jobs are usually multidimensional and not just simple tasks.  1 2 3 4 5 8

2. Jobs include frequent problem solving.  1 2 3 4 5 8

3. People are constantly learning new things on the job.  1 2 3 4 5 8

## Process Management and Measurement Systems (PM)

1. Process performance is measured in your organization.  1 2 3 4 5 8

2. Process measurements are defined.  1 2 3 4 5 8

3. Resources are allocated based on process.  1 2 3 4 5 8

4. Specific process performance goals are in place.  1 2 3 4 5 8

5. Process outcomes are measured.  1 2 3 4 5 8

## Interdepartmental Dynamics (ID)

### (PLEASE CIRCLE <u>ONLY ONE</u> NUMBER FOR EACH QUESTION)

| Completely Disagree | Mostly Disagree | Neither Agree Nor Disagree | Mostly Agree | Completely Agree | Cannot Judge |
|:---:|:---:|:---:|:---:|:---:|:---:|
| 1 | 2 | 3 | 4 | 5 | 8 |

### *Interdepartmental Conflict*

1. Most departments in this business get along well with each other.     1 2 3 4 5 8

2. When members of several departments get together, tensions frequently run high.     1 2 3 4 5 8

3. People in one department generally dislike interacting with those from other departments.     1 2 3 4 5 8

4. Employees from different departments feel that the goals of their respective departments are in harmony with each other.     1 2 3 4 5 8

5. Protecting one's departmental turf is considered to be a way of life in this business unit.     1 2 3 4 5 8

6. The objectives pursued by the marketing department are incompatible with those of the manufacturing department.     1 2 3 4 5 8

7. There is little or no interdepartmental conflict in this business unit.     1 2 3 4 5 8

### *Interdepartmental Connectedness*

1. In this business unit, it is easy to talk with virtually anyone you need to, regardless of rank or position.     1 2 3 4 5 8

2. There is ample opportunity for informal "hall talk" among individuals from different departments in this business unit.     1 2 3 4 5 8

3. In this business unit, employees from different departments feel comfortable calling each other when the need arises.     1 2 3 4 5 8

4. Managers here discourage employees from discussing work-related matters with those who are not their immediate superiors and subordinates.
   1 2 3 4 5 8

5. People around here are quite accessible to those in other departments.
   1 2 3 4 5 8

6. It is expected that communications from one department to another will be routed through "proper channels."
   1 2 3 4 5 8

7. Junior managers in my department can easily schedule meetings with junior managers in other departments.
   1 2 3 4 5 8

## Organizational Performance (OP)

**(PLEASE CIRCLE <u>ONLY ONE</u> NUMBER FOR EACH QUESTION)**

| Completely Disagree | Mostly Disagree | Neither Agree Nor Disagree | Mostly Agree | Completely Agree | Cannot Judge |
|---|---|---|---|---|---|
| 1 | 2 | 3 | 4 | 5 | 8 |

### Measures of Esprit de Corps

1. People in this business unit are genuinely concerned about the needs and problems of each other.
   1 2 3 4 5 8

2. A team spirit pervades all ranks in this business unit.
   1 2 3 4 5 8

3. Working for this business unit is like being part of a family.
   1 2 3 4 5 8

4. People in this business unit feel emotionally attached to each other.
   1 2 3 4 5 8

5. People in this business unit feel like they are "in it together."
   1 2 3 4 5 8

6. This business unit lacks an "esprit de corps."
   1 2 3 4 5 8

7. People in this business unit view themselves as independent individuals who have to tolerate others around them.
   1 2 3 4 5 8

## *Overall Performance (5 = excellent, 1 = poor)*

1. Please rate the overall performance of your business unit last year.                1 2 3 4 5 8

2. Please rate the overall performance of the business unit last year relative to major competitors.                1 2 3 4 5 8

## General Questions Needed for Analysis and Reporting of Results

Please circle your answers to the following questions.

1. What is your industry?

   1. Electronics
   2. Transportation
   3. Industrial Products
   4. Food and Beverage/CPG

   5. Aerospace and Defense
   6. Chemicals
   7. Apparel
   8. Utilities

   9. Pharmaceuticals/ Medical
   10. Mills
   11. Semiconductor
   12. Other _____

2. What is the approximate size of your entire company (number of employees)?

   Small <1,000 _____ Medium 1,000–10,000 _____
   Larger >10,000 _____

3. Within what function do you work?

   1. Sales
   2. Information Systems
   3. Planning and Scheduling
   4. Marketing

   5. Manufacturing
   6. Engineering
   7. Finance
   8. Distribution

   9. Purchasing
   10. Other _____

4. What is your position in the organization?

   1. Sr. Leadership/Executive
   2. Sr. Manager
   3. Manager
   4. Individual Contributor

Contact Information: (Optional)

Name _____

Title _____

Company _____

Address _____

City/State/Zip _____

Phone _____ Fax _____

E-mail _____

# EXHIBIT A.2 SUPPLY CHAIN ASSESSMENT SURVEY

## Supply Chain Management

> *Definition: the process of developing decisions and taking actions to direct the activities of people within the supply chain toward common objectives.*

The purpose of this survey is to capture the current status of your decision activities necessary for the successful operation of your supply chain. This survey attempts to capture YOUR OPINION concerning what is done, how often, who does it and how it is done.

Thank you for your participation in this survey.

Please return all completed questionnaires to:

Kevin McCormack
2232 Baneberry Dr.
Birmingham, AL 35244
Tel. 205-733-2096
Fax 205-733-2094
kmccorm241@aol.com

## Decision Process Area: Plan (Includes P1: Plan Supply Chain, and P0: Plan Infrastructure)

Please circle your answer concerning this supply chain decision process area using a range of:

> 1 — never or does not exist, 2 — sometimes, 3 — frequently, 4 — mostly, 5 — always or definitely exists

Please put an "X" on any question you are unable to answer.

1. Do you have an operations strategy planning team designated? ...
   ..................................................................................1 2 3 4 5

2. Does this team have formal meetings?..........................1 2 3 4 5

3. Are the major Supply Chain functions (Sales, Marketing, Manufacturing, Logistics, etc.) represented on this team? ...........1 2 3 4 5

4. Do you have a documented (written description, flow charts, etc.) operations strategy planning process? ..............................1 2 3 4 5

5. Is there an owner for the supply chain planning process?............
..................................................................................1 2 3 4 5

6. Has the business defined customer priorities?................1 2 3 4 5

7. Has the business defined product priorities?..................1 2 3 4 5

8. When you meet, do you make adjustments in the strategy and document them?..............................................................1 2 3 4 5

9. Does the team have supply chain performance measures established?.................................................................................1 2 3 4 5

10. Does the team look at the impact of their strategies on supply chain performance measures?...........................................1 2 3 4 5

11. Does the team use adequate analysis tools to examine the impact before a decision is made?................................................1 2 3 4 5

12. Is the team involved in the selection of supply chain management team members? ...............................................................1 2 3 4 5

13. Does this team look at customer profitability?...............1 2 3 4 5

14. Does this team look at product profitability? ..................1 2 3 4 5

15. Does this team participate in customer and supplier relationships? ...............................................................................1 2 3 4 5

16. Do you analyze the variability of demand for your products?.......
..................................................................................1 2 3 4 5

17. Do you have a documented demand forecasting process?............
..................................................................................1 2 3 4 5

18. Do your information systems currently support the Demand Management process?..............................................................1 2 3 4 5

19. Does this process use historical data in developing the forecast? .
..................................................................................1 2 3 4 5

20. Do you use mathematical methods (statistics) for demand forecasting?................................................................................1 2 3 4 5

21. Does this process occur on a regular (scheduled) basis? ..............
..................................................................................1 2 3 4 5

22. Is a forecast developed for each product?....................1 2 3 4 5

23. Is a forecast developed for each customer?....................1 2 3 4 5

24. Is there an owner for the demand management process?..............
..................................................................................1 2 3 4 5

25. Does your demand management process make use of customer information? .................................................................................1 2 3 4 5

26. Is the forecast updated weekly? .........................................1 2 3 4 5

27. Is the forecast credible or believable? ..............................1 2 3 4 5

28. Is the forecast used to develop plans and make commitments? .... .................................................................................1 2 3 4 5

29. Is forecast accuracy measured? .........................................1 2 3 4 5

30. Are your demand management and production planning processes integrated? ..............................................................................1 2 3 4 5

31. Do sales, manufacturing, and distribution organizations collaborate in developing the forecast? ...............................................1 2 3 4 5

32. Overall, this decision process area performs very well. .................. .................................................................................1 2 3 4 5

## Decision Process Area: SOURCE (Includes P2: Plan Source)

Please circle your answer concerning this supply chain decision process using a range of:

1 — never or does not exist, 2 — sometimes, 3 — frequently, 4 — mostly, 5 — always or definitely exists

Please put an "X" on any question you are unable to answer.

1. Is your procurement process documented (written description, flow charts)? ...............................................................................1 2 3 4 5

2. Does your information system support this process? .....1 2 3 4 5

3. Are the supplier interrelationships (variability, metrics) understood and documented? .................................................................1 2 3 4 5

4. Is a "process owner" identified? .......................................1 2 3 4 5

5. Do you have strategic suppliers for all products and services? ...... .................................................................................1 2 3 4 5

6. Do suppliers manage "your" inventory of supplies? .......1 2 3 4 5

7. Do you have electronic ordering capabilities with your suppliers? .................................................................................1 2 3 4 5

8. Do you share planning and scheduling information with suppliers? .................................................................................1 2 3 4 5

9. Do key suppliers have employees on your site(s)?........1 2 3 4 5

10. Do you "collaborate" with your suppliers to develop a plan?
.................................................................................1 2 3 4 5

11. Do you measure and feedback supplier performance?..1 2 3 4 5

12. Is there a procurement process team designated? ..........1 2 3 4 5

13. Does this team meet on a regular basis?.........................1 2 3 4 5

14. Do other functions (manufacturing, sales, etc.) work closely with the procurement process team members?........................1 2 3 4 5

15. Overall, this decision process area performs very well..1 2 3 4 5

## Decision Process Area: Make (Includes P3: Plan Make)

Please circle your answer concerning this supply chain decision process using a range of:

1 — never or does not exist, 2 — sometimes, 3 — frequently,
4 — mostly, 5 — always or definitely exists

Please put an "X" on any question you are unable to answer.

1. Do you have a documented (written description, flow charts, etc.) production planning and scheduling process?.................1 2 3 4 5

2. Are your planning processes integrated and coordinated across divisions?...........................................................................1 2 3 4 5

3. Do you have someone who "owns" the process? ..........1 2 3 4 5

4. Do you have weekly planning cycles?............................1 2 3 4 5

5. Are supplier lead times a major consideration in the planning process?..........................................................................1 2 3 4 5

6. Are supplier lead times updated monthly? ....................1 2 3 4 5

7. Are you using constraint-based planning methodologies?..............
.................................................................................1 2 3 4 5

8. Is shop floor scheduling integrated with the overall scheduling process?..........................................................................1 2 3 4 5

9. Do your information systems currently support the process?.........
.................................................................................1 2 3 4 5

10. Do you measure "adherence to plan?"...........................1 2 3 4 5

11. Does your current process adequately address the needs of the business? ................................................................................1 2 3 4 5

12. Do the sales, manufacturing and distribution organizations collaborate in the planning and scheduling process? ...............1 2 3 4 5

13. Is your customer's planning and scheduling information included in yours? ................................................................................1 2 3 4 5

14. Are changes approved through a formal, documented approval process? ................................................................................1 2 3 4 5

15. Are plans developed at the "item" level of detail? .........1 2 3 4 5

16. Overall, this decision process performs very well. .........1 2 3 4 5

## Decision Process Area: Deliver (Includes P4: Plan Deliver)

Please circle your answer concerning this supply chain decision process using a range of:

1 — never or does not exist, 2 — sometimes, 3 — frequently, 4 — mostly, 5 — always or definitely exists

Please put an "X" on any question you are unable to answer.

1. Is your order commitment process documented (written description, flow charts)? ...........................................................1 2 3 4 5

2. Do you have a Promise Delivery (order commitment) "process owner?" ................................................................................1 2 3 4 5

3. Do you track the percentage of completed customer orders delivered on time? ................................................................................1 2 3 4 5

4. Are the customer's satisfied with the current on time delivery performance? ................................................................................1 2 3 4 5

5. Do you meet short-term customer demands from finished goods inventory? ................................................................................1 2 3 4 5

6. Do you "build to order?" ....................................................1 2 3 4 5

7. Do you measure customer "requests" versus actual delivery? ........ ................................................................................1 2 3 4 5

8. Given a potential customer order, can you commit to a <u>firm</u> quantity and delivery date (based on actual conditions) on request? .......... ................................................................................1 2 3 4 5

9. Are the projected delivery commitments given to customers credible (from the customer's view)?.........................................1 2 3 4 5

10. Do you promise orders beyond what can be satisfied by current inventory levels?................................................................1 2 3 4 5

11. Do you maintain the capability to respond to unplanned, drop-in orders?.......................................................................1 2 3 4 5

12. Do you automatically replenish a customers inventory? ................. ........................................................................................1 2 3 4 5

13. Do the sales, manufacturing, distribution and planning organizations collaborate in the order commitment process? ......1 2 3 4 5

14. Do your information systems currently support the order commitment process?..............................................................1 2 3 4 5

15. Do you measures "out of stock" situations? ....................1 2 3 4 5

16. Is your order commitment process integrated with your other supply chain decision processes?......................................1 2 3 4 5

17. Is your Distribution Management process documented (written description, flow charts)? .................................................1 2 3 4 5

18. Does your information system support Distribution Management? ........................................................................................1 2 3 4 5

19. Are the network inter-relationships (variability, metrics) understood and documented?..............................................................1 2 3 4 5

20. Is a "process owner" identified?........................................1 2 3 4 5

21. Are impacts of changes examined in enough detail before the changes are made? ..........................................................1 2 3 4 5

22. Are changes made in response to the loudest "screams?" ............. ........................................................................................1 2 3 4 5

23. Are deliveries expedited (manually "bypassing" the normal process)?.......................................................................1 2 3 4 5

24. Do you use a mathematical "tool" to assist in distribution planning? ........................................................................................1 2 3 4 5

25. Can rapid replanning be done to respond to changes?.................. ........................................................................................1 2 3 4 5

26. Is the Distribution Management process integrated with the other supply chain decision processes (production planning and scheduling, demand management, etc.)? ..................................1 2 3 4 5

27. Does each node in the distribution network have inventory measures and controls? ..........................................................1 2 3 4 5

28. Do you use automatic replenishment in the distribution network? ...............................................................................................1 2 3 4 5

29. Are process measures in place? .....................................1 2 3 4 5

30. Are they used to recognize and reward the process participants? ...............................................................................................1 2 3 4 5

31. Overall, this decision process area performs very well................... ...............................................................................................1 2 3 4 5

## Common Themes Within Each Supply Chain Decision Process Area: Strategies, Tactics and Philosophy Components that are Common Across the Supply Chain

Please circle your answer to the following questions in regards to your opinion of the OVERALL supply chain.

1. Your supply chain processes are documented and defined ...

Not at all ............a little .......... somewhat........... mostly ...........completely
    1                    2                    3                 4                 5

2. Your supply chain organizational structure can be described as ...

Traditional
Function- ............a little .............. some.............. mostly ..............entirely
  Based           Process           Process           Process          Process-
                                                                        Based
    1                  2                  3                 4                 5

3. Your supply chain performance measures can be described as ...

Traditional
Function- ............a little .............. some.............. mostly ..............entirely
  Based           Process           Process           Process          Process-
                                                                        Based
    1                  2                  3                 4                 5

4. People in the supply chain organization can be generally described as …

Totally............a little ......... somewhat.......... mostly...............entirely
Internally      Customer-       Customer-       Customer-       Customer-
Focused         Focused         Focused         Focused         Focused
1               2               3               4               5

5. Your information systems currently support the supply chain processes …

Not at all............a little ......... somewhat.......... mostly...........completely
1               2               3               4               5

6. Does the demand for your product vary?

Not at all............a little ......... somewhat........... often ...............always
1               2               3               4               5

7. Jobs in the supply chain can generally be described as …

"Limited"                                                        "Broad"
Task-...............a little ......... somewhat.......... mostly..............Process-
Oriented        Process         Process         Process         Oriented
1               2               3               4               5

## Relative Performance

Please rate the overall performance of your business unit last year.

Poor .................Fair...............Good .............Very Good...........Excellent
1               2               3               4               5

Please rate the overall performance of your business unit last year relative to major competitors.

Poor .................Fair...............Good .............Very Good...........Excellent
1               2               3               4               5

Compared to your major competitors, your overall inventory Days of Supply (DOS) are:

Poor .................Fair...............Good .............Very Good...........Excellent
1               2               3               4               5

Compared to your major competitors, your overall cash-to-cash cycle times are:

Poor ................. Fair................ Good .............Very Good............Excellent
  1                2                3              4              5

Compared to your major competitors, your delivery performance vs. commit date is:

Poor ................. Fair................ Good .............Very Good............Excellent
  1                2                3              4              5

Compared to your major competitors your quoted order lead times are:

Poor ................. Fair................ Good .............Very Good............Excellent
  1                2                3              4              5

## General Questions Needed for Analysis and Reporting of Results

Please circle your answers to the following questions.

1. What is your industry?

   a) Electronics
   b) Transportation
   c) Industrial Products
   d) Food and Beverage/CPG
   e) Aerospace and Defense
   f) Chemicals
   g) Apparel
   h) Utilities
   i) Pharmaceuticals/ Medical
   j) Mills
   k) Semiconductor
   l) Other _____

2. Within what function do you work?

   a) Sales
   b) Information Systems
   c) Planning and Scheduling
   d) Marketing
   e) Manufacturing
   f) Engineering
   g) Finance
   h) Distribution
   i) Purchasing
   j) Other _____

3. What is your position in the organization?

   a) Sr. Leadership/Executive
   b) Sr. Manager
   c) Manager
   d) Individual Contributor

Contact Information: (Optional)

Name _____

Title _____

Company _____

Address _____

City/State/Zip _____

Phone _____ Fax _____

E-mail _____

# Appendix B

# REGRESSION AND COEFFICIENT ALPHA ANALYSIS RESULTS

Regression and coefficient alpha analysis were run in order to examine the quality and the explanatory power of the survey instrument. Basically, the analyses were run to answer the question of whether the survey questions can explain SCM performance in each SCOR category.

Table B.1 lists the results of regression and coefficient alpha analysis of the questions in each SCOR category that had a correlation to performance above 0.5. In each case, the number of questions above 0.5 is shown versus the total questions in the category. For example, the PLAN category had 12 questions out of 31 that were used in the regression and coefficient alpha analysis. In each case, the dependent variable in the regression equation was the self-assessed performance question in each category.

R squared, or the coefficient of determination, is a number produced in the analysis that indicates the goodness of fit of a linear model. In this case, it indicates the fit of the linear relationship between the questions

**Table B.1   Regression and Coefficient Alpha Analysis Results**

| Category | Plan | Source | Make | Deliver |
|---|---|---|---|---|
| Questions >0.5/Total Questions | 12/31 | 8/14 | 7/15 | 7/30 |
| R squared | 0.84 | 0.82 | 0.72 | 0.73 |
| Coefficient alpha | 0.94 | 0.88 | 0.88 | 0.89 |

that were above 0.5 correlation and the performance questions. R squared also indicates the proportion of the variation in the dependent variable explained by the model. For example, 84% of the variation in PLAN performance is explained by the 12 questions with a correlation above 0.5.

Coefficient alpha analysis measures the internal consistency of a set of measures or survey questions meant to represent a certain concept; this analysis is used to assess the quality of the questions and the survey instrument. A low coefficient alpha indicates that the sample of items performs poorly in capturing the construct or concept, and a large alpha indicates that the test correlates well with true scores; 0.7 is generally suggested as the lowest point below which a survey instrument becomes suspect.

The data in Table B.1 indicate a solid survey instrument (alphas of 0.88 to 0.94) that represents the concepts of SCM in all areas of the SCOR model. In addition, the R squared results show a high percentage of explanation (0.72 to 0.84) is contained in the questions above 0.5 correlation in all areas of the SCOR model.

Figure B1 depicts the results of regression analysis using the individual components of BPO. The R squared, or the coefficient of determination, is listed for each relationship as well as the Beta coefficient. This number indicates the relative importance of the variable in the relationship. In Figure B1, both the R squared and Beta coefficients are fairly strong, suggesting a relationship between BPO and SCM performance.

Overall, our research has shown that BPO is a critical factor in SCM. When an organization's SCM becomes more business-process-oriented, performance will improve. This is true for the old economy linear supply chain as well as the new economy, networked e-supply chain. The logical evolution of BPO is to extend it to supply chain networks, which is the the subject of Appendix D.

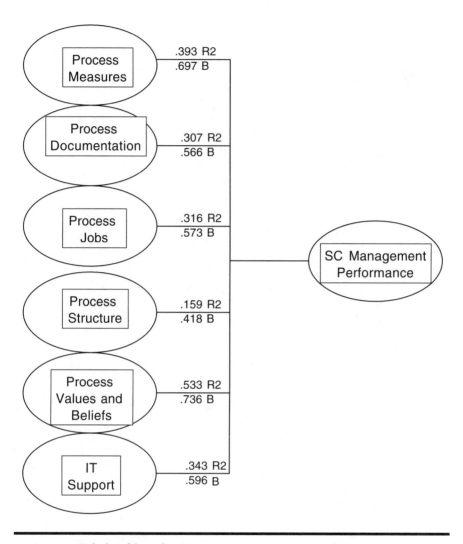

**Figure B1    Relationships of BPO Components to SCM Performance**

# Appendix C

## EXTENDED SUPPLY CHAIN VS. INTERNET USAGE CORRELATION RESULTS

**Table C.1    Digital Technology Correlations to Customer Integrating Practices**

DT1    Do your customers interact with you though the Internet (e-mail, on-line chat)?
- P25 (.445) Does your demand management process make use of customer information?
- D4 (.409) Are the customer's satisfied with the current on-time delivery performance?
- D12 (.447) Do you automatically replenish a customer's inventory?

DT2    Do your customers gather information about you (and your products) through the Internet?
- D4 (.473) Are the customers satisfied with the current on-time delivery performance?

DT3    Do your customers place orders for your goods and services through the Internet?
- P6 (-.383) Has the business defined customer priorities?

DT4    Do you gather customer data (usage, forecast, ideas, complaints) though the Internet?
- M13 (.480) Is your customer's planning and scheduling information included in yours?
- D12 (.447) Do you automatically replenish a customer's inventory?

*Note:* Significant correlations are shown in parentheses.

**Table C.2   Digital Technology Correlations to Supplier Integrating Practices**

| | |
|---|---|
| DT5 | Do your suppliers interact with you though the Internet (e-mail, online chat)? <br> ■ S6 (.447) Do suppliers manage "your" inventory of supplies? |
| DT6 | Do you gather information about your suppliers (and their products) through the Internet? <br> ■ S6 (.428) Do suppliers manage "your" inventory of supplies? |
| DT7 | Do you place orders for your suppliers' goods and services through the Internet? <br> ■ S6 (.556) Do suppliers manage "your" inventory of supplies? <br> ■ S8 (.397) Do you share planning and scheduling information with suppliers? <br> ■ S7 (.352) Do you have electronic ordering capabilities with your suppliers? |
| DT8 | Do you gather supplier data (performance, forecast, ideas) though the Internet? <br> ■ S6 (.404) Do suppliers manage "your" inventory of supplies? |

*Note:*  Significant correlations are shown in parentheses.

# Appendix D

## SC NETWORK MODEL AND SITUATIONAL FACTORS — DETAILED SURVEY QUESTIONS

### EXHIBIT D.1: SC NETWORK MODEL COMPONENTS AND OUTCOMES — DETAILED SURVEY QUESTIONS

The purpose of the attached survey is to gather data for a study investigating the relationship between Supply Chain Network Management (SCNM) and organizational performance.

SCNM is the process of simulating, responding to, and controlling exceptions to planned and unplanned events in the supply chain.

SCNM consists of five business processes:

Monitor
Notify
Simulate
Control
Measure

SCNM moves from a single enterprise controlling multiple processes to multiple enterprises that control a single process distributed across trading partners.[1]

Thank you for your participation in this survey.

Please return all completed questionnaires to:

---

[1] Maloni, M. and Benton, W.C., 2000, Power influences in the supply chain, *Journal of Business Logistics,* vol. 21, No. 1.

Kevin McCormack
2232 Baneberry Dr.
Birmingham, AL 35244
Tel. 205-733-2096
Fax 205-733-2094
kmccorm241@aol.com

The following questions ask you to comment on your organization. What we wish to know is how you perceive your organization regarding how the organization is structured toward getting work done. Please agree or disagree with each statement using the following scale:

**(PLEASE CIRCLE ONLY ONE NUMBER FOR EACH QUESTION)**

| Completely Disagree | Mostly Disagree | Neither Agree Nor Disagree | Mostly Agree | Completely Agree | Cannot Judge |
|---|---|---|---|---|---|
| 1 | 2 | 3 | 4 | 5 | 8 |

# PROCESS VIEW (PV)

**(PLEASE CIRCLE ONLY ONE NUMBER FOR EACH STATEMENT)**

| Completely Disagree | Mostly Disagree | Neither Agree Nor Disagree | Mostly Agree | Completely Agree | Cannot Judge |
|---|---|---|---|---|---|
| 1 | 2 | 3 | 4 | 5 | 8 |

The average employee views process management as a key to monitoring supply chain events.

Process terms such as input, output, process, and process owners are used in discussing supply chain network management issues.

Processes shared with supply chain trading partners are defined and documented to support supply chain network management.

The business processes in our organization are sufficiently defined to facilitate supply chain network management with our trading partners.

The business processes in our trading partners' organizations are sufficiently defined to facilitate supply chain network management in our organization.

Supply chain network management business processes are defined and documented (monitor, notify, simulate, control and measure).

## PROCESS JOBS (PJ)

Supply chain network management (SCNM) jobs are multidimensional and interact with the entire supply chain network of trading partners.

Supply chain network management is used by supply chain trading partners for joint problem solving on multidimensional jobs.

Best practices on supply chain network management are constantly shared among trading partners to improve process performance.

Supply chain network management jobs are identified.

These SCNM jobs have broad authority to take action anywhere in the supply chain.

## PROCESS MANAGEMENT AND MEASUREMENT SYSTEMS (PM)

The performance of supply chain network processes is measured in your organization.

Supply chain network process measurements are defined.

Supply chain network resources are allocated based on process needs.

Specific supply chain network process performance goals are in place.

Supply chain network process outcomes are measured.

## PROCESS STRUCTURES (PS)

SCNM process owners are identified.

An SCNM team is operating.

This SCNM team includes team members from our trading partners.

Supply chain network management is organized around the SCNM business processes (monitor, notify, simulate, control and measure).

The SCNM team has the authority to make real time decisions that impact the entire supply chain.

SCNM team members are involved in selecting other SCNM team members.

## PROCESS VALUES AND BELIEFS (PVB)

The management of the supply chain trading partners emphasizes SCNM.

The SCNM team is empowered rather than controlled.

Supply chain trading partner management emphasizes improving how work gets done.

Customers are asked about SCNM process performance.

The SCNM team members are well informed and trained.

SCNM team members work toward achieving common goals.

## TECHNOLOGY SUPPORT (TS)

Our information systems allow the SCNM team to respond to unplanned events on an exception basis.

Our information systems support the *monitoring* of supply chain network processes.

Our information systems support the *notification* of SCNM team members when supply chain network process events or issues occur.

Our information systems support the *simulation* of supply chain network processes.

Our information systems support the *control* of supply chain network processes.

Our information systems support the *measurement* of supply chain network processes.

## OVERALL PERFORMANCE
## (5 = EXCELLENT, 1 = POOR)

Please rate the overall performance of your supply chain network last year.

Please rate the overall performance of the supply chain network last year relative to major competitors.

## MEASURES OF SUPPLY CHAIN NETWORK
## ESPRIT DE CORPS

People in this supply chain network are genuinely concerned about theneeds and problems of each other.

A team spirit pervades all ranks in this supply chain network.

Working in this supply chain network is like being part of a family.

People in this supply chain network feel emotionally attached to each other.

People in this supply chain network feel like they are "in it together."

This supply chain network lacks an "esprit de corps."

People in this supply chain network view themselves as independent individuals who have to tolerate others around them.

## INTERNAL SITUATIONAL FACTORS — SUPPLY CHAIN
## NETWORK POWER MEASURES[1]

(Scale 1 — Completely Disagree to 5 — Completely Agree)

### Expert Power

The lead company in this supply chain network is an expert in the industry.

We respect the judgment of the lead company's representatives.

The lead company retains business expertise that makes it likely to suggest the proper things to do.

### Referent Power

We really admire the way the lead company runs its business so we try to follow its lead.

We often do what the lead company asks because we are proud to be affiliated with it.

We talk up the lead company to our colleagues as a great business with which to be associated.

### Legitimate Power

The lead company has the right to tell us what to do.

Because the lead company is our customer, we should accept its requests and recommendations.

### Legal Legitimate Power

The lead company often refers to portions of an agreement to gain our compliance on a particular request.

The lead company makes a point to refer to any legal agreement when attempting to influence us.

The lead company uses sections of our sales agreement as a "tool" to get us to agree to its demands.

### Reward Power

The lead company offers incentives when we were initially reluctant to cooperate with a new program.

We feel that by going along with the lead company, we will be favored on other occasions.

The lead company offers rewards so that we will go along with its wishes.

### Coercive Power

If we do not do as asked, we will not receive very good treatment from the lead company.

If we do not agree to its suggestions, the lead company could make things difficult for us.

The lead company makes it clear that failing to comply with their requests will result in penalties against us.

## Other Measures

### Commitment

Our firm is committed to the preservation of good working relationships with the lead company.

Our firm believes in the lead company as a partner.

Our relationship with the lead company could be described as one of high commitment.

### Conflict

Sometimes the lead company prevents us from doing what we want to do.

The lead company does not have our best interest at heart.

We often disagree with the lead company.

### Conflict Resolution

The discussions we have with the lead company in areas of disagreement are usually very productive.

Our discussions in areas of disagreement with the lead company create more problems than they solve.

Discussions in areas of disagreement increase the strength of our relationship.

### Cooperation

Our relationship with the lead company is better described as a "cooperative effort" rather than an "arms length negotiation."

Overall, our firm and the lead company perform well together in carrying out our respective tasks.

We feel that we can count on the lead company to give us the support that other suppliers receive.

### Trust

The lead company is concerned about our welfare.

The lead company considers how its actions will affect us.

We trust the lead company.

### Performance

The performance of the entire supply chain has improved as a result of our relationship with the lead company.

The efficiency of our relationship with the lead company has improved the lead company's performance.

Without the lead company, our performance would not be as good as it is with it.

## COMPETITIVE EDGES SURVEY INSTRUMENT

Listed below are nine areas on which supply chain networks can develop competitive edges on which to compete in the marketplace. Please rank them in the order of importance based upon the *current* strategies of your supply chain network. A rank of 1 denotes that the area is most critical to the supply chain network's competitive position, while a rank of nine denotes it is least important. Please use each number (1 through 9) once.

| | |
|---|---|
| _____ | Due Date Performance |
| _____ | Field Service |
| _____ | Innovation |
| _____ | Lead Time |
| _____ | Price |
| _____ | Process Flexibility |
| _____ | Product Flexibility |
| _____ | Product Introduction Responsiveness |
| _____ | Quality |

The following is a brief explanation of each concept. The **price** on which a firm can compete is based on environmental factors such as market turbulence and competitive intensity. Product and service attributes based on actual market requirements must be established in order to develop a competitive edge in the area of **quality**. **Lead time** refers to the time between recognition of the need for an order and the receipt of goods by the customer. Firms competing on lead time must continually reduce their order cycles. To compete on **due date performance**, firms must consistently deliver goods based on promise dates determined by the customer. **Product and process flexibility** refer to a firm's ability to configure and adapt their products and corresponding processes to conform to changing customer requirements. **Field service** organizations can provide a competitive edge through their ability to respond to post-sale problems encountered by the customer. **Innovation** refers to a firm's ability to offer creative solutions to its customers that lead to a distinct market advantage. Finally, firms that can rapidly **respond to customer needs by introducing new products** can exploit first-mover advantages via the competitive edge of product introduction responsiveness.

## External Situational Factors — (Environmental Factors)[2]

(Scale 1 — Completely Disagree to 5 — Completely Agree)

### *Market Turbulence*

In our kind of business, customers' product preferences change quite a bit over time.

Our customers tend to look for new products all the time.

Sometimes our customers are very price sensitive, but on other occasions, price is relatively unimportant.

We are witnessing demand for our products and services from customers who never bought them before.

New customers tend to have product-related needs that are different from those of our existing customers.

---

[2] Kohli, A.K. and Jaworski, B.J. (July 1993). Market orientation: antecedents and consequences, *J. Mark.*

We cater to many of the same customers that we used to in the past.

## Competitive Intensity

Competition in our industry is cutthroat.

There are many "promotion wars" in our industry.

If one competitor can offer a particular product or service, others can match readily.

Price competition is a hallmark of our industry.

One hears of a new competitive move almost every day.

Our competitors are relatively weak.

## Technological Turbulence

The technology in our industry is changing rapidly.

Technological changes provide big opportunities in our industry.

It is very difficult to forecast where the technology in our industry will be in the next 2 to 3 years.

A large number of new product ideas have been made possible through technological breakthroughs in our industry.

Technological developments in our industry are rather minor.

# GLOSSARY

**Advanced Planning and Schedule (APS):** Applies knowledge and advanced technologies (usually advanced mathematics and computing technology) to achieve improved plans that take into account most of the factors and constraints that limit the ability to deliver a product or service on time.

**Alignment:** The proper positioning of parts in relation to each other. In a network this is strategy, goals, objectives, measures, business process orientation (BPO), etc.

**APICS:** The Educational Society for Resource Management, an international, not-for-profit organization.

**Benchmarking:** The systematic comparison of process performance, practices, and attributes for the purpose of process improvement.

**Best Practice:** A way of doing things that has been shown to lead to superior results or outcomes.

**Business-to-Business (B2B):** The interactions between separate, legal business entities.

**Business Process:** A collection of activities that takes one or more kinds of input and creates an output that is of value to the customer. A reengineered business is composed of strategic, customer-focused processes that start with the customer and emphasize outcome, not mechanisms.

**Business Process Change (BPC):** A strategy-driven organizational initiative to improve and (re)design business processes to achieve competitive advantage in performance through changes in the relationships between management, information, technology, organizational structure, and people.

**Business Process Orientation (BPO):** Emphasizes process, a process-oriented way of thinking, customers, and outcomes as opposed to hierarchies.

**Business Webs:** Network configurations proposed to reflect the interconnected roles and activities within a cross-enterprise supply chain making the historical legal and organizational structures no longer the basis of competition.

**Chaotic Network:** The set of supply chain players is potentially different for each order fulfilled. Trading exchanges, business-to-business (B2B) e-commerce, and business-to-consumer (B2C) e-commerce over the Internet are examples.

**Chassis Groupings:** Provide the framework or foundation for achieving process capability, predictability, and maturity.

**Coefficient Alpha Analysis:** Measures the internal consistency of a set of measures or survey question meant to represent a certain concept and is used to assess the quality of the questions and survey instrument.

**Communications Matrix:** Identifies a set of relevant issues (e.g., products, technologies, markets, etc.) and then identifies the individuals (by function) who have relevant expertise on that particular issue. Provides valuable information regarding where relevant expertise resides within the partnering firms and helps direct interactions in a much more focused way.

**Competitive Intensity:** The behavior, resources, and ability of competitors to differentiate themselves in a market.

**Coordination Theory:** A body of principles about how activities can be coordinated and how actors can work together harmoniously.

**Collaboration:** Forms, behaviors, constructive conflict, and creative integration in order to achieve a common goal.

**Collaborative Planning and Forecasting:** A collaborative business relationship based on exchanging information to support the synchronization of activities to deliver products in response to market demand. Sometimes includes replenishment of materials (CPFR).

**Commitment:** Actions and values of key supply network decision makers regarding continuation of the relationship and a willingness to invest resources in the relationship.

**Competitive Edges:** Product or service characteristics whose improvement leads to a strategic advantage in a specific market or market segment.

**Cooperation:** Where supply chain network actors are working jointly to achieve mutual and individual goals.

**Core Processes:** The value-added activities that support and facilitate the customer life cycle, represent the foundation of most businesses, and the value for which customers pay as well as the essence of most businesses.

**Correlation Analysis:** Identifies the statistically significant relationship between variables. A "0" means no relationship and "1.0" means a perfect relationship. The closer a correlation is to 1, the stronger the relationship.

**Demand Management:** A management process that integrates supply and demand information for the purpose of optimizing operations.

**Dependence:** Willingness on the part of supply chain network actors to invest and dedicate resources for the purpose of strengthening business relationships.

**Digital Orders:** Orders placed for goods or services via electronic methods.

**Downstream (in the Supply Chain Network):** Close to the marketplace.

**Electronic Data Interchange (EDI) Technologies:** Technologies that enable "electronic document interchange," conforming to published EDI standards.

**e-Commerce:** Transacting between parties electronically, usually over the Internet.

**e-Hub:** Information flows among a supply network partners are completely automated using this approach.

**e-Marketplace:** An Internet-based marketplace in which people or businesses "meet" electronically to trade or negotiate with others for the sale/acquisition of products or services.

**e-Procurement:** The acquisition of goods or services using the Internet.

**Enabling Processes:** Processes that are key to the achievement of critical business goals such as online order processing, which enablers and Internet retailers require in order to exist.

**Engine Groupings:** Provide the power and control mechanisms for achieving higher performance levels and efficiency. Both are required to achieve sustainable maturity levels.

**Esprit de Corps:** The feeling of belonging to a group and the strong identification with the group goals and purpose.

**Extended Supply Chain:** Extending outward beyond company boundaries to customers and suppliers, and connecting with them by use of Internet technologies supporting integrating practices.

**Framework:** A basic conceptual structure; a frame of reference.

**Globalization:** The process of making something (business, product, service, etc.) worldwide in scope or application.

**Holistic:** Relating to or concerned with complete systems instead of the analysis of dissections or parts.

**Horizontal Corporation:** Described as eliminating both hierarchy and functional boundaries. It is governed by a skeleton group of senior executives from finance and human resources. Everyone else is working together in multidisciplinary teams that perform core processes, such as product development, with only three or four layers of management between the chairman and the "staffers" in a given process.

**Information Exchange:** The nonrecursive flow of transactional and other data that help facilitate supply (demand) chain strategy planning as well as the flow of goods and services across the supply chain network.

**Interfunctional Conflict:** Tension among departments arising from the incompatibility of actual or desired responses.

**Interdepartmental Connectedness:** The degree of formal and informal direct contact among employees across departments.

**Interorganizational Connectedness:** The degree of formal and informal direct contact among employees across organizations or partners across a network.

**Information Exchange (Sharing):** The purposeful sharing and exchange of information between trading partners in a network. Attributes include intensity, quality, and openness.

**Institutionalization:** A critical aspect of process maturity, when a practice is part of the routine, completed every time, and not an exception.

**Integrated Supply Chain:** A seamless supply chain of close collaborative relationships with integrated data and business processes. These are internal integration, customer integration, relationship integration, technology and planning integration, measurement integration, and supplier integration.

**Integrating Practices:** Integrating mechanisms within a company and with supply chain partners that include cohabitation, shared employees, shared information, and shared secrets. Integrating practices can be further divided into practices that extend outward to suppliers and practices that extend outward to customers.

**Interactions (Interfirm):** The searching, coordinating, and monitoring that people and companies do when they exchange goods, services, and ideas. The key activities of managing a supply chain or what is now becoming a trading partner network. They are the friction of the economy; they represent a major cost of managing a supply chain, representing 80% of a supply chain manager's activity.

**Interaction Costs:** The money and time expended whenever people and companies exchange goods, services, or ideas.

**Interaction Friction:** The force that resists successful interactions. This resistance requires energy to overcome resulting in costs, both economic and personal (frustration).

**Interaction Capability:** The amount and quality of interactions that can be sustained.

**Interaction Connectivity:** The available number of possible connections with which to interact.

**Interoperate:** Interaction between entities in order to perform an operation (combined outcome).

**Internet Economy:** Economic activity impacted and enabled by the universal information network — the Internet — connecting customers, suppliers, and resellers. Also known as the digital economy.

**Internet Technologies:** Technologies that are network-based and have communication/information transfer as their main function (e-mail, online chat, file transfer, shared programs).

**Intraorganizational Collaboration:** Joint activities among people and across units focused upon common goals.

**Interfunctional Coordination (Cooperation):** The coordinated utilization of company resources in creating superior value for target customers

**Interdepartmental Dynamics:** Consists of *conflict* and *connectedness*. Conflict pertains to the extent to which the goals of different departments were incompatible and tension prevailed in interdepartmental interactions and connectedness captures the extent to which individuals in a department were networked to various levels of the hierarchy in other departments.

**Kaizen:** The overriding concept behind good management; a combination of philosophy, strategy, organization methods, and tools needed to compete successfully today and in the future.

**Keiretsu:** A network of businesses that own stakes in one another as a means of mutual security, especially in Japan, and usually including large manufacturers and their suppliers of raw materials and components. The Keiretsu is characterized by cross-ownership of equity, ties with major banking entities, and product-market ties with other firms in the group.

**Logistics:** The process of planning, implementing, and controlling the efficient and cost effective flow and storage of raw material, in-process inventory, finished goods, and related information, from the point of origin to the point of consumption, for the purpose of conforming to customer requirements.

**Main Supply Chain Thread:** The primary route of a product's physical flow through a supply chain network.

**Management:** The process of developing decisions and taking actions to direct the activities of people within an organization; planning, organizing, staffing, leading, and controlling.

**Market Turbulence:** The rate of change in the composition of customers and their preferences.

**Midstream (in the Supply Chain Network):** Close to the transformation (make) process.

**Model:** A structural design or an example. A system of postulates, data, and inferences presented as a description of an entity or state of affairs. A description used to help visualize something that cannot be directly observed.

**Networked Corporation:** An economic organization based upon a trading partner network, not the corporation.

**Networked Economy:** The supply chain or trading partner network is the dominant organizing principle, not the corporation.

**Networked Supply Chains (NCS):** A network of interenterprise supply chain events connected through a private or public eMarketplace.

**Nominal Trading Partner:** Any independent organization that provides an essential material or service within the supply chain network, but where financial success is largely independent of the end-to-end financial success of the network. Generic parts suppliers, second-tier distributors, wholesalers, less-than-truckload (LTL) carriers, freight forwarders, customs brokerage services, commercial banks, credit card services, wireless services, and Internet service providers are all examples of nominal trading partners.

**Operations Strategy:** The process of developing and setting broad policies and plans for using the production resources of the firm to best support the firm's long-term objectives and competitive strategies.

**Opportunistic Behaviors:** Relationship behaviors that take advantage of a situation at the expense of another party.

**Orchestrators:** The dominant company in a supply chain network, many times the one close to the demand or customer.

**Order-Qualifying Criteria:** Product or service attributes that allow firms, and in this case networks, to be considered as potential suppliers of the product.

**Order-Winning Criteria :** Product or service attributes that provide a competitive advantage for a firm or network.

**Organizational Culture:** The pattern of shared values and beliefs that help individuals understand organizational functioning, and thus provides them with the norms for behavior in the organization.

**Outsourcing:** Shifting responsibility and ownership of an activity to an outside company.

**Perspective:** The interrelation in which a subject or its parts are mentally viewed.

**Process:** A specific ordering of work activities across time and place, with a beginning, an end, and clearly identified inputs and outputs a structure for action.

**Process Centering:** Refocus and reorganize around processes or building an organization with a business process orientation.

**Process Control:** The difference between process targets and actual and the variation (range) around these targets.

**Process Documentation:** A clear understanding, documentation, and agreement of what is to be done in a business process. This is usually achieved through process design and mapping sessions, or review and validation sessions with process teams.

**Process Effectiveness:** The achievement of targeted results and the ability to raise targets.

**Process Flow Diagram:** Tool used for defining the steps of a process in order to better understand the importance and value of each step to the customer as well as identify potential fail points.

**Process Jobs:** Jobs that reflect the assignment of broad process ownership and authority (cross functional or cross company).

**Process Management and Measurement:** Measures that include aspects of the process such as output quality, cycle time, process cost, and variability compared with the traditional accounting measures.

**Process Management:** Viewing the operation as a set of interrelated work tasks with prescribed inputs and outputs. Provides a structure and framework for understanding the process and relationships and for applying the process-oriented tools. Establishing control points, performing measurements of appropriate parameters that describe the process, and taking corrective action on process deviations.

**Process Maturity:** Proposes that a process has a lifecycle that is measured by the extent to which the process is explicitly defined, managed, measured, controlled, and effective.

**Process Maturity Model:** A model depicting increasing levels of process maturity.

**Process-Oriented Structure:** An organization structure that deemphasizes the functional structure of business and emphasizes the process, cross-functional view. A dynamic view of how an organization delivers value.

**Process Predictability:** Measured by the variability in achieving process cost and performance objectives.

**Process Values and Beliefs**: Customer-focused, empowerment, and continuous-improvement-oriented values and beliefs (culture).

**Process View:** The cross-functional, horizontal picture of business involving elements of structure, focus, measurement, ownership, and customers.

**Reengineering:** The development of a customer-focused, strategic business-process-based organization enabled by rethinking the assumptions in a process-oriented way and utilizing information technology as a key enabler.

**Regression Analysis:** A general statistical technique used to analyze the relationship between a dependent variable and independent variables.

The objective is to predict a dependent variable from one or more independent variables.

**Relationship:** A state of affairs existing between those having relations or dealings such as trading partners in a network.

**Relationship Commitment:** Commitment between partners that comprises three facets: a desire to develop a stable relationship; a willingness to make short-term sacrifices to maintain the relationship; and a confidence in the stability of the relationship.

**Relationship Cooperation:** The activity that both the customer and supplier are working jointly on to achieve mutual and individual goals. Involves coordinated activities between supply chain actors aimed at producing desirable results for all firms. It takes three forms: cooperation in development; technical cooperation; and integration of management.

**Relationship Dependence:** A willingness to invest time and dedicate resources for the purpose of establishing and strengthening a business relationship.

**Relationship Enablers:** Key behaviors, enhanced by BPO, which minimize relationship decay and strengthen the bonds that lead to long-term supply network relationships. The relationship enablers consist of trust, commitment, dependence, and cooperation.

**Relationship Trust:** A trustworthy customer or supplier is one that displays the following characteristics: does not act in a purely self-serving manner; accurately discloses relevant information when requested; does not change supply specifications, standards, or costs to take advantage of other parties; and generally acts according to normally accepted ethical standards.

**Reverse Stream (in a Supply Chain Network):** The flow from the customer to the supply chain network; return, repair, and refurbishment.

**R-Squared, or the Coefficient of Determination:** A number produced in regression analysis that indicates the goodness of fit of a linear model. In this case, it indicates the fit of the linear relationship between the questions that were above 0.5 correlation and the performance questions. R squared also indicates the proportion of the variation in the dependent variable explained by the model.

**Situational Factors:** Factors that may determine the success of a network and are an aspect of the unique circumstances of the network, such as market conditions, business purpose of the network, technological dynamics, and relationship dynamics.

**Static Network:** A single set of suppliers, factories, wholesalers, and retailers defining a supply chain network that fulfills orders for customers and creates value for shareholders.

**Supply Chain:** The global network used to deliver products and services from raw materials to end customers through an engineered flow of information, physical distribution, and cash.

**Supply Chain Event Management (SCEM):** The process of simulating, responding to, and controlling exceptions to planned and unplanned events in the supply chain. SCEM moves from a single enterprise controlling multiple processes to multiple enterprises that control a single process distributed across trading partners.

**Supply Chain Management (SCM):** The process of developing decisions and taking actions to direct the activities of people within the supply chain toward common objectives.

**SCM (Integrated):** Involves designing, managing, and integrating a company's own supply chain with that of their suppliers and customers. Integrated supply chain management encompasses all activities associated with the flow and transformation of products from the raw materials stage through delivery to the end customer.

**SCM (Traditional):** Focused on the management of the supply chain for a single company. SCM often involves just the management of suppliers, with the use of coercion in most cases, by the large companies that dominate the chain. Management's objective is to work with a supplier that can provide low-cost, high-quality, and on-time delivery.

**SCM Costs:** All costs related to management of the supply chain including: material acquisition costs, order management costs, finance and planning costs, supply chain information technology, and administrative costs (i.e., inventory carrying costs included in asset management).

**Supply Chain Networks (SCN):** Groups of supply chains that are voluntarily connected and cooperating for the purpose of serving a specific market or set of customers.

**Supply Chain Network Integration:** The close coupling of all activities associated with the flow and transformation of products from the raw materials stage through delivery to the end customer.

**Supply Chain Operations Reference (SCOR™):** A model, developed by the Supply Chain Council (www.supply-chain.org) that breaks the supply chain into the core processes of Plan, Source, Make, Deliver, and Return (further defined by more detailed process models within each component area); a "common language" for supply chains.

**Supply Chain Partnership Management:** The process of developing, monitoring, managing, and maintaining strategic alliances between supply chain members that complement and support the business goals and objectives of each trading partner.

**Supply Chain Power (Interfirm):** The ability of one firm (the source) to influence the intentions and actions of another firm (the target). *Reward* — the ability of the source to mediated dividends to the target. *Coercion* — the ability of the source to mediated punishments to the target. *Expert* — the perception that one firm holds information or expertise that is valued by another firm. *Referent* — one form desires identification with another for recognition by association. *Legitimate* — the target believes in the inherent right of the source to wield influence. Legal legitimate æ the target believes in the legal right of the source to wield influence.

**Supporting Processes:** Processes that are not as insignificant as their position on the map might imply. They are shown at the bottom of the map because they are the furthest from the customer. Human resource management would be an example of a supporting process in a consulting company. Information systems frequently serve as a supporting process for many companies today.

**Supply Chain Strategy:** The process of developing and setting broad policies and plans for using the supply chain resources of entire supply chain to best support the long-term objectives and competitive strategies of the chain.

**Sustaining Processes:** These processes may not result in direct customer interactions, yet are critical to the operation of the business, such as product research and development.

**System Perspective:** Becoming aware and interacting with the environment in a complementary way. Thinking in system terms: input, output, transformation, measurement, feedback, and control.

**Switched Network:** A network where, from time to time, a new trading partner is brought into the network, while another is taken out.

**Teams:** Groups of individuals who work together to develop products or deliver services for which they are mutually accountable.

**Technological Turbulence:** The rate of technological change in a market.

**Trading Communities:** A group of people or businesses that come together for the common purpose of engaging the exchange of goods or services.

**Trading Partner:** An independent organization that plays an integral role within the supply chain network, and with a business fortune that depends on the end-to-end success of the supply chain network. Tier-one distributors, manufacturing centers, contract manufacturers, and third party logistics (3PL) service providers are good examples of trading partners.

**Transaction Costs:** The costs associated with an exchange (transfer) of a product or service.

**Transaction Cost Theory:** Suggests that firms organize internally those exchanges that might otherwise be conducted in markets due to the costs associated with an exchange (transfer) of a product or service in the market (costly negotiating and monitoring costs that may accompany exchanges conducted within the market).

**Trust:** A willingness to rely on supply network exchange partners, which is predicated on the confidence and believability of their intentions.

**Unbundled Corporation:** The disassembled corporation creating networks of outsourced business processes.

**Upstream (in the Supply Chain Network):** Close to the supply base.

**Value Chain:** A systematic way of examining all the activities a firm performs and how they interact to provide competitive advantage (see Figure 2.3). This chain is composed of "strategically relevant activities" that create value for a firm's buyers.

**Value:** A trade-off between the benefits received compared with the costs (both economic and noneconomic) incurred in purchasing and using a product or service.

**Value Proposition:** A "shared" understanding between the firm and customers or an implicit "contract" between company and customer, listing all products, programs, services, and target customer, as well as the effect of these offerings on the customer's business.

**Vendor Managed Inventory (VMI):** A "just-in-time" technique whereby a supplier of goods is able to access the inventory records of a customer to determine whether to make a shipment to that customer. The vendor may be able to replenish the inventory stock and update the customer's inventory records accordingly.

**Vertically Integrated Businesses:** Companies organized to minimize the total costs of transformation and interaction through the ownership of suppliers and sometimes customers.

**Vertical Organization:** An organization with members who look up to bosses instead of out to customers. Loyalty and commitment is given to functional fiefdoms, not the overall corporation and its goals. Too many layers of management can slow decision making and lead to high coordination costs.

**Virtual Companies:** Market organizations based upon networks (relationships and agreements, not ownership).

# INDEX

## A

Ad hoc level of maturity, 50, 57–61
Advanced Planning and Scheduling (APS), 124, 201
Advertising Display Company (ADC), 99
Alignment, 5–6, 142–144, 201
    downstream, 106
    midstream, 105–106
    network, 93, 94–96
    reverse stream, 106–107
    of rewards, 142
    strategic, 105–107, 142
    upstream, 105
    of values and beliefs, 135
AMR Research, 71
APICS, 201
APICS membership, 114
APICS principles, 105–129
    SCOR™ model and, 116
    summary of, 116–117
    Value Principle, 127–128
    Variability Principle, 119–122
    Velocity Principle, 117–119
    Visualize Principle, 125–127
    Vocalize Principle, 122–125
Arcs, 109

## B

*Battle Studies, Ancient and Modern* (du Picq), 25
Behaviors, opportunistic, 206
Benchmarking, 201

Best practice, 201
Bullwhip effect, 94–95
Business process, 201
Business process change (BPC), 201
Business process orientation (BPO), 5–6, 9–30, 201
    as compared with functional, 12–13
    from concept to measurement, 21–23
    definition, 21–23
    impacts of, 23–26
    integrating with supply chain design, 117–119
    networked corporation and, 26–28
    overview of concept, 10–12
    process and value creation, 13–15
    in 1990s: organizational design, 19–20
    in 1990s: technology enablement, 16–19
    within supply chains, 114–117
Business-to-business (B2B) interactions, 69–85, 201, *see also* Extended supply chains; Internet
Business webs, 202

## C

Capability, interaction, 204
Capability and Maturity Model (Carnegie Mellon University), 48
Cases
    customer relationship management, 147–155
    supply chain maturity, 56–64
    value creation (Envera™ example), 157–160

Cash flow, 109
Cash-to-cash cycle time, 120–121
Channel masters, *see* Orchestrators
Chaotic networks, 113, 124, 126–127, 128, 202
Chassis groupings, 202
Cisco Systems, 4, 91–92
Coase, Ronald, 88
Coefficient alpha analysis, 202
Coefficient of determination (R-squared), 208
Coercion power, 139, 196–197, 210
Collaboration, 202
    interorganizational, 205
Collaborative planning, forecasting, and replenishment (CPFR), 71, 126–127, 202
Commitment, 97–98, 197, 202
    relationship, 208
Communications matrix, 202
Competencies, logistic, 71
Competitive edges, 202
    survey instrument, 198–200
Competitive infrastructure, 117–119
Competitive intensity, 140–141, 200, 202
Competitor orientation, 10
Conflict, 118, 121, 197
    interfunctional, 23–24
    survey questions, 171
Conflict resolution, 197
Connectedness
    interdepartmental, 23–24, 204
    interorganizational, 204
    interplane, 121
    intraplane, 121
    survey questions, 171–172
Connectivity, 11–12, 89–90
    interaction, 204
Continuous improvement, 119
Control, process, 47, 206
Cooperation, 98, 197–198, 202
    relationship, 208
Coordination, interfunctional, 205
Coordination theory, 202
Core processes, 202
Corporations
    horizontal, 19, 203–204
    networked, 26–28, 206
    unbundled, 211
    vertically integrated, 19, 211
Correlation analysis, 203

Costs
    interaction, 204
    transaction, 210
Coty Corporation, 95
Criteria
    order-qualifying, 138, 206
    order-winning, 138, 206
Culture, organizational, 206
Customer relationship management, case study, 147–155
Cycle time
    cash-to-cash, 120–121
    order-to-delivery, 119–120
    order-to-reorder, 119–120

**D**

Data analysis, 77–81
Davenport, Thomas, 11, 16–18
Decision process, survey questions, 173–182
Defined level of maturity, 50, 61–63
Dell Computer, 120–121, 141
Dell, Michael, 131
Demand management, 83, 203
Deming Flow Diagram, 11, 13–14
Dependence, 98–99, 203
    relationship, 208
Digital orders, 203
Disruptive technologies, 141
Documentation, process, 207
Downstream, 203
Downstream alignment, 106
Due date performance, 138, 199
du Picq, Col. Ardant, 25
Dynamics, interdepartmental, 205

**E**

EBITDA (earnings before interest, taxes, depreciation, and amortization), 25
e-commerce, 203
Economy, networked, 206
Educational Society for Resource Management, *see* APICS entries
Effectiveness, 47
    process, 207
e-Hub (Cisco Systems), 91–92, 203

Electronic data interchange (EDI)
    technologies, 70, 94, 203, *see*
    *also* Internet
e-marketplace, 203
Enablers, relationship, 208
Enabling processes, 203
Engine groupings, 203
Enterprise Resource Planning (ERP), 124
Envera™, 157–160
e-procurement, 203
Equivalent throughput, 125
Esprit de corps, 24–25, 93, 118–119, 125,
    136, 203
  survey questions, 172, 195
Ethyl Corporation, 157, *see also* Envera™
    case study
European sample functions, 79
European sample industries, 78
European sample positions, 80
Event management, 134
Expert power, 139, 195, 210
Extended level of maturity, 52
Extended supply chain, vs. Internet usage
    results, 189–190
Extended supply chain management, 203,
    *see also* Internet
  background, 70–72
  concepts and measures, 73–77
  conclusions and implications, 83–84
  data gathering and results, 77–81
  Internet and, 69–85
  proposed variable relationships, 72
  results and findings, 81–83
  scope and organization of study, 72
Extensible markup language (XML), 135
External (environmental) situational factors,
    140–141, 199–200

## F

Federal Express, 96
Field service, 138, 199
Flexibility, product and process, 138,
    199
Flow
  physical, 104
  types of, 109
Flow sequences, 109–112
Ford, Henry, 9, 12, 87
Ford Motor Company, 9, 87–88
Forrester Research, 71

Framework, 203
Friction, interaction, 88–89, 204
Fuji Corporation, 95
Functional orientation, 12–13, 18

## G

General Motors, 88
Genesis Solutions, 5
Gerstner, Lou, 27
Gillette Company, 99
Globalization, 203
Global performance measurement, 125–127
Goldart's Theory of Constraint, 122–124
Gummesson, Evert, 96

## H

Hammer, Michael, 11, 16, 17
Holistic, 203
Horizontal corporation, 19, 203–204

## I

Information exchange/information sharing,
    93, 94–96, 204
Information flow, 104–105, 109
Information standards, 143
Information technology, 16–17
Innovation, 138, 199
Institutionalization, 204
Integrated level of maturity, 50, 63–64
Integrated Supply Chain Management, 3
Integrated supply chains, 204
Integrating practice measures, 73–77, *see*
    *also* Survey questions
Integrating practices, 73–74, 204
Interaction capability, 204
Interaction connectivity, 204
Interaction costs, 88–91, 204
Interaction friction, 88–89, 204
Interaction platforms, 143
Interactions (interfirm), 204
Interdepartmental connectedness, 23–24,
    204
Interdepartmental dynamics, 205
Interfunctional conflict, 23–24
Interfunctional coordination, 205
Internal situational factors, 137–140

Internet
    as enabling factor, 131
    impact of, 26–27
    usage correlations to supply chain
        management performance, 73,
        81–83
Internet economy, 205
Internet technologies, 205
Interoperability, 143–144
Interorganizational collaboration, 205
Interorganizational connectedness, 204
Interplane connectedness, 121
Intraplane connectedness, 121
Inventory
    total system, 125, 126
    vendor management (VMI), 71, 83

**J**

J.C. Penney, 98
Jobs
    in network structure, 135
    process, 22, 192–193, 207
    survey questions, 170, 192–193

**K**

Kaizen, 205
Keiretsu, 205

**L**

Lead time, 138
    quality, 199
Learning, organizational, 4–6
Legal legitimate power, 139, 196, 210
Legitimate power, 139, 196, 210
Leveraging worldwide logistics, 119–122
Linked level of maturity, 51–52
Logistic competencies, 71
Logistics, 119, 205
Loops, 109

**M**

Main thread, 104–105, 110, 205
Management, 32, 205
Manufacturing Resource Planning (MRP),
    126

Market orientation, 10
Market turbulence, 140–141, 199–200, 205
Maturity
    process, 45–51, *see also* Process maturity
    supply chain, 45–67, *see also* Supply
        chain maturity
Maturity level, 47–48
Maturity model, 45, 49, *see also* Supply
        chain maturity
Maytag Corporation, 3–4
McKesson Corporation, 94
Measures
    integrating practice, 73–77
    shared, 135
Michigan State University supply chain
        model, 71
Midstream, 205
Midstream alignment, 105–106
Model/modeling defined, 205–206
Models
    Michigan State University supply chain,
        71
    process maturity, 207
    supply chain (SC) network, 131–145

**N**

Nervous system of supply chain network,
        135
Net value creation, 127–128
Network alignment, 93, 94–96
Network dynamics, 112–114
Networked corporation, 26–28, 206
Networked economy, 206, *see also* Supply
        chain networks
    information exchange and network
        alignment, 94–96
    interaction costs, 88–91
    interactions and relationships, 87–102
    multilevel interoperation, 91–94
    relationshiop enablers, 96–99
Networked supply chains, 206
Network orchestrators, 3–4, 27, 108–109,
        141–142, 143, 206
Networks
    static, 208
    supply chain, 103–129, *see also* Supply
        chain networks
    switched, 210
Network supply chains, 71
Nominal trading partners, 107–108, 142, 206

North American sample functions, 79
North American sample industries, 78
North American sample positions, 80

# O

Operations strategy, 206
Opportunistic behaviors, 206
*Optimizing the Supply Chain,* 5
Orchestrators, 3–4, 27, 108–109, 141–142, 143, 206
Order-qualifying criteria, 138, 206
Order-to-delivery cycle time, 119–120
Order-to-reorder cycle time, 119–120
Order-winning criteria, 138, 206
Organizational charts, 12–13
Organizational culture, 206
Organizational design, 19–20
Organizational learning, 4–6
Organizations, vertical, 211
Outsourcing, 90, 206
Overall performance, survey questions, 173, 195

# P

Partners
    nominal trading, 107–108, 142, 206
    strategic trading, 142
    trading, 107, 141–142, 210
Partnership management, 134
Penney, J.C., 98
Perfect order, 125
Performance, 198
    overall, 195
    survey questions, 173, 182–183
Performance measurement, 135–136
Perspective, 206
Physical flow, 109
    backward and forward, 104–105
Porter, Michael, 11 E.14–15, 31
Power, 139–140
    survey questions, 195–197
    types of, 209–210
Predictability, 47
    process, 207
Price, 138, 199
Process, 206
Process centering, 206
Process control, 206

Process documentation, 207
Process effectiveness, 207
Processes
    supporting, 210
    sustaining, 210
Process jobs, 22, 207
    survey questions, 170, 192–193
Process management and measurement
        systems, survey questions, 170, 193
Process maturity, 207
    concepts and foundations, 45–48
Process maturity model, 207
Process-oriented structure, 207
Process owners, 18
Process predictability, 207
Process structures, survey questions, 193–194
Process thinking, 16
Process values and beliefs, 118–119, 121, 207
    survey questions, 194
Process view, 17, 22, 118, 119, 121, 135, 207
    survey questions, 170, 192–193
Procter & Gamble, 98
Product and process flexibility, 138, 199
Product introduction responsiveness, 138
Production orientation, 10
Product orientation, 10
Push/pull boundary, 126

# Q

Quality lead time, 199
Questions, survey, *see* Survey questions

# R

Reengineering, 11, 16, 18–19, 207
Referent power, 139, 196, 210
Regression analysis, 207–208
Regression and coefficient alpha analysis
        results, 185–187
Relationship, 208
Relationship commitment, 208
Relationship cooperation, 208
Relationship dependence, 208
Relationship enablers, 96–99, 208
    commitment, 97–98
    cooperation, 98

dependence, 98–99
trust, 96–97
Relationship marketing, 93–94
Relationship trust, 208
Responsiveness, product introduction,
138
Return on assets (ROA), 12
Reverse stream, 208
Reverse stream alignment, 106–107
Reward power, 139, 196
Rewards, alignment of, 142
Rockefeller, John D., 87
RosettaNet, 135
R-squared (coefficient of determination),
208

## S

SCOR model™, 31–43, 74–75, 209
APICS principles and, 116
data collection, 34–35
relationship correlation with
performance, 40–42
relationship identification, 35–40
supply chain management and BPO,
31–34
Selling orientation, 10
Shared measures, 135
Short, James, 11
Situational factors, 137–141, 208
external (environmental), 140–141,
199–200
internal, 137–140
survey questions, 191–200, 195–198
Sloan, Afred P., 9, 12
Smith, Adam, 12
Southwest Airlines, 25
Standard Oil, 87, 90
Static networks, 112–113, 208
Strategic alignment, 142
Strategic Management Group (SGM), 5
Strategic trading partners, 142
Strategy
operations, 206
supply chain, 210
Structure, process-oriented, 207
Structure component of model, 135
Suboptimization phenomenon, 20
Supply chains, 209
defined, 32

extended, 69–85, *see also* Extended
supply chain management;
Internet
integrated, 204
networked, 206
Supply chain event management (SCEM),
209
Supply chain integration (Lee model),
71–72
Supply chain management (SCM), 209
defined, 31, 32
integrated, 209
traditional, 209
traditional vs. integrated, 1–4
Supply chain management maturity, 45–67,
*see also* Process maturity
ad hoc level, 50, 57–61
assessment of, 48–50
BPO components in model of, 52–56
business performance and, 64–66
conclusion and future prospect, 66
defined level, 50, 61–63
extended level, 52, 66
implementation case studies, 56–64
integrated, 50, 63–64
levels of, 50–52
process maturity and, 45–48
Supply chain management performance,
correlations to Internet usage,
81–83
Supply chain network integration, 209
Supply chain (SC) network model, 131–145
application of supply chain network,
141–144
concepts and components, 134–135
external factors, 132
focus of, 141–144
internal factors, 132
performance measurement, 135–136
situational factors: external
(environmental), 140–141
situational factors: internal, 132, 137–140
survey questions, 191–200
Supply chain networks, 103–129, 209
alignment with business strategy,
105–107
business process orientation (BPO)
within, 114–117
classifying players, 107–109
flow sequences, 109–112

global performance measurement, 125–127
identifying main thread, 104–105
integrating BPO with, 122–127
integrating BPO with design of, 117–119
leveraging worldwide logistics, 119–121
nervous system of, 135
net value creation, 127–128
network dynamics, 112–114
supply/demand synchronization, 122–125
Supply Chain Operations Reference (SCOR™) model, *see* SCOR™ model
Supply chain optimization, 4–6
Supply chain partnership management, 209
Supply chain performance, 31–42, *see also* Supply chain management
Supply chain players, 107–109
Supply chain power (interfirm), 209–210, *see also* Power
Supply chain strategy, 210
Supply/demand synchronization, 122–125
Supporting processes, 210
Survey questions, 22–23, 73–77, 169–184
Sustaining processes, 210
Switched networks, 113, 210
System perspective, 210

**T**

Teams, 210
Technological turbulence, 141, 200, 210
Technologies
disruptive, 141
Internet, 205
Technology enablement, 16–19
Technology support, survey questions, 194
Texas Instruments, 16, 17
Total system inventory, 125
Trading communities, 210
Trading partners, 107, 210
nominal, 107–108, 142, 206
strategic, 142
Transaction costs, 210
Transaction cost theory, 210–211
Triggers, 110

Trust, 96–97, 198, 211
relationship, 208
Turbulence
market, 140–141, 199–200, 205
technological, 141, 200, 210

**U**

Unbundled corporation, 211
United Parcel Service (UPS), 98
Upstream, 211
Upstream alignment, 105

**V**

Value, 211
Value chain, 14–15, 211
Value chain economics, 158–159
Value creation, 13–15
Envera™, 157–160
Value Principle, 127–128
Value proposition, 211
Vanilla Fields example, 95
Variability Principle, 119–122
Velocity Principle, 117–119
Vendor management inventory (VMI), 71, 83, 211
Vertical corporation, 19
Vertical integration, 9–10
Vertically integrated businesses, 211
Vertical organization, 211
Virtual companies, 211
Visualize Principle, 125–127
Vocalize Principle, 122–125
Von Hippel, Eric, 95

**W**

Wal-Mart, 98
Webs, business, 202
Welch, John ("Jack"), 19
Whirlpool Corporation, 3–4

**X**

Xerox, 95
XML (extensible markup language), 135